D1436878

# I HATE TO-MORROW

*Books by the same Author*

THE FACE OF FRANCE
MIRRORS OF MOSCOW
AMERICAN SCENE
PACIFIC SCENE
STORM OVER INDIA
THE STRANGE LIFE OF WILLIE CLARKSON
SCOOPS
ROUND THE WORLD FOR NEWS
MEDITERRANEAN CRISIS
    ETC.

# I HATE TO-MORROW

*An*
*Autobiographical Experiment*

In Twenty-three Chapters
and a Prologue

*by*
HARRY J. GREENWALL

THE BOOK CLUB
111, CHARING CROSS ROAD
LONDON, W.C.2

*This Edition 1940*

MADE AND PRINTED IN GREAT BRITAIN BY
EBENEZER BAYLIS AND SON, LTD., THE
TRINITY PRESS, WORCESTER, AND LONDON

# CONTENTS

## PROLOGUE

## Book I

## Book II

# CONTENTS

## Book III

## Book IV

# PROLOGUE

THIS BOOK'S main objective is to relate in narrative form the story of one man's struggle and at the same time to vindicate Disraeli's pronouncement, too often forgotten, that man, through his own exertions alone, can extricate himself from any given circumstances. A publisher, perhaps in facetious mood, suggested I should entitle this book "*My* Struggle", but I was adamant; I had no wish to compete with a person whose book of like title forms the bible of those whose lives are devoted to the glorification of making Life in the future tense unhappy.

My book begins in the last days of the reign of Queen Victoria, days to look back upon now with a certain melancholy regret. As a small boy struggling in the throng near Marble Arch, I saw the Queen's funeral procession pass on its way to Paddington station and ultimately Windsor. Riding in that procession I saw a man on a horse who some years later was to make Europe shiver and tremble; he was the Kaiser Wilhelm. Another passage of years, and I saw him again, this time a broken old man walking through the forest near his place of exile in Doorn.

If we could see the to-morrow which we are told never comes! I saw Germany as an arrogant and proud country dreaming of the overthrow of Britain, during the miserable, and for us, uncertain days of the Boer War; I never went there again until Germany had bitten the dust, when she was starving in defeat, but again and again I went back to Germany when she was girding up her loins to fight again. While I have been writing this book, the tramp of German soldiers has been growing louder; German armoured cars and tanks and aeroplanes rattle and roar across stricken Europe; the peace I knew in my youth melted in the furnace of war; the aftermath has been nothing but a slow preparation for further slaughter.

In a desk near to hand I have a handful of coloured cards which gave me entry to the Peace Conferences which built up the world in which we live: The Palace of Versailles; the Palace of St. Germain; dog-eared and crumpled they lay with others which mention Washington, Sèvres, Lausanne, the Hague, and Geneva. I was present at all these meetings; I heard all the lies told, all the promises made and broken. I saw and heard His Majesty King George V open the Naval Conference in London, then the World Economic Conference, held in London, and when on that rainy day I heard a sad voice repeating: "the life of His Majesty the King is slowly moving to its end", I thought of King George, a naval officer who never expected a throne, coming from his convalescence to open the Naval Conference. He stood in front of a temporary throne and read his speech; then the throne was removed by lackeys, and in place of the King, there stood Mr. Ramsay MacDonald, the poor boy who had made good.

Struggle, struggle, everlasting struggle, but to what green altar do we fight our way? Do we, the People, care for Empires, for glory, for power, or do we all spend our lives in the mute pursuit of Happiness?

# PROLOGUE

That, surely, is the answer: contentment, and all that it brings, which means: Happiness.

At the time of writing there are men who seek to rule the world through power; they have forgotten the lesson of history, and still more, they have forgotten the lesson of their own lives. These men who believe in brute force as a means to rule rose from humble beginnings, and through their struggles reached places of eminence, but although their eyes may be fixed on far horizons, they forget that over the horizon there is always to-morrow.

H.J.G.

Paris, July, '39.

IN
MEMORY
OF MY
MOTHER

# BOOK I

# CHAPTER I

## PRIORY DENE

WHEN ALICE put him to bed that evening, she told him his mother would be back from her honeymoon in the morning and would bring him a lovely present. He remembered Alice very well, memory aided perhaps by a faded picture he kept for years, showing himself as he was then, a very small boy wearing a three-cornered hat, standing close to a seated Alice; her hands folded across her lap held one of his. He remembered realistically when that photograph was taken. He had gone with Alice and his mother to the Military Tournament at the Agricultural Hall in Islington, and somewhere near there, while his mother was away, the picture was taken. He had been born in North London. His was a photographic memory made up of odd pictures which bore no relation one to the other. There was Alice, a short little woman with a pale pasty face and eyes like currants stuck in a pudding. Then there was the incident of the dog which came along and took a sponge cake out of his hand; he was riding in a three-wheeled perambulator and wearing a white pelisse and he insisted that he was being trundled in a certain direction, with the sea on the left; his amazed mother said it was impossible to remember that, because that occurred when they were living at Brighton and he was not more than two-and-a-half. Other memories must have been helped by his mother, with nobody else to talk to but her small son and Alice. There was for instance the story of the death of his father which happened when he was five months old. His mother was ill; there was a mysterious burglary in the house, and his father died of heart failure. It was a mystery which was never cleared up, partly perhaps because a young ne'er-do-well brother of his mother's was staying in the house at the time; he went abroad soon afterwards. He was always going abroad, to America, to Canada, to South Africa, to Australia and then coming back and getting into serious trouble and then going away again. He formed a sinister shadow hovering around the family, but there were other shadows.

His mother? Alice said she was coming back from Antwerp, wherever that might be, and she was bringing with her a new uncle, which sounded very nice and exciting, and then in a few days they would be leaving the lodgings and moving across the way to Priory Dene.

They had been in lodgings for a few days only, Alice and the little boy, because they had been staying with his grandmother, who lived in a house in Maida Vale, a house with a lovely garden with a hammock in it. Aunt May, mother's sister, used to swing all day, it seemed, in that hammock. Grandmother was a nice old lady (a comparison of ages proved subsequently that she was a woman in the early forties at this time) who wore a sort of bright mauve dress with a cameo brooch at the neck. Grandmother, he was told, had been very rich and mother and Aunt May used to ride horses and grandmother had "kept her carriage" when mother was first married to father. It

4

was nice to snuggle down to sleep and think of this lovely
to-morrow and the new uncle and the lovely present.

Here was his mother with the present which alas he
so soon forgot, and here was the new uncle, whom he
was told to call "daddy", but he was too shy to do so
and he called him uncle for a long time, at least until
his stepsister was born. When he was quite small and
indeed until his half-sister and half-brothers arrived
on the scene, his stepfather was kind to him;
while they stayed in the lodgings his mother and
"uncle" had a bedroom on one floor, and the little
boy and Alice slept on the next floor, but every morning before "uncle" went away to his work in Hatton
Garden he would go upstairs and play with the little
boy, and he would do the same when he came home
in the evening. The little boy had great games with his
stepfather and remembered him for years as a smiling
good-looking man with a long body and short legs
and a big chest. He wore a close-clipped moustache.
While mother was getting Priory Dene ready, the
small boy and Alice used to go walking in the nearby
streets in St. John's Wood, where milkmaids with
many petticoats carried the milk in two big pails
slung from a sort of harness across their shoulders; it
was like the wooden trays in which butcher's boys
carried meat, with a curved middle to fit round the
back of the neck. Then there were other strange
things to be seen in the neighbourhood, not only
German bands which played at street corners, and
many Punch and Judy shows, but Jack-in-the-Green,
a man covered with branches of ivy who used to dance
on May Day. There was lots of fun for a little boy at
the moment, when the firing of guns announced the
birth of a son to the Duke and Duchess of York.

("Won't the old Queen be pleased?"), and the little boy and his Nanny, Alice, and his mother and his new "uncle" moved across the road to Priory Dene.

From the night-nursery window with bars across it, the little boy could look out to see the lodgings where he had been living, the red house with the pointed roof, just like the one he built up with nursery bricks; the white and blue tiles between the topmost window and the roof, and they were still there fifty years later, when the little boy passed that way again. Priory Dene was the corner house of a row of houses which retired gently from the main road in Maida Vale and which called itself Priory Road. In almost the first house in the road lived a family called Tripp where a daughter was born who later burst upon the world as an actress called June. Towards the middle of the base of this triangle of which Priory Dene formed one angle, was another old house in which a family lived named Aschenberg; they published music; in the mind of a small boy behind the bars of the window was a picture from the front page of the score of Puccini's *Vie de Boheme*, of Mimi in the snow outside one of the gates of Paris, which he must have seen one day when he was taken into the Aschenberg's shop. At the apex of the triangle was a jolly old house where an author named Max Pemberton lived. The small boy from Priory Dene when he grew older, used to play with the author's two sons, one of whom in after years became a colleague on the same newspaper, until he crashed to death one foggy night in an aeroplane accident in the wilds of Cumberland. Across the road from Priory Dene was a school called Henley House, which had its day of fame, because it was there that a boy named Alfred Harmsworth went to school, and this young Harmsworth, the neighbourhood knew, had just started an orange-covered weekly called *Answers*.

Looking over the low garden wall which separated the back garden from Greville Road, the small boy used to see some mornings a bent figure wearing spectacles riding a horse. That was Israel Zangwill.

When the family of three moved into the new house, everything seemed fine and happy, but there came a dreadful change which the little boy could not understand. There was loud shouting and often his mother was in tears. Then the clouds would roll away and everything was happy again.

In the afternoons grandmother would come and sit and play with her grandson; the little boy when he had moved away forgotten, used to hear his mother say how she wished she had a little girl, and if she had, now nicely she would dress her; it did not seem to make sense, because it was a well-known fact that little boys and little girls were purchased already dressed.

At other times grandmother would sit there crying, and mother would cry too. Grandmother had to give up her house in Maida Vale and go to live in a boarding-house. Then early one Christmas morning grandfather appeared. Mother's father had come from America and materialized like a conjuring trick. He was a thin little man, he walked as if he had a poker down his back; his head was bald, his eyes blue and watery, and he wore side-whiskers. He seemed to be always wearing a frock-coat. The rows started all over again; it was clear this was a house of warring Montagues and Capulets. The small boy became a sort of whipping boy; he was a messenger, small as he was, who had to tell his mother from his "uncle" that

7

his grandfather was not to come to the house any more, but he used to come still, in secret, and there were whispered conversations behind the closed drawing-room door. It appeared that the child's mother called "uncle's" family low; they came from the East End, and they had no manners. One sister of "uncle's" was married to a man who played the violin in the Gaiety orchestra; he used to come to Priory Dene sometimes on Sundays, with another sister who was married to a cigar-maker.

Then all of a sudden, mother's sister, Aunt May, went to South Africa where she had two brothers living; then other members of mother's family came along. There was Uncle Moss, who had been a dental mechanic but who had become stone deaf through having had scarlet fever; his hair and his face were white as snow; his head looked as if it were made of wax and he spoke in a veiled voice, as people do who have not heard a human voice for years and have forgotten the sound. He had the smile which deaf people often carry as a permanency. His favourite joke was to ask everybody: "You like Paris?" Uncle Moss lived alone in lodgings on a small pension given him by a sister. The pension was small, but not so small that the deaf old man could not have six-penny bets; that was all he did, to buy the papers and write down his bets and give them to a passing runner.

Then there was another Uncle Moss who had been a great swell in his day; he had been a Colonel in the Honorable Artillery Company, but when Albert Edward Prince of Wales became Honorary Colonel of the Regiment, Uncle Moss had to resign, because he was in trade. His firm had made a famous brand of lamp. To be in trade was so low, of course. And anyhow, Uncle Moss had no money any more; he had two daughters, Cousin Jenny and Cousin Lizzie, who kept a small boarding-house in Bayswater. She was always falling asleep; she would take a nap before and after a meal, and sometimes mother would take her to the Metropolitan Music Hall, where she would sleep peacefully, even though the delightful Mr. George Robey was singing his naughtiest songs.

Cousin Jenny, her sister, was married to a man who was paralyzed and wore blue spectacles and was wheeled about in a chair.

There were other cousins, a whole bunch of women cousins of mothers. *They* had been very rich too, but their father died and left nothing; they all had to go out to work. One went to live in Paris, and the youngest was a clerk in the City—a terrible comedown of course, but she married in later life; she married a blind man who hawked tea round the neighbourhood. He was a cheerful man; he always used to know what the weather was like, even though he had always been blind.

"Uncle" or daddy had a father and mother who used to come sometimes in a slow jogging horse omnibus all the way from the East End to Priory Dene. His father and his mother had lived long in Holland, Dutch was their native tongue and they spoke it to their son. Their ancestors had been driven out of Portugal during the Inquisition; they had settled in Holland and then in London. They were very poor indeed and lived by exploiting a small delicatessen shop in White's Row, Whitechapel. Daddy had a favourite brother called Jack who had looked after him when he was young, before he went to South

Africa. One Sunday Jack walked all the way from the East End to Priory Dene; he had put on his best Sunday suit, but he went to the side door and the cook said no, nothing to-day, thank you, and Jack was so nervous that he did not go to the front door, but he had gone and stood at the corner of Goldsmith's Place opposite Priory Dene all the afternoon, hoping he would see his brother and attract his attention, but he did not, so he walked all the way home again.

More glamorous persons and much richer, in the millionaire class, came to Priory Dene sometimes; these had originally come from Whitechapel, but they were now preparing to live in Park Lane. Daddy had gone out to South Africa, to Kimberley in the diamond boom time. He had gone with two brothers named Isaacs who changed their name to Barnato; they had been a music-hall act before they found diamonds. With the Isaac brothers went their cousins, the Joels, Jack and Solly, whose mother used to keep a fried fish shop in Whitechapel. Now they were all "home", and mother wrapped up the fish and chips for the last time and went to live in a fine house, 6, Marble Arch. All the troop, with the exception of daddy, had made fortunes, but he just tagged along with them, ran their errands for them, sold them jewellery which they gave away.

Occasionally on a Sunday morning a hansom cab would come jingling up to Priory Dene and Solly Joel would jump out and ring the bell and say that he had just come to smoke a cigar with his old friend; then the two, daddy and Solly Joel would go into the drawing-room and shut the door. Sometimes daddy wanted to give his old friend a treat and show him that even he knew what was what, then he would send

the maid to the wine cellar to get a bottle of the
"boy"; and would whisper to the servant to open the
bottle just outside the door, left artfully ajar so that
Solly Joel should hear the pop of the champagne cork.

Daddy never minded what he spent on things for
his friends and himself, but when the house-keeping
bills were put in front of him on a Friday morning, he
raised hell. Sometimes mother would say the bills
were not ready, and so postpone the bad quarter of an
hour, but the music had to be faced, and she faced it
always with a bad grace. Sometimes the rows were so
fierce of an evening that mother would put on her
bonnet and ram a hat on her small son's head and drag
him off for the evening. Sometimes they would go to
the Metropolitan Music Hall in the Edgware Road,
or sometimes to the West London Theatre, in a street
off the Edgware Road, where they played blood and
thunder melodrama, and changed the "bill" every
Monday night. It was this way that the small boy,
who had been christened Henry James, began to pick
up a liking for the theatre. In his early years he knew
quite a lot of the gossip; he knew for instance that the
pretty fair-haired girl who sold programmes in the
Metropolitan was the sister of the girl who sang ballads
and whose name on the programme was Amy Clevere,
who lived with the resident manager. The programmes
were prime; there was Marie Lloyd and George
Robey as a Chinese laundryman which in itself was
quite a coincidence because the ne'er-do-well uncle
just suddenly turned up from nowhere and opened
the first Chinese laundry London ever knew, but unfortunately there was a spot of trouble; the laundry
closed down and the uncle vanished from circulation
for a time, but not for long, because he was heard of

again in Cape Town, where he had taken the christian
and surnames of his young nephew and made himself
a baronet.

When all was quiet at Priory Dene, daddy would
take his stepson with him in the morning to Hatton
Garden, where in a back street he had a small factory
for the cutting and polishing of diamonds brought to
London from Amsterdam and Antwerp. The half a
dozen workmen were all Dutch; three or four of them
stood at a bench, each in front of a steel wheel revolv-
ing at a dizzy speed. A diamond was imbedded in a
blob of soft metal which the workmen kept on the
spinning wheel with weights. Other men stood round
the bench rubbing two sticks together. Imbedded in
cement in the head of each stick was a diamond; the
men rubbed one diamond against the other.

Every morning a "pirate" horse omnibus would
stop for a few moments outside Priory Dene; daddy
would go out and take his seat on the "knife-board"
next to the driver. When Lord Rothschild sent a
present of game to the drivers and conductors, they
would sport on their whips the Rothschild racing
colours, just as they wore Oxford or Cambridge blue
at Boat Race time. People were all for wearing
emblems of some kind in those days, and most people
wore a posey of Beaconsfield's favourite flower on
Primrose Day. Going down to Hatton Garden vied
with being taken to the Metropolitan Music Hall by
mother, but it was a bit better, because theatre-going
was always in connection with a row at home, though
that had its compensation, because in trying to get
home late enough for her husband to have gone to
bed, mother would sometimes take Henry James to
have a dozen oysters, bought and eaten from a

coster's barrow lit by flaring naphtha lights. Hatton
Garden meant being taken down into that romantic
underground café, the African, where there was
always a rattling of dominoes on the marble-topped
tables; where there were queer-looking men, all wearing top hats, who went into a huddle and showed one
another what looked like bits of polished glass wrapped
up in rice paper; it *was* rice paper, but the "glass"
were valuable unpolished diamonds. People used to
drift up to daddy and ask: "Is this your boy?" and he
inevitably answered: "This is my wife's boy." Most
of the curious looking men were Jews, but there was
one who was not, a big jovial man named Tom Evans,
who used to joke with the Jews in Yiddish which he
had picked up in Hatton Garden.

There used to come to Priory Dene at irregular
intervals, the son of Henry James's father by his first
wife, a young man in the late twenties, twenty-one
years older than Henry James and approximately the
same age as Henry James's mother. He had, it was
said, bitterly resented the second marriage of his
father with whom he lived on bad terms, as the saying
is, and had, according to his stepmother, actually
taken the blankets from the bed of his dead father and
sold them. A Freud might be able to explain the
strange complex of this man for bed linen. Years
later he married and after fifteen years his wife went
off with another man; he divorced her. The home
broken up, the deceived husband sold most of his
belongings, but stored some in an old-fashioned hotel
in central London; then he roamed from Paris to
Nice and from Nice to Ostend, yet every autumn he
would arrive back in London and go to this old-
fashioned hotel where he would instruct a servant to

have his trunk brought down. From the trunk he would take bed-linen, have the hotel linen stripped from the bed which was remade with his own; then he would sleep between these sheets for a night or two, and then have the linen returned to the trunk and the trunk returned to the box-room; then he would resume his wanderings.

Henry James began to be aware of his own personality; he asked his mother why daddy always referred to him as his wife's boy. Then he was told the story of his birth. He learned too that he was a ward in Chancery and that once a year his mother had to produce him in Court to prove that he was alive, because he had inherited £3,000 from his father. This money was locked up in things called Consols until the time when Henry James would be twenty-one; in the meantime, said his mother, she had the interest on his money; although he did not of course know what that meant, but later he was to know much more about that and many other things concerned with it.

There came a time when his mother seemed very low-spirited; she cried a good deal and Henry James was left alone with Alice who was also very cross nowadays. Then one morning Alice told him to come downstairs and see his new sister. Henry James whom they used to call Harry was taken to the front bedroom and there in a white wicker armchair, near the foot of the bed, was a morsel of humanity wrapped in a shawl, that was the sister, the girl for whom mother had prayed.

Things seemed to go wrong before the new baby was very old. Harry used to be taken sometimes in an omnibus to see his grandfather, who was always asking his grandson what was the capital of Ceylon, and what was the capital of the United States. One day Harry noticed a big building and asked what it was and was told it was the Imperial Institute. When he reached home he said he had seen it, and his stepfather asked when, he said that very afternoon. Then his stepfather knew that he and his mother had disobeyed and had been to see his grandfather. There was a big row.

Soon after the stepsister was born, they sent Harry to a kindergarten where he learned how to count red and white beads on a wire frame, and many years later he saw Chinamen and Negroes, Russians all in their own countries, counting intricate figures just as he had learned to count at the Kilburn kindergarten.

It was soon after the birth of the first half-brother, in the second series, was born, that daddy struck Henry James for the first time. All his life long he will remember the first blow, which like other blows subsequently struck came when there were no witnesses. Henry James was sitting on the floor in the dining-room at Priory Dene, looking at some books he had found in the sideboard. His mother was out. His stepfather came into the room, and walking past the boy on the floor, struck him a blow on the side of his head; saying nothing, he walked across the room and sat in his favourite armchair and began to read. Henry James's photographic memory does not recall the title of the book, but to this day he remembers that the name of the author was Marion Crawford. What strange tricks memory plays.

The little boy went creeping up the winding stairs to the nursery to Alice who sat by his side while he cried himself to sleep. Alice told him not to tell his mother and he did not. He cried again very soon because Alice went away. Alice wanted to go home to her own father who lived near Ipswich. That was the first sorrow the little boy knew, and it is as real and as poignant to him now as it was all those years back. He would neither eat nor sleep, but his sobs used to heave him up as he lay in bed with a night-light next to him, a flickering night-light that made fantastic shadows on the ceiling. Early in the morning before Alice or the other servants were up, the little boy used to creep downstairs and curl himself up outside his mother's bedroom, afraid to go in, because of his step-father, that once laughing man who had now turned into a growling menace. Mother did not know what to do. She said a new Nanny was coming and she was bringing him a beautiful present, but this did not appease him much. He remembers as if it were yesterday, his mother coming to the nursery one afternoon, tiny snow-flakes still on her, and she gave him a Noah's Ark.

The departure of Alice was followed by a series of new Nannies, all of whom brought presents, but there was obviously something wrong with life, some unseen person, God perhaps, who was unkind. There were fresh scenes at Priory Dene when the ne'er-do-well uncle turned up again and mother had to go to some prison or other to see him. Then life became more horrible and cruel on account of external things. There was talk at home of murder and tales perhaps not best fitted to the mind of a little boy whose imagination was already overheated.

When his parents were out in the evening and the baby in its bed in the night nursery on the top floor, Henry James had the whole darkened house to him-

self. The warm kitchen in the basement was his only
refuge; the little boy used to creep in there and listen
to cook and Jane discuss the Whitechapel murders.
It was fascinatingly horrible, the tales of the women
found dead in the dark street, and blood, blood everywhere. It seemed that anybody might be murdered,
their throats slit from ear to ear, the pillow soaked in
blood, because Jack might take it into his head to
enter a house, particularly a lonely house like this,
and murder us all in our beds. Is the chain on the
hook, Jane? And don't forget to take it off before we
goes up to bed, otherwise They won't be able to get in,
and now run off to bed, Master Harry. Master Harry
would wait and hope that one of them would go up
with him, but nobody did; then he would go up alone,
up the stone steps from the basement to the first floor;
that was all right, because the gas jet lit the staircase
up to the turn, then it was dark, dark, and the stairs
creaked.

The really bad part was passing the big window at
the turn of the carpeted stairs, because you could see
out into Greville Road where the fog made the gas-
lamp at the corner look all ghostly. One night just as
Master Harry was passing that window, a newsboy
came down the hill shouting: "'Orrible murder, another 'orrible Ripper murder"; the child fled panic-
stricken upstairs, while a voice going Kilburn-wards
continued to shout of the 'orrible murder.

Life was cruel in Priory Dene; kindness had gone
out of life altogether. Daddy had complete command
now; mother's family was poor, but daddy was doing
well in Hatton Garden; he was riding high; he could
laugh and sneer at "that old bankrupt" as he called
his father-in-law, but even daddy had a brief moment

of gentleness. Mother and her first-born were sitting in the dining-room sticking stamps in Harry's album, when there was the sound of a key in the front door—a sound never heard in the afternoon. Daddy came in slowly and said to mother that he had some bad news to tell; May was very ill. She had married the previous year in Johannesburg. She had had a baby, the baby was dead and May.... Mother jumped up screaming: "May is dead, my darling sister is dead". Daddy smoothed a crumpled telegram over the stamp album.

Henry James was sent to day school, but when the first holidays came round he did not do as the other boys did: he did not have holidays like them; he was made a boarder during holiday time because his parents went away and daddy did not want him home with his stepsister and brother.

After one more term it was decided to send Henry James to school at Ramsgate, small as he was still, nervous and high-strung; he had already learned many things they do not teach in school and one thing was something he was afraid to tell anybody about because it seemed so awful and wicked. Henry James discovered that by holding his breath and doing what is to-day called concentrating, he could become a double person, he was able to project himself outside his little body and see himself from outside; the second personality, the one that went outside was strong and could do things that he could not do when he was just one person, and as you will have guessed that Henry James is the author of this story, who unfortunately can no longer take those wonderful rides into limitless space and feel strong and powerful and capable of all things, Henry James will become the Ego and compère of this story.

I was unhappy at the thought of leaving home, not because home was the happy place where other boys seemed to live, but I loved my mother dearly and understood how she felt. Her story I knew thoroughly like some book I had read over and over again until I knew the story by heart. I knew she had married the second time, when I was a little more than three years old, because of her family. Her brothers, three of them, had borrowed money my father had left her and she had nothing to live on but the income from my money and that was not enough for both of us. I can see her as I write: a very proud-looking woman who looked fearless, but in reality she was as weak as water. She wanted to inspire affection and everybody did love her and took advantage of her good nature. Tradesmen robbed her barefacedly; everybody cheated her, and she laughed and ended on a sob.

My mother adored her family, they could do no wrong, although she knew her father had an unofficial wife and two unofficial children; her youngest and favourite brother was "no good", as they say; her eldest brother had married a lady from the Empire promenade and had tried to cut his throat while on his honeymoon at Brighton. Then he and his wife were reconciled to the family; they went to South Africa where after some years the uncle fell in love with a married woman and again tried to commit suicide, but his wife stuck to him all through his life and made him a marvellous wife. After many years in Africa he came back to London, completely "broke". My uncle borrowed £70 on his wife's jewellery and started a business which did well; when it did very well his wife died. He went to pieces. My mother was a woman of over sixty then and she had lost the sight of one eye entirely and had cataract in the other, but her indomitable spirit never left her and she would go to her brother's place of business and if he was not there and she thought he should be, she would go round the nearby public houses and wait for him and take him home. These things of course happened after I was packed off to Ramsgate.

My stepfather and my mother took me to the station where the head master, the Reverend Blank, was awaiting his charges. He was a short, lame man, and I remember my stepfather whispering: "Squeers" to my mother. I had not then begun to read Dickens and did not understand the allusion to the cruel head master, but before many weeks had passed I was to learn of the character of this merciless man who was in charge of about sixty boys.

Blank throughout term time was never seen without his cane, a slim wangee. Limping along he would take a slash at a passing boy, perhaps on the assumption that if the boy was doing nothing wrong at the moment he was sure to do something sooner or later. When the head master saw a boy standing on a form put there for some minor fault, he would slash at him, beating him about the body. Once after he had slashed a boy all over the body and there were several angry-looking welts across the boy's back, the boy's mother was announced. The head master's two daughters took the boy away and gave him milk and cakes and begged him not to tell his mother; they bribed him successfully. Once when we were being drilled in the playground, a boy was stood outside the ranks by the drill-sergeant because of inattention. The head master came out, as usual with his cane, and began to thrash the boy. A woman at a window

in a house overlooking the playground shouted abuse
at him and screamed she would tell the authorities.
The head master did not care; no inspector ever came
his way. We lived in an atmosphere of abject fear.
One of my school companions who stayed but a very
short time was named Belisha. In grown up life I
worked with him on the same newspaper until he
became a member of the Cabinet. His name to-day
is Leslie Hore-Belisha. There used to come back
sometimes an old boy, who looked morose, and who
used to play the piano to us. His name was Alphonse
Courlander; fifteen years afterwards I succeeded him
as Paris correspondent of the *Daily Express*.

When I went back to Priory Dene for the holidays,
I found I had a new baby stepbrother; but there was
another visitor: a seedy looking man was sitting in the
drawing-room looking at the red plush family album
which contained a photograph of Olga Nethersole,
who was supposed to be so like my mother. Nobody
told me who the seedy looking man was, but when I
was a little older I was told he was the "man in
possession", the broker's man. Things were going
wrong, my mother was in debt everywhere; she tried
to live in good style to please her husband; but she did
not have sufficient housekeeping money, although in
fairness to her husband it must be recorded that no
sum would have been sufficient; her money melted,
and the calls on her from her father were without mercy.

The broker's man did not stay long; my mother
recovered her spirits and took me to the annual
pantomime at the Grand Theatre, Islington, where
the genial Harry Randall was always the "Dame".
Sometimes during the holidays my mother would
give me a shilling and my omnibus fare and I would

go off to a matinée at the Oxford or the Tivoli and sit up in the gallery and see Dan Leno and Marie Lloyd and Little Tich and all the other stars of the day. I had fourpence a week pocket-money but a big appetite for entertainment. Every Saturday night my mother and stepfather went to the theatre, and I was alone all through those holiday Saturday nights. Kilburn Town Hall where they used to have Poole's Panorama from time to time became the Theatre Royal with good plays every week, but when the neighbourhood "went down", as they used to say, the theatre became a cheap music-hall. I could get in for threepence, but I never had threepence; when I was alone, my stepbrothers and sister asleep, and the servants downstairs, I used to steal into the day nursery where there was a moneybox on the mantelpiece; it was shaped like a red letterbox and it had V.R. in black letters in the front. I became a thief. I worked three pennies through the slit, then creeping downstairs I would go out to the music-hall and be home and in bed before my mother returned. It was the old type of music-hall; the serio-comic woman singer in silk tights with a contralto voice; red-nosed comedians with baggy umbrellas and songs about the lodger and twins. Very vulgar, but very human.

The Kilburn Music-hall afterwards became a cinema managed or owned by a local young man. Now he is a big figure in the British cinema world, famed as Sir Albert Clavering.

For breakfast at the Ramsgate school we were given a mixture of tea, coffee and cocoa; whatever was left over in one of the three steaming tin jars was poured into the others, so the breakfast beverage was always a surprise. The main dish was a small sardine, but there was plenty of moist bread and margarine. The midday meal consisted of tasteless meat, white haricot beans which rattled like pieces of metal when they dropped on a plate, and potatoes. The meal finished up with a suet pudding and a dollop of jam. For the evening meal the tables were laid with glasses of water and platters of bread and butter. The head master, with cane, used to come in unexpectedly sometimes and sit near the door and watch each boy as he filed past him up to bed. One night I secreted a piece of bread and butter beneath my buttoned coat. I must have trembled involuntarily as I passed the head master. "What have you there?" he thundered at me. Like a rabbit hypnotized by a snake, I produced the piece of incriminating evidence and had my hands lashed with the cane.

There were a few so-called parlour boarders who lunched at the Rev. Blank's table and took their evening meal in his private dining-room with his family. One term I slept in a dormitory on the first floor of the private house section of the building. Every night as we boys went up to bed, we could see delicious smelling victuals going in to the dining-room; how our mouths watered. One night, after I had been thrashed for hiding a slice of bread, I succumbed to temptation. There was an open dish of lovely floury potatoes standing unattended on a tray outside the dining-room door; the maid's attention was distracted. *Passant regardant*, as they say in heraldry, I seized a hot potato in my fingers and stuffed it into my mouth as I began to climb the stairs. There were merry voices on the other side of the dining-room door; the voices were suddenly louder, as I turned to see the door open and the head master framed against the light, looking at me. He said nothing; but ten minutes later he was in the dormitory laying into me with the cane.

Another boy and I, he is a prosperous underwriter at Lloyds now, made up our minds to run away to London; we had no money and no idea of the way, but we both knew the way to Margate, which is four miles distant from Ramsgate. One half holiday, directly after lunch, we climbed the playground wall and started off, running and walking the four miles. We spent the afternoon in Margate and then made up our minds to return and take our beating. We jog-trotted back all the way, climbed the wall back into the playground and crept into the dining-room as the boys sat down to bread and margarine. Our absence had not been noticed.

During the holidays I used to beg to be taken away, but my stepfather would not hear of it. Then he paid his first visit, an unexpected one, to the school. He saw the filthy latrines, the unkempt appearance of the boys, compared with the lovely private house and well-kept garden which the parents were always shown when they "inspected" the school. My stepfather told my mother to remove me at once. She did, and I believed the gates of heaven were opening for me, but I was wrong.

# CHAPTER II

## VALE, VICTORIA

I SAW Queen Victoria for the first time in June, 1897, when she drove to St. Paul's for the celebration of her Diamond Jubilee. London was very rich in those days, and very poor too, but, as people used to say: "God bless the rich, the poor can work," and work they did and how they used to drink. Every bank holiday was a drunken orgy, and of course the public houses were open all day during the week days. On bank holidays the streets were full of drunken women, fighting with each other when they were not fighting the men. Opposite Priory Dene was a short street of slum houses; what battles went on there. The women either wore men's caps or black straw hats called boaters, pinned with long pins to their piled-up hair. Before they fought, they carefully unpinned their hats, because part of the fight consisted of getting the fingers entwined in the hair and tugging. People liked to laugh a lot in those last years of the Victorian era, but they liked tears too; the Princess' Theatre in Oxford Street was the home of melodrama, often translated from the French, which provided laughter and tears. "Two Little Vagabonds" was a play typical of the public taste at the time when the old Queen drove through the streets of her capital to St. Paul's. My grandfather used to tell stories about the Queen's younger days, when she was not so popular, because

she hardly ever stayed in London. My grandfather
said there was some comic paper of the period which
published a picture of the Queen driving past Buck-
ingham Palace and poking her coachman in the back
as she asked him, pointing with her umbrella: "Who
lives there?"

Queen Mary in those days was known as Princess
May of Teck. She was engaged to the Duke of
Clarence, who died, and then she became engaged to
his brother and married him and became the Duchess
of York. In thousands of nurseries throughout England, there was a picture called Four Generations.
There was the old Queen seated and nursing a baby
(the future King Edward VIII); beside her stood
two bearded men: her son, Albert Edward Prince of
Wales and his son, the future King George V.

We moved from Priory Dene to a large house in
Maida Vale, a corner house with a mews behind it.
There were as many fights there as there had been in
Goldsmith's Place, the street of slum houses already
mentioned. The nursery on the top floor, like other
nurseries of the period, had the walls covered with
pictures from the Christmas annuals; *Pears* was a
favourite; it produced the famous Bubbles; but
perhaps just as famous were the pictures in *Tit Bits'*
*Annual*; they had what they called companion pictures.
One year would be the picture of a boy from a fish
shop, a basket full of succulent looking salmon and
other fish; the boy was delivering the fish to a large
house, he left his basket for a moment while he took a
look at *Tit Bits*; meanwhile a cat crept up and began
to eat the fish.

We had to wait a whole year for the sequel:
the boy sees the cat and jumps up in alarm

and tries to throw his cap at the retreating animal.

Hatton Garden and the diamond trade prospered exceedingly at this time; there were grand parties in Maida Vale and six weeks holiday in the summer at the seaside. When the time of the Jubilee came round, my stepfather took my mother and myself to see the procession from a room which he shared with some friends in the Borough; his own pleasure was damped because one of his friends with whom he went to South Africa in the early eighties, Barney Barnato, committed suicide by jumping overboard from a ship while *en route* to London for the Jubilee. Barnato, born in Whitechapel, became a millionaire, and was building himself a house in Park Lane when he went crazy. Barnato was the foundation for several stage characters; Willie Edouin played the part of a millionaire called Hoggenheimer, in a play called "The Girl from Kays". He had a catch phrase: "I'm not rude, I'm rich." When Beerbohm Tree played the principal part in "Business is Business", a translation of "*Les Affaires sont Les Affaires*", Tree also had the eccentric millionaire in mind, and by clever stage play created the suggestions that the millionaire he was portraying had at some time been a conjuror, which was what Barnato had been: an illusionist. He was, I believe, the originator of the "Missing Lady" act. I loved the theatre and more particularly back stage. With a cousin I made the acquaintance of Willie Clarkson; we used to roam about his storerooms in his Wellington Street premises. Many years later I became Clarkson's biographer.

Looking backwards, a pleasant but useless thing to do, I can understand how that year 1897 was the top notch of England's glory. It was two years before the beginning of the Boer War. John Bull looked up and saw no cloud across the sky. England had the greatest navy in the world, and even if the nations were jealous of England, what of it? The Jubilee must have been the outward sign of Britain's prosperity. Detachments of troops from every colony and possession marched in front of the old Queen. Behind her carriage rode proud Indian princes, rubies of fantastic size in their turbans and ropes of pearls round their necks. On one side of her rode her son, the elderly Prince of Wales, and on the other Lord Wolsey, Commander-in-Chief of her forces, and the Queen, sitting on a springed cushion, bowed to the right and left, smiling beneath her lace parasol, the Queen of the greatest Empire since the time of the old Romans. But the twilight was nearer than anybody knew.

Although there were signs of outward prosperity, life at home was no better. I went to day school, University College School in Gower Street, where I found that I was absolutely unfitted for school work there. The foundation I had had at Ramsgate was puerile; I could read and write, but my writing was shocking. The money my mother received from the Court of Chancery was more than sufficient to pay for my schooling; I cost my stepfather nothing at all; but he could not abide me, he never had a kind word for me and it seemed that every mouthful of food I ate in his presence was too much. He would take no notice of me, except if I spoke, and then he immediately contradicted. He wanted to show my mother and me too that I was a perfect fool. I was moved out of the nursery. A third half-brother had now been born and I had a room to myself on the same floor as the room shared by my mother and my stepfather, which adjoined a dressing-room used by him. Often and often I used to hear my stepfather shout from his dressing-room to my mother in her bedroom: "You had better see that your boy has his money properly invested, because he will never be able to earn his own living; he is a complete blockhead."

Blockhead, blockhead, blockhead, round and round and round, like a kitten chasing its tail, like a never-ending saga of sadness, I was a perfect fool; I must be, because he said so, he was successful, so he knew. He was very clever, he said so himself; if he had not been a diamond merchant, he would have been a great engineer, he told my mother, who told me. Now he was making money, he changed his style of life, he came home in the evening when he liked; sometimes he would arrive about seven-thirty and rave because the dinner was not ready; other nights he would come in at nine o'clock. If my mother dared to ring for a maid to serve dinner, he would stop her and shout: "We will ring when I tell you to, not before."

Maids in those days were slaves; they stuck it then, but they would not nowadays. There was a nurse, the cook and two other maids in the house; the maids shared a room on the top floor. They came down at six-thirty in the morning and spent their days in the basement; there was a steep flight of stone stairs going up to the first floor and then another steep flight from the first to the second floor; every scuttle of coal had to be carried up by hand; every bit of food had to be carried up; the maids never went to bed before eleven or eleven-thirty at night. My stepfather became fastidious with his food. My mother sat opposite to him trembling, waiting for him to pronounce judgment on the first mouthful; if it was all right, there was peace for the remainder of the evening.

There were still money troubles; my mother was always short of money to pay her tradesmen's bills, because she was still giving money away, as well as food, which went from our house to any distressed people in the neighbourhood of whom she knew. There was always my grandfather in the background, she used to see him in secret at an office he had, where he ran an estate agency, in a street off lower Regent Street. He would come to the house in the mornings sometimes, after his son-in-law had gone to Hatton Garden, and my mother would give him money, although he had an allowance from a rich sister, a widow who lived in Russell Square with a female companion, a gurgling pug dog called Nellie and a brougham. Aunt Louisa, the hope of the family, my great aunt who walked with an ebony stick, like the old ladies in plays. She was austere and frightening, but as I was to discover late in life, as silly as her pet dog.

My grandmother died while she was living separated from my grandfather; she was living in a boarding-house in a street off the High Road, Kilburn; but he went gaily on living until he was nearly eighty-five. It is told how when he was around eighty, one of his sons said to him: "Guv'nor, tell me, at what age does a man cease to want a woman," and my grandfather replied: "I don't know, my boy."

Members of the family came and went, trundling out in horse omnibuses from the East End, to see my stepfather, and from Russell Square, from Bayswater and from nearby Maida Vale, to see my mother. Uncle Moss, with his sly twinkling eyes, probably thinking of the winners of the three-thirty but asking you in a mocking voice: "Do you like Paris?" and Cousin Lizzie, falling fast asleep whenever she sat down, or awake, peering through her pince-nez at a world which never seemed to be quite right.

Every morning with my school bag I would be sent off to Gower Street, I had to walk or take the omnibus to Edgware Road, and then to use my season ticket on the smoky, sulphurous underground. I was given fourpence a day for my lunch, which I spent on sweets and fruit at the school tuck shop; I used to walk to Edgware Road and back to save the pennies to buy newspapers. I joined the School Cadet Corps, attached to the London Rifle Brigade whose head-quarters were in Bunhill Row, in the City, where we used to go and drill one night a week with the Brigade. My, I can still smell the hops from some nearby brewery in the Bunhill Row district.

In the summer I went to the Public School Camp at Aldershot, and was there during the first part of the Boer war, when Sir Redvers Buller, after the Colenso fiasco, was brought back and put in command at Aldershot. I was very tiny for my age and must have looked comic in a towering shako and cock's feathers and a full pack and carbine, when Sir Redvers, look-ing very beery and unsteady on his legs, inspected us one church parade. He stopped in front of me and tried to get me into focus, and blustered, all in one word: "Howold'sthatboy?"

There were letters to the papers from indignant parents because we went out for a night attack with the Regulars and were knee-deep in water all night, but we were different from the Harrow Corps in adjacent lines. When the officer of the day came round and asked if there were any complaints, a Harrow youth complained that the ginger beer bottles had burst.

London was grand during the Boer war, fiercely patriotic. We all wore buttons with the photographs of our favourite generals, and we all had khaki handkerchiefs and ties. The evening papers used to come out with posters announcing victories in battles which were never fought; the war was so far away that people thought of it as a sort of picnic, although when there were a series of bad defeats and Roberts and Kitchener were sent "out" people did begin to take things seriously for a bit, but not for long. The City of London Yeomanry, the C.I.V.'s for short, and called in the city: "Chamberlain's Innocent Victims" (that meant Joe Chamberlain) went to South Africa but they soon came back. Our Cadet Corps was posted as a guard of honour in King's Street, leading to the Guildhall, where the home-coming regiment was to be given the Freedom of the City. The regiment was supposed to arrive at the Guildhall about midday, but it came straggling along in twos and threes about tea-time. Long before then, we boys, almost fainting with hunger and fatigue, as we had paraded in the early morning with a heavy kit, had our ranks broken by the surging crowd, but we were cheered when we read the next morning that the crowd had broken through the ranks of the Regulars lining the route and prevented the C.I.V.'s reaching the Guildhall at the scheduled time.

The school was told that the old Queen wanted her subjects to see her and that she would undertake several drives through the streets of London. The Boer War and its defeats and its scandals had taken a heavy toll of the old lady's reserve of energy. In the autumn of 1900 we boys left school early to go into a street near Albany Street, and there see the Queen drive past. That was the second and last time I saw her, very old looking and very frail, hardly moving as the open carriage swayed, and looking as if she were waiting for the end.

A few weeks after this drive which left a deep impression in the minds of all those who saw it, my stepfather's mother died. His father was already dead. I sat next to him in the funeral carriage. He cried all the way and told us he had one regret concerning his mother. Once when he was small and lived in White's Row in Whitechapel, he was playing with the boys and saw his mother coming along from the market carrying a basket of provisions and he made the boys move into another street, pretending not to see his mother coming because he was ashamed of her.

In January 1901 Queen Victoria died. I remember that winter evening, when the bells tolled the passing of the Queen; my mother and I stood by an open window in the hall and listened to the bells; my mother began to weep softly. While she was crying my stepfather came home, the sound of his key grating in the lock always gave me near-heart failure. He asked my mother why she was crying and she told him. He burst into a rage because she was crying for the death of Queen Victoria, but when his mother died, he said, she never shed a tear.

While the Boer War was still raging arrangements were made for me to go to school in Germany, near Hanover; my mother had fixed up with the parents of

another boy that I should go with him. We were both
to go to a boarding school and my mother and the
father and mother of the other boy were to go to
Germany with us. When my mother saw the school
she did not like it, it was more like a prison than a
school. She suggested to my friend's parents that we
should be placed with a private family of whom she
knew in Hanover, and that we should attend a day
school. It was agreed. I went to live with a music
teacher named Rose and his family in the Nikolai-
strasse in Hanover, opposite the English church. I
shared a room with my friend and went to a school
across the Jahrmarkt, a school consisting of two rooms
with large peat-heated white porcelain stoves; the
windows were always closed throughout the whole
winter. I can still smell the almost indescribable smell,
a mixture of badly washed humanity, sweat-soaked
clothes and slates which were washed with spittle. In
that drowsy atmosphere I sat in class and listened to
words not one of which I understood. The master
droned on, occasionally breaking out to swear at a
boy "*donnerwetter, noch ein Tausend noch einmal,*" which
sounded fairly complete. In the flat where I lodged,
there were the father and mother and three children,
a boy and two girls, the younger always walking
around the flat with her filthy dirty panties hanging
down. Her mother could never forget that she was
not born to take in lodgers and would tell at every meal
how she came from a good family. Her husband used
to prowl around and every time he saw me he would
exclaim automatically: "Write me a couple of hundred
sentences". I did not learn much German at this
stage, but I began to learn about Life. My friend and
I used to see every afternoon about five o'clock a

number of women walking slowly along the pavement outside the house in which we were living; my friend asked me what they were doing, dragging their feet along so slowly and stopping every few paces. I said that these women must be the wives of workmen meeting their husbands on the way home from work, and I believed what I said. It was not until I heard my German schoolmates calling them "Louis's" (why I don't know) that I learned the truth. None of my German school companions knew any English, but many knew enough of English obscenity.

As the Boer War dragged along to a close, and the path to victory became more difficult, so did the presence of English boys in Hanover become difficult. We were followed in the streets and jeered at; people used to shout words about the brave Boers and the cowardly English. I got a black eye while attempting to answer words with blows. Then I obtained permission to leave the little school where I was learning nothing and go to an Oberrealschule where they did teach. I was completely humiliated when I was made to attend the English class, when the master, a Herr Fischer, used to show off his knowledge by addressing me in what he thought was English. He used to greet me thus: "Hello, mixed pickles W.C." Then he would reminisce about a visit which he said he had paid to London. He told the class about a comic paper called, he said, *Pickpocket*, and it was only years afterwards I discovered he meant a paper of those days called *Pick-Me-Up*. At this school I mixed with both German and foreign youths much older than myself; they were great dandies, some of them. One, a boy named Wulf, was the son of the famous circus proprietor of those days; the circus used to go to the

Crystal Palace once a year and Wulf told us that his father lived in a palace, that he was so constipated he had a lavatory fitted up as a library. Another boy was the son of the Chief of Police of Pretoria, a Boer; it was exciting to be on friendly terms with an enemy. All these dandies had their girl friends and they lived in rooms "on their own" and went to cafés where I was not allowed to go, except with Herr Rose, who never went anywhere. On Sundays I had to walk miles through the forests, tramping with all the members of the Rose family, and then we sat in a beer garden, drinking coffee and eating cakes which Frau Rose had brought with her. Sometimes I used to slip away to a beer garden on my own and listen to the military band and the conversations. Young as I was, I was rising sixteen, I began to understand the German jealousy and hatred of England; the burden of conversation was always the same: One day . . . . The day . . . . I used to hang about "back stage" whenever I could, especially at the Mellini Music Hall, a famous one in those days, where I used to meet all the best known American and Continental "turns". Carl Hertz, the Illusionist, used to take me back to his "digs" and teach me his tricks. That was grand. In the summer my mother and my stepfather came to Germany. Although when I was at Ramsgate they were often in the neighbourhood, my stepfather never allowed my mother to see me, so I never expected to see her in Germany. She came as I say, but later I learned that she even came to Germany while I was there, to see an oculist, but she never came to see me. This holiday in Germany was a happy one though; my stepfather said he did not like the Ger-

mans; I knew afterwards that he had made his own
plans in England, and he went back home. My mother
and I wandered along the Rhine, and had a happy
time together. She said she was glad my future was
assured; my stepfather was going to take me into his
own business in Hatton Garden. "My future" always
worried my mother and me, for we both knew, we
had been told it so often, that I was absolutely stupid
and could never amount to anything; now everything
seemed all right, my mother had in effect paved the
way for me to become a diamond merchant, because
she had encouraged me to learn about precious stones,
and that jovial Tom Evans of Hatton Garden had
given me an ivory and morocco case which contained
a set of various precious stones, cut and uncut; it was
very attractive, but not as valuable as I thought,
because I pawned it some years later and did not
obtain much for it.

I stayed on in Hanover for a year, then I thought I
would give my mother a surprise by arriving a day
earlier than she expected. I wore, I remember, a
broad-brimmed black hat, we all affected those in our
circle in Hanover, as I walked up the garden path to
the front door, I heard my mother exclaim through
the open window: "Good God, there's Charlie." She
was talking to my grandfather. Charlie was the name
of the ne'er-do-well brother of my mother's.

I was hoping to start work at once in my stepfather's
business, but nothing happened. I could never speak
to him, never ask him anything direct, so anything I
wanted to know from him had to be asked through my
mother, and she had to choose her moment and her
words very carefully. Finally she managed to ask him
when I could start working with him; the answer was

that I was not going to work with him. His was a purely personal business, so he said, which may have been true, but my hopes were dashed. I was sure to be a failure. I had nothing to look forward to at all. Then one day my stepfather came home and said I was to go to work as a clerk with a firm of chartered accountants named Bowden, Smiles & Co. in Lawrence Poultney Hill, just off Cannon Street, in the City of London. I was not a clerk, I was an office boy. My job was to take the letters to the post, after copying them in the press; how I hated that part of my work, damping the sheets and putting in a piece of carbon paper and then putting the letter-book beneath the press, and turning it and smudging the letters and being cursed by the head clerk. I was paid ten shillings a week, but there must have been some sort of an arrangement for the firm to teach me something about accountancy, because I was sent sometimes with a clerk out on an audit. My firm specialized in auditing the books of firms engaged in the electrical engineering trade, but they had one very good account, that was Mainprice and Lord, a firm of chain wine stores, with headquarters at New Cross.

One bitterly cold winter I was sent with a clerk to do the audit at New Cross. It was way down below zero when we arrived and set to work in the wine cellars where the firm kept the account books. I can see that clerk plainly, he looked more like a fox than most foxes do, and he taunted me with being a "gentleman" which, God knows, I was not, and not knowing anything about my job, which was entirely true. I wrote very badly and untidily, and I could not add up properly; I hated the work anyway. We were so cold that we could not hold our pens; the youths working in the cellars, whistling cheerfully while they bottled and corked the wine, looked at us curiously. We went out to lunch at an A.B.C. and came back more frozen than ever. About four o'clock one of the youths came over with a bottle and said: " 'Ave a drop of this, it will warm yer up." We 'ad, I should say had some of whatever it was, port, I think, and then another good fellow brought us something else, I guess it was brandy; then several fellows brought over bottles, so we kept having drops of this and that and felt decidedly better and warmer for it. A whole army corps of youths came with thousands of bottles and stood all round us while we kept on having drops. We sang with them, then it seemed that the work became lighter; the figures were no longer difficult to control; they added themselves up, but not that alone: they danced quadrilles; they joined hands down the middle and set to partners, as I tried to explain to my companion who was crooning gently to his books, telling the figures to be good little fellows and not to jump about so.

But all of a sudden it was time to go home; it seemed that the next minute I was in bed in Maida Vale. Disgrace attended me all around. I said I did not like the work, anyhow, which was quite true. Once again I was at a loose end, doing nothing, lounging round the house, an utter, utter failure.

I read *David Copperfield* and saw a fancied likeness to myself; but David turned out a success; where was I going to achieve success? I tried to become a commercial traveller with a firm of fancy goods manufacturers, on a commission basis, but I was no good, quite definitely no good; I never sold a thing. I must have been so miserable looking that no buyer ever wanted to talk to me, let alone buy from me; in the jargon of to-day, I had an inferiority complex, badly; I was no good and I knew I was no good. I might as well die, and often I wished I could. This bedroom of mine was my supreme refuge; I used to sit in the morning room for a few minutes after supper, then kissing my mother good night would go up to my room. It was bitterly cold there; of course I had no fire or any sort of heat. The room was lit by a gas jet, from near the window; my bed was near the door: it was not easy to read. Often it was so cold I was afraid to get undressed; I would lie on my bed and fall asleep; then wake up frozen and have to undress anyhow. To add to my general misery I became a victim of rheumatism, although I was only seventeen I was crippled; sometimes my ankles were in such a state I could not walk; the pain in my shoulders prevented me raising my arms.

In my bedroom was a big brown wardrobe in which my stepfather kept his clothes. When he came in the first thing in the morning to fetch a suit, he managed to do his daily good deed by cursing me; he always managed to find something for which he could curse me. When I was crippled and moved with difficulty, that was his big moment, I was shamming, of course. One morning he asked me some question or other; when I replied he said: "Who do you think you are, the bloody Prince of Wales?" (he was referring to the gentleman who became George V).

There was a far away branch of the family, cousins of my mothers, with whom my mother had not been on friendly terms, but while I was in Hanover, they had become reconciled. That family consisted of father and mother and daughter; she was sweet. I fell in love with her and intended to marry her; we adored each other. Her father had inherited a wholesale bag and trunk business from his father-in-law, who was also his uncle. He took pity on me when he saw me moping about, doing nothing but hang around his daughter. One day he asked me if I would like to go into his business, in Red Cross Street. I jumped at the opportunity. I was to start at ten shillings a week, but if he had offered me five I should have accepted it just the same.

Once again I became a city gent. My mother allowed me to have a pound a week of my own money, so with thirty shillings a week income, I was passing rich, but there was a snag. I was put into the counting house, where I was no good at all. Then I was made a warehouseman; though all of us had to work pretty hard, I as a relation was expected to stay on until eight and later at night and all Saturday afternoons. I struggled up ladders with trunks on my back and piled them up; I could do that without falling down the ladder after I learned the knack. I went up and down the stone staircase with huge leather trunks on my back, and worked as a nigger is supposed to work, but does not. My cousin was very old-fashioned, when he saw I was carrying a cane to business, he said it looked bad; he told me I should carry an umbrella. I did not care; I struggled along and had my salary raised to fifteen shillings a week, but I knew I was getting nowhere; if I stayed on I might be a warehouseman all my life. My mother used to say to me: "Make yourself indispensable." Yes, but how? I did not know, all I knew was to work hard.

There were a number of "cards" working in that warehouse in Red Cross Street. There was a fellow named Bolton, the head packer, who had a bitter sense of humour. "I dreamed I was dead last night," he used to relate, "straight I did, and I went to Heaven and there was St. Peter, and St. Peter says to me, he says,: 'where have you been working,' and I spoke up to St. Peter and I says, 'where have I been working,' I says, 'I have been working for twenty years at Lyons & Co. in Red Cross Street. Then St. Peter says 'Bolton, come in, you must be tired'."

Tired we were, all of us and I especially. Then other combers began to swell around me. Matters at home were going from bad to worse. There were always rows about money. My stepfather sometimes used to relate the lunches he ate at the "Bell" in Holborn; he used, he said, to dip his fork in some caviare and then spear an oyster and swallow it. No wonder my mother on the allowance he made her found it passing difficult to cater on that standard; she tried valiantly, but rarely did she please him. For herself, she never asked a thing, which was fortunate, because she would not have had it. When she was almost in rags and needed a new dress, one of her woman friends who was not afraid of my stepfather, one of the rare ones, had to go and plead for a dress for my mother.

I noticed my mother was crying now more than ever, and I begged and nagged her to tell me what was the matter, what was more especially the matter now. She had pawned her jewelry and she was afraid my stepfather would find out. She, as a diamond merchant's wife, had numerous pieces of jewelry; I do not know whether it was all very valuable, but it was pretty. I remember quite a number of bracelets, also a red enamel heart with a frame of diamonds round it, and a diamond in the centre; yet another heart entirely composed of diamonds; then there was a profile of a woman cut from a moonstone, with a diamond hat and a diamond bodice. Pretty they were, all these things, and some of them must have been valuable, as we shall see.

The jewels were pawned with a firm called Thompson, in the High Road, Kilburn. The manager was a man named Hart, who was kind to my mother, so she said. She pleaded with him to lend her some of the jewels over the week-end; he did. Then she would send him a bottle of port as a present, or something for his wife. I was brought into service, now I knew the skeleton in the cupboard. I used to go and ask for the jewels and take them back to the pawnshop myself early Monday morning before I went to Red Cross Street. There were dramatic moments, however. Sometimes on a Saturday night, when my mother and my stepfather were dressing to go to the theatre, my stepfather would call out to my mother from his dressing-room: "Maud, I haven't seen you wearing that little heart brooch lately." Then my mother would fetch me and whisper and I would creep down the stairs and go out of the side door so that I should not be heard and run up the High Road and see Mr. Hart and borrow the heart brooch and come running back to my mother who would casually pin the brooch on her bodice and say nothing.

When the demands of my grandfather became too exigent, I had to make a trip during the week as well, to pawn a piece of jewelry for my mother so that I could bring back some ready money; the same thing used to happen when a tradesman became too insistant, threatening a summons. In the daytime I used to work, harder and harder, later and later, because

I wanted to be something like a success; then the storm burst.

In order to keep on friendly terms with some of the buyers in Wood Street, my cousin would give them cases of wine and he always had whisky and soda on tap in his private office, in case a buyer should drop in on his way home; some of these buyers in those days were very heavy drinkers. I was working in the warehouse late one night, packing up some order for the morrow, while in my cousin's office a buyer who was drunk when he called was continuing to drink. My stepfather arrived on his way to Liverpool Street where he was taking the night service to the Continent; he wanted to see my cousin about something or other; he came face to face with the drunken buyer. I heard nothing of what happened in the office; I went on packing. My stepfather came out and as he passed me he said: "You are leaving here at the end of the week."

That was the end of all my hopes for a fine future, my hopes of marrying my cousin and perhaps one day succeeding to the business. I went home and told my mother. I was to leave on the following Saturday, and I made up my mind to kill myself that Saturday night. I bought a length of rubber tubing which I was going to fix to the gas jet; it seemed quite simple, but I made one miscalculation, I did not know how fast the express delivery of letters could be. I had a bad attack of rheumatism that week. I went home early on the Saturday and wrote a letter of farewell to my cousin. My mother and stepfather went to the theatre, I said I was going to the Metropolitan Music Hall in Edgware Road. I remember that the pain in my ankles was so bad that I could not stand up at the end of the programme, but had to be helped up by an attendant. Then I went home to commit suicide. In the hall I found waiting for me, my cousin. My letter had been received too early, or too late, I am not sure which.

Once again I was branded as a failure; once again I heard disputes concerning myself; I was no good and my mother should see that my money was properly invested, when at the age of twenty-one I came into possession of it, because never would I be able to do anything in life, that was definite. My mother did not answer; what could she answer? My stepfather now took another decision: I was to be articled to a tailor; he found one who would take me; he had premises nearly next door to Queen's Hall. There I was sent, to be an articled apprentice. I found there was no business doing, or rather not much, certainly not enough to enable me to learn anything about the tailoring trade, but such few suits and ladies' costumes as the tailor did make, I had to deliver on my bicycle. I went skidding along all over the tramlines of North London, but I learned nothing; trade decreased so rapidly that I was not surprised when I arrived one morning and found the shop closed and the tailor in the bankruptcy court.

Once again I had nothing to do, nothing but to watch my mother cry. Matters seemed worse and I wanted to know what was particularly the matter. Gradually I obtained the story. Mr. Hart was leaving the pawnbrokers; and it was not likely that the new manager would be as complacent as Mr. Hart. My mother would not be able to borrow her jewelry over the week-end, and my stepfather would be sure to find out. I asked my mother how much she owed the pawnbrokers; she did not know. Was it a hundred pounds? Oh, more. Was it two hundred pounds? Yes, it might be about that. Then I took a decision. I went to the pawnbrokers and I said I had come from my mother who wanted to redeem all her jewelry; what was the amount owing? The pawnbroker asked me to take a seat while he looked through his books. Then he handed me a slip of paper on which was written these figures: £424. I was staggered, flabbergasted. I told my mother, but she did not seem very impressed. I was nineteen years old now. I said that somehow I would find the money and redeem her jewels. I started walking into the offices of West-End moneylenders and asked them to lend me the money. I explained I was a ward in Chancery and had £3000 to come to me in two years time, but no moneylender would do business with me. Then I remembered a very rich cousin of my mother's, the son of one of the original founders of the De Beer's Company. To him I went and told the whole story. He was sympathetic, he agreed to lend me the money for the purpose of redeeming my mother's jewels. He made me insure my life for the sum of £1000, in his favour. He made me sign a document which bound me to pay the premium on the insurance every year and two-and-a-half per cent per annum on the £424 he lent me, and the document said I was to repay the capital sum when I received my money at the age of twenty-one. He was doing business with a minor and he was right to take precautions. I took his cheque and cashed it and went to the pawnbroker and said that I had the money with me, in notes. I wanted I said to take the jewels away at once. I took them wrapped up in a pocket handkerchief which I stuffed into my pocket and walked on air all the way home to Maida Vale.

My mother was in the nursery with my young stepbrothers. I said I wanted to speak to her for a minute. She came outside on the landing and stood by a wooden gate which prevents small children falling downstairs. I handed her the handkerchief and told her to look inside. She burst into tears and hugged and kissed me. I asked her to promise me she would never pawn her jewels again, and she swore on her children's heads she would not. I was satisfied, happier than I had ever been, before or since.

My stepfather came home that night and said I was to be apprenticed to another tailor, one Alexander Cameron, at 19 Old Burlington Street. Cameron was a Scot from Coldstream. He was a hard-working little man who never quite caught up with his debts. He wore pince-nez and was very nervous. He owned a gold watch and chain; the watch never, during the two years I stayed with him, worked, but it had its uses. When a customer was choosing a suit and asked the price, Cameron would dash down the tiny shop, dash back and look at the face of his stilled watch and say: "£4 5s. 6d."

We were a curious crew in that little shop which consisted of a tiny show room on the ground floor with a miniature fitting-room at the back, and a basement where the assistant and I worked. There was another youth named Hempson, who combined the job of a bookkeeper and errand-boy. His mother was a wardress in Holloway jail. The assistant's name was William Drakeford, the son of a tailor in India. Drakeford, who comes again into this narrative, in circumstances certainly unusual, was religiously inclined and would have long discussions with me; but sometimes we would both go to a music hall, then Drakeford would say it was possible to serve both God and Mammon. Drakeford was engaged to a girl living at Ashford, in Kent, and saw no prospect of marrying her. But marry her he did. I never saw her then, but I thought I knew her, and when years afterwards I did see her, when she was living in Turkey, I realized I never knew her at all. When Drakeford left he was succeeded by a young man who was sentenced to six weeks imprisonment for stealing one of Cameron's suits instead of delivering it. He was succeeded by another young man who was blackmailed for years by a nurse he and I met one evening walking across Hyde Park.

Upstairs over the shop was living a Dr. Jackson Lang, a handsome man who was medical advisor to the National Sporting Club and the Actors' Association, so we prisoners in the basement used to see a lot of high life going up and down the stairs. Among our customers was Ben Davies, the tenor.

My stepfather was among our customers too. Then the rich aunt in Russell Square offered to pay for a frock-coat suit for my grandfather, who was her brother. I used to see my grandfather sometimes when I went out to tea. I fetched him in his office off Lower Regent Street, and took him to tea at a Lyons. He used to borrow half-crowns from me quite affably, but he taught me chess. My grandfather talked about the suit and ordered it from Cameron, but never paid him and he owed the money for two years. After I left, Cameron took a judgment summons out against him.

Sometimes I would go to have a cup of tea at the

public-house opposite the shop, kept by a cheerful
fellow named Freeman. He used to say his new house
was near the training grounds. The Metropolitan
trains behind. We were, as you will notice, simple
folk, but we had loads of fun. There was an old
broken-down actor who used to come round singing.
He had a song with a lugubrious chorus which went
something like this:

"It's money, it's for money that the parson
     says his prayers,
It's money, money, money everywhere."

That always started another argument with Drakeford.

Time was getting on; I was nearing the end of my
two years' apprenticeship, and nearing the time when
I should come into my inheritance, and nearing most
of all the moment when I should have to repay my
cousin the money I had borrowed to redeem my
mother's jewels. I had no idea what I should do when
I became of age, but I had heard of a tailoring job in
Paris, and flirted with the idea of trying to get it.
Then a bombshell burst. My mother told me that as
a great favour to me my stepfather would take my
money and invest it in his business. I was horrified.
For two years, from the age of nineteen to twenty-one,
when most of the young men I knew were having a
good time, prior to embarking on the more serious
things in life, I had been handicapped with a debt I
had assumed. I had to pay out of the interest I
received on my own money, the interest on the loan
from my cousin and the insurance premium; I had
very little left over, a few shillings only for my clothes

and amusements. I was looking forward to a freer, easier life when I came into my money; now I was not to see a penny of it, except such interest as my step-father liked to pay me. More particularly, what was I to tell my cousin? My mother did not know. I went again to my cousin and begged him to allow me to go on paying interest on the loan, and to let the loan continue for awhile; he agreed, but I was sick at heart. My twenty-first birthday was a day of horror and despair.

One of the South African uncles, whose marriage I have referred to, was now back in London. I told him the story of my despair and of my difficulties. His advice was: "Whenever you can lay your hands on a few bob, I advise you to get out of this." I thought of the job in Paris, rushed to get particulars and arranged to go over and spend a Sunday there and try and fix up the job.

# CHAPTER III

## SO I WENT TO PARIS

I FELT I was free at last, because life and adventure lay before me. I was escaping to Paris from bonds which had held me prisoner since babyhood. I had little doubt about getting that job, whatever it was worth, but in any case I was to receive £75 a year interest from my stepfather in return for the use of my money in his business. As against that, out of the money I was to get as income, I had to pay interest on the loan from my cousin and the annual premium on the life-insurance contracted in his favour. Nevertheless . . . twenty-one . . . Paris.

I wrote to the tailor in Paris; he had an establishment in the rue Royale; he told me to call on him at eleven o'clock on a Sunday morning. There were Sunday excursions to Paris in those days via Newhaven and Dieppe. The third class return fare was seventeen shillings; one left Saturday night and returned Sunday night, a whole day in Paris! What is the use of going to Paris unless you can spend a night there, leered my friends, but I did not care. I thought of Paris as the great unknown; beautiful girls . . . tall trees . . . a winding river . . . a quiet retreat overlooking the water, but it took me exactly thirty years finding that retreat overlooking the trees and the river.

I started out for Paris one rough night in October

51

1908. There were paddle steamers only then, and the crossing of the Channel took about five hours, five hours of misery and hopeless sea-sickness. Then a short railway journey and Paris. Paris in the dawn.

Because it was Sunday, the centre of the city was quiet, but it was Sunday in Paris. Everything and everybody seemed so happy; people looked like they were really enjoying themselves. It was a St. Martin's summer that October, and the sun was shining, the trees were golden and bronze; I was like a man suddenly ejected from prison into paradise. As I walked through the sunny streets, watching the happy looking couples, I thought of my own home in London. I saw my mother sitting opposite my stepfather, humbly watching him eat the first mouthful of food, watching to see what he would say and do; whether he would stamp out of the room, or whether he would say nothing at all, which would be an indication of his approval.

I remembered the party which had been given by my mother and stepfather shortly before I came away. It appeared that my grandfather had informed my mother that his unofficial wife had threatened to go to the house and create a scene. I was instructed by my mother to remain in the hall, pretending that I was there to look after the lights, in case a fuse blew out; in reality to rush to the front door if the lady materialized.

I walked about Paris from the dawn until it was time for me to go in and interview my prospective employer. I just wandered, thrilled every moment, when I discovered a street named as it was at the time of Dumas's romances. I stood and almost ate the Louvre up with my eyes; I pictured d'Artagnan fighting the Cardinal's Guards on the stairs. I made up my mind, whether I secured this job or not, I was coming back to this city to live.

I found my prospective employer a big fat man who did not speak a word of English; my French was sketchy and school-boyish. What to do? *Sprechen Sie Deutsch?* he asked. He was an Alsatian and spoke German. I was saved.

His was a beautiful big place, which scared me by its grandeur. It seemed that a salesman who could speak English was required. I could speak English, but heaven knows I was no salesman; I did not tell the fat man that. In the end he engaged me at the princely salary of one hundred francs (£4) per month. Well, that was £48 a year to be added to my seventy-five—a little less than £2 10s. a week, out of which I had to keep myself and pay the interest on the loans, which worried me like a toothache, and the yearly insurance premium, as well. Could it be done? Let us see, I said to myself.

I found the Place de la Concorde and crossed it into the past. I wandered into the rue de Lille and found a small hotel where on the top floor was a room, but there was no gas and no electric light; there was however a red stone floor which delighted me. The room was cheap so I took it and arranged to occupy it in a fortnight's time. Then I walked back to the Boulevards, had some lunch at a Duval's, wondering whether the meat was horseflesh, just as a good Englishman should. Then I saw they were playing the Belle of New York at the Olympia Theatre opposite, and I went into the promenade, to be picked up by a hundred, or so it seemed, pretty ladies. Then I came out and fought my way through squads of guides, all offering meant-to-be alluring entertainment. I walked along telling myself I was in Paris and I was coming back. I saw people drinking pretty looking drinks and I sat down in the open air, which in itself was wonderful, and ordered myself something or other. The whole time inside a band was playing, I mean inside me. I was happy, happy, happy.

I went back to London that night, completely intoxicated by Paris. I said good-bye to Cameron and my mother and was growled at by my stepfather. Then I took a single ticket to the Gare St. Lazare.

Again the dawn, and a drive in a horse-drawn cab to the rue de Lille where I found a letter from my mother. Poor soul, she wished me she said all sorts of good luck and hoped that I was at the beginning of a prosperous career.

The next morning at eight I went to work. There was an Irishman employed as a cutter and a Chilian salesman who spoke fluent English; the Irishman resented an Englishman coming into the business; the Chilian used to come back from lunch kissing the tips of his fingers and giving intimate and embarrassing details of how he had spent his lunch time: two hours. The boss used to gather the staff round him when no customers were in the place and then call me to listen to his abuse of England; unfortunately I could understand French well enough to know what he was saying, but could not speak it sufficiently well to answer his more or less amiable insults, so I was forced back on German, which was not so good.

My work was very light but very boring. All I had to do was in effect to clear up the mess; the salesmen opened up lengths of cloth to show customers and left them lying about. I had to roll them up again, very neatly; and I am not neat.

Often we had to go to the shop on Sunday mornings, and we always had to stay late in the evenings to put everything away. The job was not overpaid at the rate of four pounds a month. I found the going hard. I had to get up in the bitter cold, because my little room was unheated, and often I had to break the ice in the water jug before I could wash. There was no bathroom in the house, I had to go to a public bath place. The Chilian took me once to a Turkish bath; I wish I could recall where it was, somewhere near the Place de la République I think. After the bath, all the bathers sat round in a big room and had drinks while the masseurs gave a sort of café chantant. That was fun.

I did not have much fun, I did not have enough money for fun. My girl friends were all of the midinette type, because it was not expensive to entertain them. I had a cup of black coffee and a *croissant* for breakfast, standing up at the zinc bar in a cheap café; as the junior, I had to go last to lunch which I took either at a Duval's or a Chartier, when I found this style of place was cheaper. I used to eat well, plus a quarter of a bottle of red wine, for one franc, twenty-five centimes or about tenpence. Often I went without dinner because I did not have enough money. I tried the experiment of frying an egg on a spirit stove, but discovered that nature did not intend me to be a cook. I was very homesick, homesick for my mother and not for my home; but I made up my mind to stick it out, lonely as I was.

Cousin Lizzie of an earlier chapter had given me a note of introduction to a man who had been the Paris agent of her father's; the letter I noticed was worded rather in the style of the daughter of the manor; perhaps the poor faded lady in Bayswater forgot that her father had died broken in pocket as well as in heart. I had no idea then about Paris addresses, so when I saw Faubourg St. Denis on the envelope, I did not realize this was a business quarter. As it was a Sunday morning I felt exceptionally lonely. I thought maybe if I went along some good soul would insist on keeping me to lunch.

I found the address was an office and it was shut. Perhaps my look of disappointment made the kindly *concierge* write down another address which I understood was a home address; but I did not know that Montmorency was a residential suburb someway out of Paris. However, faint heart never won a Sunday lunch, so I took the train from the Gare du Nord and after losing myself many times, I arrived, and sure enough it was lunch-time, because when I was put in a small room to wait, I heard all the joyful sounds of a Sunday meal in progress. After a decent interval during which perhaps he had a liqueur with his coffee, the Paris agent, a frail old man, came into the room and looked at me. He inquired after the man whose agent he had been. I said he had died some ten years ago. The agent regretted. I said it was a pity; the agent tried to delve into the past to recall whether the gentleman had any family; I said that the writer of the letter was, as she claimed, his daughter. The old man peered at the letter and said indeed, yes. Then he looked at me again and said the next time I came to Paris I must certainly come and see him; I said that was too kind and went out into a world of stepchildren and dead cats.

That evening as usual I took my candle from a stand in the lobby and walked up six flights to bed. I heard voices speaking English and knew how a lonely mariner feels when he spies a sail. I knocked at the door and found two young Englishmen; they were teachers at a language school, paid six pounds a month. Millionaires!

They did not like the hotel either and were for moving to another, in the rue Boissy d'Anglas, a stone's throw from the Madeleine. I noted the address. That evening they suggested that I should eat where they were in the habit of eating, in a dairy in the rue Ste-Anne. I went and for the next year ate there twice a day. It was marvellous, that little *crémerie*, where I kept my serviette in a ring labelled thirty-six and as Monsieur thirty-six I was known to everybody; they were nearly all "regulars"; we all knew each other and each other's business. The *patronne* was Madame Pauline Rabier, known to us as Madame Pauline. Her husband was the brother of Benjamin Rabier, the famous animal artist, the Cecil Aldin of France, but this brother had been a circus acrobat and sometime during his career he had fallen on his head, which was not much good any more; he could not work so he used to sit around and watch his bustling wife and her servant, the red-cheeked Rosalie. Madame Pauline, tall, thin faced, with her black hair piled high on her head, was our mother confessor. An outsider coming in might think we were all on terms of bitter enmity with her, but that was just our way. The tiny kitchen was at the back of the little shop and we, the "regulars", would walk in, kiss Rosalie on both cheeks and ask what there was for lunch. When a customer got "gay" with the serious-looking Rosalie, Madame Pauline would call out: "*Ca finira avec un enfant*" and by Jove, in the end she was right.

Life became better for me when I found my feet in the rue Ste-Anne. Then it became better still when I gradually came on friendly terms with a young Englishman who used to call, as commercial traveller at my place of business; he represented a well-known English firm selling tailors' trimmings, and lived in a small pension back of the Folies Bergères. He was engaged to a red-haired girl who lived in Dulwich, but for reasons which will become clear in a moment, he did not marry her. Paris intervened.

The Englishman, H. went with me to the *crémerie* in the rue Ste-Anne and, as my friend, he became known as Monsieur thirty-six *bis*. In this little place where we were so friendly with the girls who so out-numbered us that we had to entertain them in turn, we met another Englishman, who was teaching English. H. and he became very friendly. The teacher lost his job or threw it up and borrowed some money from H. saying his mother was sending him some. The money did not arrive, so H. and I lent the young fellow some money to go home and fetch the money; he was to take a return ticket, when he left London, and to give the return half to H. who wanted to go to London but had not got the money. Our young friend returned, *minus a return ticket*; his story was that he had had no time to take a return ticket; that set me thinking, but H. still believed in him. The young man said he had been racing at Long-champs and was winning a lot of money and would pay his debts in a day or so; we had guaranteed his bill at Madame Pauline's. Then he appeared with a story that while he was watching the racing results being stuck up outside the Matin building, his pocket was picked and all his money stolen. That put H. and I in "Dicky Street" as they say in the North of England.

While our swindling friend was in London, H. and I met two German girl students. I moved to the rue Boissy d'Anglas, where every night, when I went back to the hotel I had to run the gauntlet and wave away platoons of pretty ladies who offered their services. One enterprising damsel chased me up the stairs and moved so much quicker than I that I became panic-stricken and locked myself in a lavatory.

H. fell heavily for his German girl. I went back to London for a few days to see my mother. The morning I arrived back in Paris, H. came to see me. His face as pale as my bed-sheet. He said that unless he could raise X pounds immediately, he would have to go to prison. Unbeknown to me, he and the English teacher, had been visiting Enghien casino; he had lost, and had "borrowed" money from office funds. Then he had gambled again to win the money he had "borrowed", with the usual result; could I help him?

I took everything I had, silver brushes, tie pins, two cigarette cases, a gold watch and chain, another fancy chain, all twenty-first birthday presents; I took everything I had of any likely value to the Mont de Piété, *chez ma tante*, as the French call the national pawnbrokers. I handed the total received to H. and begged him to put the money back and cut out the gambling. He had written to his fiancée of his plight; she poor girl was in a panic. She wrote to me and I replied telling her there was no need to worry; I said H. had had a severe lesson, but I was wrong. Soon after I left Paris, he fell in love with an English teacher and kicked over the traces again. He wrote me: ". . . Paris did it, but funnily enough, I don't hate Paris; I love it."

My mother did not approve of the way I was living, exaggerated tales about me had reached her. She had been writing me to return to London. I wanted to stay in Paris, but I agreed to give up my job and go back and discuss matters with her.

My mother wanted me to stay in London for good. She said I had been living a "fast" life in Paris (on less than thirty shillings a week!). I had other ideas; I wanted to go back to Paris, to draw my money out of my stepfather's business and buy a partnership in Paris. I was checkmated by my stepfather, who knew somebody in the City who had a tailor who wanted a partner with money in order to start a business in the West-End. I was to be that partner. I was not consulted at all. £1000 of my money was transferred from my stepfather's business, and I found myself in business in Savile Row, with a partner who lived in Holloway and whose wife took in lodgers. I was to be paid £2 a week, and a share of the profits, if any.

# CHAPTER IV

## IN SAVILE ROW

MY PERSONAL financial situation when I was embarked on the sea of West End tradesmanship was precarious. For years, as I have related, I was used to hearing myself described as a blockhead whose money must be well-invested, because I should never be able to earn my own living, but I never suspected that my stepfather's business would be regarded as the ideal place for investment. When I ceased to be a ward in Chancery, my holdings in "old" Consols were sold; they had been purchased at par, but the sale resulted in a loss of £500; £1,000 put into the Savile Row business reduced my total to £1,500, of which £500 was mortgaged to my cousin because he had lent me the money to redeem my mother's jewellery. I could therefore count on possessing £1,000 of my own. . . . My knowledge of tailoring was practically nil, and my interest in it was on a level with my knowledge; I was supposed to keep the books, but my knowledge of book-keeping was elementary, to say the least; I was also supposed to be a salesman and assistant fitter, but I did not appreciate the honour of helping customers on and off with their trousers. The truth of the matter was I was homesick, homesick for Paris.

I began business in Savile Row in the summer, when

my family was away at the seaside and I was alone in the house, except for a caretaker. In order to satisfy my craving for Paris and things Parisian, I used to go to the Café Royal and drink absinthe, although never had I drunk absinthe in Paris; I used to eat in French restaurants in Soho, just for the pleasure of talking French. Then I met Jeanette. . . . Jeanette accosted me one evening in Piccadilly Circus, outside the London Pavilion. Had she addressed me in English I should have ignored her, but she spoke French, and so there was magic in her words. Jeanette was a Belgian, which was a disappointment, but it did not matter very much; she spoke French. I asked her to go with me to Earl's Court Exhibition; she said if I would give her five pounds, she would, and I, poor little fool, I gave her five pounds, or rather promised I would give it to her in the morning, and did. The Earl's Court Exhibition of the Edwardian days! the military bands, the cool summer evenings, the innocent merriment of the days when there were no cinemas. Heigho!

I thought at the beginning of our acquaintance that Jeanette lived in Gower Street; she had a sitting-room and bedroom there, but that was her work room; she pretended as long as she could. Then I found out. I fell completely head over heels in love with Jeanette, that flower of the London pavements. She moved in a heavily scented atmosphere of Trèfle Incarnat; she was over rouged; her eyelids were too black; she had brown snapping eyes, a retroussé nose and golden hair, real golden hair. She was completely vulgar, and I loved her to distraction.

I never had any intention of marrying her, but I wanted to "save" her, if that is the correct expression. I wanted to take her off the streets. I wanted her to go back to her job, which was millinery, and she promised she would. Then I found out.

I found out that Jeanette lived in a back room in Soho with a Polish working tailor who had not worked for years. Jeanette worked to keep him. He was her "protector". She was afraid of him, and with reason. I saw the bruises on her body, and I wanted to kill the man who had caused them. Hanging over my head was the debt to my cousin, who sent me cryptic messages occasionally, asking when I intended to repay the money. I had the Savile Row shop where I spent most of the daylight hours, but that debt and that shop became unreal. Jeanette was my real life. Then I begged her to let me see this man who terrorised her, but she would not; all the time she was asking me for money which I gave her. We used to lunch and dine together in a little French restaurant in Dean Street, and it was not until years after that I learned that those who saw me there, including the *patron* and the two waiters, thought I was the *souteneur*.

Summer was over, and the family back in Maida Vale; no longer were my nights or even my evenings free. I had to be home to dinner, which took place at any hour my stepfather chose, but always too late for me to go out afterwards, and, besides, old as I was, in the early twenties, and nominally at least a West-End shopkeeper, I was tied with invisible strings. Sometimes I would get away, plead I was asked out by a friend, and then I would spend a few hours with Jeanette. Sometimes I would go down town unexpectedly and meet her pacing Coventry Street. One night in Shaftesbury Avenue I saw her in a hansom cab with a man, driving towards Gower Street. I ran all the way behind that cab and came panting upon her outside her door and thrust money into her hands and begged her to tell the man to go away. I abased myself in this sordid love affair, but I loved her so much.

I could not stand the idea of her living with this pimp; when I could, I haunted Soho and eventually met the man, a greasy, middle-aged individual. I affronted him, and expected he would draw a knife, or attack me in some manner. It was an anti-climax, for he ran away.

I begged and prayed Jeanette to give up this life and promised I would support her until she found a job. She consented. I was in a heaven of happiness. She found a room just off Tottenham Court Road; a girl friend of hers arranged to be drinking with the man while Jeanette went to her Soho room and removed her things. It all worked out according to plan. I used to see Jeanette at odd moments; she said she was looking for a job. About a week after she took the room I had a curious feeling that something was wrong. Pleading an engagement with a friend, I went West to Piccadilly Circus and then walked along the north side of Coventry Street. Outside the Empire Theatre I met Jeanette, with all her war paint on. I upbraided her; she boxed my ears soundly and walked on, then she turned back and burst into tears and threw her arms round my neck and dragged me to a cab. But it was no good, the spell was broken. Then I just went plumb crazy.

The only male I ever met in Jeanette's rooms was a Captain Blank, who was "just a friend". The Captain became my old Man of the Sea, and even to-day —he exists within my orbit—I am not quite sure I have shaken him off. About thirty-two, he was tall, handsome and well-dressed and had discovered the art of living on nothing a year. Once upon a time he had been in receipt of a good allowance from a father; that had ceased long before I met him. Now he was paid a few pounds a year, about £1 a month, I think, to lend his name as a "guinea-pig" director of some company. He had a room in Orange Street; his appetite was small; he stayed in bed every day until the early afternoon, which disposed of the problem of breakfast and lunch. Rising he would take two hours or so to shave and dress, but the result was worth while, oh dear yes. In a top hat, all the "nuts" wore top hats in those days, white spats, striped trousers and a morning coat, he would toddle along, as he would say, the shady side of Piccadilly, up the Burlington Arcade, to the Bristol, at the corner of New Burlington Street and Cork Street. There he would wait for somebody to buy him his first brandy and soda. The Bristol was the meeting place for the girls and the "nuts", who were young men down from the universities, young naval officers home on leave, officers up from Aldershot and Shorncliffe and although I didn't know it until a Scotland Yard man told me, "where the girls go, you find the young men, and where you find them you find the crooks after them, and us after the crooks." I fell into a nice nest of trouble.

The Captain would sit in the Bristol like a good looking spider waiting for a fly; he was the cicerone to the young men, the mentor who told them which girl was on the level, where to go, where to dine. In those Edwardian days there was plenty of money about and he had his pickings. One night in the Leicester

65

Comedy Club, a club of actors, journalists and men about town with a habitat in Green Street, Leicester Square, I met him. I had just returned to London from a raid on Paris and I was going to catch the midnight train from Paddington to Cookham, where I had a fourteen shilling a week furnished cottage. He invited himself down to the Nook for the week-end, and asked me to go with him to collect some things in Orange Street. I noticed he slunk down back streets; it was the only time I ever saw him afraid of creditors. The week-end stretched itself out week by week. I had to go to town every morning, leaving him alone. When I saw my tradesmen's books, I found sundry sums of ten and fifteen shillings for which I could not account. When I inquired I was told that my friend had developed a habit of dropping in on the butcher, the baker and the greengrocer to say I had had to rush up to town in a hurry, and had no time to cash a cheque, would they oblige. . . . The Captain certainly added to the gaiety of the Nook which I had rented to get away from home. He had a nice taste in girl friends, and my cottage was from time to time enlivened by the presence of ladies from the Gaiety and Daly's, who found the Nook handy for Skindle's. After six weeks I persuaded, or should I say bribed, him to return to Orange Street. A year or so later some friends and I found the upkeep of the Captain too expensive. This was about 1913, so we had a whip round and paid his fare to a far off land; we knew of a job there and we could think of no place further away than that spot. We gave him a good send off, and one of his Gaiety friends who had become a star and who later married an Earl helped in the entertainment. A year later War broke out, and we had him back with the local contingent. He then joined an Indian Horse regiment, sprained a ligament, or something and was removed in very great state to Indian Army Base at Marseilles where he stayed very peacefully until demobilization. Then he became secretary to an American millionaire, but there was some unpleasantness over golf clubs. Then he became a sort of public charge on his friends; but I have wandered far from those Edwardian days when Captain Blank took me under his wing.

Every night he was to be seen in "immaculate evening dress," as the reporters used to say, in the Empire promenade; if he met a willing person, there was brandy and soda and a snack at Romano's, the Globe or the Continental, where he might introduce his friend to a lady. Every other Friday there was a Ball at Covent Garden. He was there, and so was I. Nothing mattered but wine, woman and song. I was having the very best of good times, because always hanging over me was that question of the debt and then . . . the Deluge. I drank far too much; I wasn't used to strong drink and had no stomach for it. I had the habit of drinking brandies until I became tired of them, and then I turned to kummels, and then as like as not went back to brandy. The shop was merely a pest; it was not doing well but I didn't care. My partner was an unfriendly fellow who hated my stepfather with whom he quarrelled over the fit of a waistcoat, and whom he accused of ruining the business. I didn't care. I was heavily in debt and saw nothing but ruin staring me in the face. Three or four nights a week I drank too much to go back to Maida Vale, but having no money to go to a hotel, I used to go and sleep in the fitting-room in the shop, using a roll of cloth as a pillow. Once or twice a passing policeman saw a light and insisted on coming in and making me prove I had a right to be there. What a fright I must have looked, with a pale face and in dishevelled evening dress. One evening when I was going to a Covent Garden Ball I arranged to dress at the shop, but had several drinks at the Bristol first. When I arrived at the Piccadilly Grill where I was meeting my friends, a roar of laughter went up as I approached the group. In my vinous excitement, I had put on an unfinished dress coat waiting for a customer to fit on.

When I did go home, I had to be very careful to creep in. There was a circular carriage drive leading to the front steps; one pair of wooden gates was always locked, and the other often stuck and had to be forced. I arrived back one spring morning about five-thirty; the sun was coming up, the birds were twittering, and the damned gates were stuck. If I used force, they would make a noise, and my mother and step-father slept in a room on the front. I hauled myself up and was astride the gates ready to drop down on the other side when two policemen came round the corner.

"What are you doing there?" asked one.

"I'm going home," I answered with becoming dignity, as if the young master invariably returned at that hour and in that manner. "A likely story," replied the two policemen, adding "have you a latchkey?" "Certainly I have," I answered pompously but a little doubtfully. "Then let's see you use it," said the Law. I had to pull open those gates and march up the carriage drive, with the police at my heels. Then I opened the front door; removing my shoes I crept up the first flight. At the head of the stairs stood my mother, like an avenging angel: "Have you enjoyed

yourself?" she inquired in a voice of impending doom.
I mumbled a reply. Then she spoke these words of
wisdom: "I don't mind what time you come home,
but be in bed before the maids come down." That
made the deadline six-thirty.

Those jolly days in the Piccadilly Grill when De
Groot conducted the orchestra, were expensive. Blank
had introduced me to what was known in Edwardian
days as a "fast set". He had put a proposition to me;
if I would clothe him free, gratis and for nothing, he
would introduce custom. I knew that many West-
End tailors did that, so I thought we might, too, but
there was one matter I overlooked: his introduc-
tions also obtained their clothes on the never, never
system. All the crooks of London gathered round;
a "mug" had been sighted on the horizon, and I, of
course, was the "mug". One smart looking fellow
dashed in, having been introduced by Blank. He had
just arrived from India, he said, and all his clothes
had been stolen; he ordered about £50 worth of
goods, but before he came to try on his clothes, he
was in the hands of the police; he was a cardsharper,
and when he said he had just arrived from India, he
made a mistake; he had just arrived from prison.
Blank used to take me to the rooms of a friend of his in
Duke Street, St. James. The man is dead now, so I
can name him: Jack Newcombe, but, as I found out
later, that was only one of his names. He had a nice
manner, charming and polished, well travelled and
handsome. A really charming man, who eventually
cost me £500 and nearly my life.

Out of the one thousand five hundred pounds which
remained to me, I had had to put another five hundred pounds into the Savile Row business, leaving me

a balance of one thousand pounds still invested in my stepfather's business. Now I was told by my partner that another five hundred pounds was needed. I was getting scared; if I put that money in, I should have five hundred pounds left, which was due to my cousin, and the business might require more money; what to do?

At my mother's house I had met a youngish man who had married the daughter of a friend; this man told me quite frankly he saw I was unhappy and said that if there was anything he could do to help me, he would. I said I would like to consult him. He was a partner in a financial house, with an office in Southampton Row; he asked me to lunch at the Holborn restaurant and during the meal invited me to tell him my troubles. I told him the full story of my mother's pawned jewels, what I had done to redeem them, and my fears concerning the repayment. I told him also that since I had paid over the sum of four hundred odd pounds, my mother had borrowed from me various sums to pay local tradesmen and a sum of thirty pounds to pay part of the family's summer holiday; she had had the money from her husband but had spent it. G. listened to my story without interrupting. Then he said: "In our business we know a lot of what is going on. Are you sure that your mother has not pawned her jewellery again?" I laughed aloud: "Don't be silly," I said, "she promised me, she swore on her children's heads she never would do such a thing again." G. looked at me curiously. "Maybe you are quite right," he said, "but if I were you I would make sure."

I jumped on an omnibus going Kilburnwards. Not for years had I been to Thompson the pawnbroker, thank goodness, but I said to myself, I will just go in and make sure. I walked into the shop. The staff had changed; I knew nobody and nobody knew me. "I have come," I announced, "from Mrs. Blank, who asks me, her son, to find out how much she owes you." Of course, I knew they would look blankly at me and say they had never heard of her. "Take a seat a moment," said the manager politely, "and I'll let you know the exact amount." The shop became a dark cave peopled by devils. I felt weak suddenly, and quite ill. I muttered that I would come back another time and settle the matter. Then I staggered out into the street. I could have killed my mother. I will say this again, calmly and collectedly. I could have killed the person I loved best in the world. Ten minutes previously I was a young man; now I felt old and worn out. That was twenty-five years ago; since then I have roamed the world, but those few minutes in the Kilburn pawnbroker's shop brought down an iron curtain which cut me off from my youth.

I went home and asked my mother to spare me a few minutes. We went together in to the dining-room and closed the door. She stood facing me. I asked her if she recalled a certain promise she had made me some years previously. She said she did, perfectly. "I have just come from the pawnbroker's," I said. "You have done it again." "What the devil is that to do with you," she replied icily. I suppose it had nothing to do with me, except that I had had years of hell on earth, worrying, striving and trying to keep things going. There seemed nothing I could do. I did not answer my mother, but left the house, went to the Piccadilly Grill, got very drunk, and then went to the Pavilion, where I was robbed of every penny I had.

It was neatly done, because though I was absolutely conscious of being robbed, there was nothing I could do about it. I met a woman in the promenade and bought her a drink. At that time, and now still for all I know, there was a passage way beneath the stage, connected on either side with the promenade by two short staircases. The woman on some pretext or other, induced me to go through this passage with her. It was usually deserted during the performance. While we were on the last step of the first staircase, she detained me for a second, then a man I hadn't previously noticed pinned my arms, while the woman neatly and deftly removed my wallet; then they decamped, each up a different staircase. Prettily worked, as Little Tich used to say.

But what the devil, what did it matter? There was a musical comedy on at the Shaftesbury Theatre at this time called "The Arcadians". There was a song which went something like this:

> I've got a motto
> Always merry and bright
> Look around and you'll soon find
> Every cloud is silver lined
> The sun will shine
> Altho' the sky's a grey one
> I've always said to myself, I've said
> Peter Dooley, you'll soon be dead
> A short life and a gay one.

That was me, a short life and a gay one. What the hell? A few of my friends and myself used to go to the "Warrington" in the evenings, a gay spot then in Warrington Crescent, Maida Vale; it was run by a man named Cubitt Cook who used to "work" the Joel's racing commission. One of my particular chums was an ugly, charming fellow named Arthur Henry, who was destined for his father's chartered accountancy business; he used to write anonymous articles for *Punch* on the sly, and he hated the thought of going into business. When the Warrington closed, I used to walk home with Arthur Henry, while he kept on repeating: "To-morrow! God, how I hate to-morrow!" He was saved from what he hated because he obtained a commission in the Middlesex Regiment when War broke out and was killed in action within six weeks of arriving in France.

Meanwhile, something had to be done about repaying my cousin. The comedy was over, the jewels had been pawned again; it was no use going on paying interest and insurance premiums. The deluge was approaching.

The only human person from whom I could seek advice was an aunt who has already appeared in this work as the Lady from the Empire Promenade. I had begged my mother to tell her husband the truth, or, alternately, to be with me when I told him, but she would not hear of it. With one of my stepbrothers she retired to Tankerton until the storm blew over. My aunt, grand person, agreed to go with me to my stepfather's place of business in Hatton Garden and there tell him the story and ask him to let me have five hundred pounds of my own money to repay my cousin.

My stepfather liked my aunt. When we came to his office he was in a good mood for once, he joked and laughed and made things all the more difficult. Then we told him, calmly, dispassionately. I have seen a storm gather over a mountain, that was awe inspiring and something like the physical change which crossed my stepfather's face. He aged; there is no question about that, he aged. Without a word he wrote me out a cheque for £500. I deliberately exaggerated the amount owing to my cousin, because for once I wanted to have the feel of my own money, the money for which my father had worked and left to me. That £75 I got rid of very quickly. Daisy helped a lot.

I was mad again, and as cunning as a lunatic. Daisy was just a girl I had picked up and fallen for as heavily as I did for Jeanette. Daisy I met in the Bristol; she came from the country, had had a child by a man who had left her and whose mood marched in step with mine. What the hell?

I thought I was cunning but events proved I was not as cunning as I believed. I made up my mind to put that £500 in my own pocket and get away, but not very far, as we shall see.

Savile Row had dealt me one good hand, we had a customer named Norman Roe, a cousin of A. V. Roe, I believe; Roe was the editor of *Vanity Fair* and lived in lodgings near by. Roe suggested one evening that I should write a column once a week in *Vanity Fair*, called : "In Savile Row". I did, signing the column "Harlequin". I wrote that column until I disappeared with Daisy.

# CHAPTER V

## CRASH !

IF I had had any encouragement, instead of running away, I would have begun to try and earn my living as a writer. The *Vanity Fair* articles were successful and attracted attention. I used to write little sketches scribbled by hand, and show them to my mother who glanced at them amusedly and said they weren't bad but that I had better not let my stepfather know about them, otherwise there might be trouble; so I tore them up, all except one, an attempt at a short story.

My mother and I were reconciled after her retreat to Tankerton, while I faced the storm in Hatton Garden. I was now the blacksheep again. One night while my stepfather sat on the porch of the house in Maida Vale watching the summer lightning play among the laburnum trees in the garden, I approached him in fear and asked him what I should do about the £1000 insurance policy on my life which I had taken out at my cousin's behest and which, now he had been paid, he handed back to me. I knew nothing about insurance, nothing about the potential valuable asset I possessed, so humbly I asked what I should do. "I don't care a damn what you do," my stepfather muttered; I went the next day and surrendered the policy and secured, to my surprise and delight, some of the money I had paid as premiums. Daisy was delighted too, but the money was soon

75

gone, and more was needed. I started to put into operation my plan to run away and start again . . . in East Africa. Why East Africa, I really do not know. I suspect it was Jack Newcombe who put the idea into my head. All I wanted was to get away, to break completely with the present. Daisy was not the reason, she was merely the excuse. Stupefied with drink, and not knowing what I was doing, I listened to the proposition made me by Newcombe. The £500 which was to be put into the Savile Row business would be paid by cheque made to the joint names of my partner and myself. I had two or three blank cheques on our joint account; my partner had signed them so that I could deal with current financial matters while he was absent; he had some blank cheques signed by me for a similar purpose. I was to make out one of the blank cheques for the sum of £500 and draw the money in notes and I was to hand the notes to Newcombe who would obtain a banker's draft and bring me the money to Paris, where I was to go immediately I had cashed the cheque. I was quite clear about one matter only: fundamentally, I was doing nothing dishonest; it was my own money I was taking. I felt that if the money went into the Savile Row business it would be lost, just as the previous sums so invested had been lost. When Newcombe arrived with the draft, he and I were to go farming in East Africa. At that time I did not know anything about Jack Newcombe; he was many years older than myself. I looked up to him as a man of the world, and to him I had confided my troubles because he was a man of the world. I drew the money early one morning and handed the five hundred pounds to Jack at Frascatti's the same morning and left for Paris with Daisy that after-

noon. Jack was to arrive the next day. I had
arranged to stay at a certain hotel near the Gare St.
Lazare.

Nobody but Daisy and Jack knew my plans. I
intended to write to my mother before leaving Paris.
The next day I went to the Gare du Nord to meet
Newcombe; he was not on the train. I met the next
train; he did not come. I had a little money with me
but not enough to stay long in Paris unless Jack
arrived with my money. I haunted the hall porter's
desk, begging to be told the moment a cable arrived.
There were no cables. I met every train, but there
was no sign of Newcombe. I cabled to him to London
and again waited all day near the hall porter, waiting
in vain for a message; meanwhile, my money was
dwindling. Daisy was bad tempered and unhelpful. I
knew a few people in Paris, but I had never borrowed
a penny for myself and was ashamed to ask anybody
for help. The hotel people must have suspected something was wrong, because I was stopped leaving the
hotel; I could not go out unless I paid my bill, I was
told. I said I would go and get the money. I walked
about the streets and decided I would go to the shop
where I had worked for a year and ask them to lend
me a little money, enough to send Daisy back to
London. They refused to lend me any. I went back to
the hotel and gave them every penny I had and said I
would pay the remainder in two hours' time. I kept
my promise by pawning a few articles; then we
moved to a small hotel in Montmartre. When I had
paid for the evening meal I had nothing left. I was
completely stranded in Paris. I felt a criminal and
imagined that I was liable to arrest. I tried to think
of somebody to whom I could turn for help and advice

and remembered that in London I had met a man introduced by Captain Blank, a man who was the living counterpart of Micawber.

Alec Boss was always waiting for something to turn up. Life had dealt him many dirty blows but he invariably came up smiling. At this time Boss must have been in the forties. When he was very young he and his brother enlisted in a Hussar regiment and were "bought out" by their father; since then Alec had always been connected with the entertainment world, usually unfortunately. He had had some sort of a job when the Palace Theatre in London opened as an opera house—and failed. Then he had toured in the United States and France and Great Britain and Germany, but he was invariably "broke" and just as invariably happy and apparently contented. It was not of Alec Boss but of another man who resembled him in character that Hannen Swaffer remarked "he has no sense of stumer". Alec sailed gaily through life looking the perfect theatrical manager of tradition: well-dressed, monocled, dapper and cynical. He liked cigars, but if there were no cigars he would smoke cigarettes, just as he drank a glass of water when there was no champagne. His shining top hat was always tilted at a cocky angle; he caressed a silky moustache which would have well become a Ouida guardsman. Alec's French was as fluent and eloquent as his German; he had what is known as the gift of the gab to the nth degree. I will not say he could talk the hind leg off a donkey; when Alec had finished with the donkey, the poor donkey would be sitting on his rump wondering what had become of his hay.

I do not recall how many times Alec had married,

but he said he called all his wives Jane in case he talked in his sleep. Boss had latterly been associated with C. B. Cochran in exploiting a roller skating rink in Berlin; when I met him in London he was trying to float a company to start a luxurious skating rink in Paris, in the rue d'Edimbourg. In that little street I inquired for him and with the current wife I found him staying in a small hotel, quite broke but quite happy; like Micawber, about to fall back for a spring. I told Alec Boss my tragic tale. He advised me to return to London immediately; he gave me the name and address of his lawyers and suggested I should get them to get in contact with my mother; but Alec gave me something even more valuable than advice; he lent me a small sum of money from his slender store, and gave me the two return halves of two third class tickets to London. Daisy and I left Paris that night.

The return of the prodigal son was not greeted with any feasting and merriment. I walked from the station to "digs" in Orange Street and secured a room. Then I went to the City to see the lawyers. They communicated with my mother and told me I had nothing to fear, but that I must make an immediate application for a warrant for the arrest of Jack Newcombe. The next morning I telephoned to the lawyer who said my mother and my stepfather were going to his office at eleven that morning. I was there too, but neither my mother nor my stepfather knew I was there, and although I saw them, they did not see me; I was in a small room and saw their shadows reflected on the ground glass window in the door, as they passed along the corridor to the lawyer's office.

When I went to Vine Street police station to inquire concerning the procedure for taking out a warrant, an inspector took me to the "Rogues Gallery" and asked me to identify Jack Newcombe. They had three pictures of him, full face, right and left profile. Then they showed me his police record. Jack Newcombe, I know now, was the illegitimate son of a famous industrialist in the Midlands. He had served in a "crack" cavalry regiment but had to leave on account of card debts. His father had paid his enormous debts many times, but in the end had refused to have anything more to do with him. Then Jack Newcombe, with several other names, embarked on a life of crime and served three prison sentences; confidence trick offences and offences connected with card sharping. I said in a previous chapter of this book that Newcombe cost me five hundred pounds and nearly my life. I have explained the five hundred pounds; if it had not been for the sound common sense of Daisy, who told me that she cared absolutely nothing about me or what happened to me, my life would have been forfeit in Paris.

The warrant for the arrest of Jack Newcombe was issued at Marlborough Street, and then I went to Maida Vale to face the music; but I threw a bombshell when I asked for my last five hundred pounds. I told them I wanted to invest it in the Paris skating rink in which Alec Boss was interested. Paris was calling me again.

There were legal complications concerning the Savile Row business. I had to begin a libel suit against my partner, and have since had reason to regret that I agreed to settle this matter out of court. The partnership was dissolved, but I stuck to my guns and demanded that I be allowed to invest my own money where I wanted to invest it. In the end my insistence prevailed and I purchased 500 shares in the skating rink, with the proviso that I was to be paid £6 a week as secretary to the rink. Then I packed my trunk and returned to Paris and took a room in a small hotel nearly opposite the site where the rink was going to be—one day.

I was still a little crazy, however; the first week-end I was in Paris I dashed back to London to pay a surprise visit to Daisy. She was away for the week-end, her embarrassed landlady told me. Then bit by bit I gathered the full sordid story. Fooled again, I returned to Paris, a wiser if a sadder young man.

I found the skating rink in a very backward condition. Alec Boss was an entertaining person and he could keep one in fits of laughter, but he was no organizer, and if ever there was a man with a hoodoo, that man was Alec Boss. When the rink failed, as of course it did, Boss went to London; one day in a train going somewhere or other he met a man who said he had a business in Berlin and wanted an Englishman to manage it, would Boss like to be that man? Boss accepted a very good job and went to Berlin. A few weeks later War broke out; Alec was interned in Ruthleben prison camp for about three years.

When Boss had the idea of starting a rink in Paris, it was a very good idea, so good in fact that several other people did start rinks and made money, while our rink was being got ready. We had strikes among the builders; we were short of money, and when eventually the parquet flooring was ordered from Liverpool and paid for and was coming to Paris, all the way by water, the great Paris Floods started; the steamer could not pass under the Seine bridges. There was the floor and there were we waiting for it; meanwhile expenses were piling up. The company was short of money; my £6 a week was never paid me after the first few weeks. I had to be satisfied with what I could persuade Boss to let me have.

One day when I was working in a little office in the incompleted rink, a stranger came in, an Englishman. Very mysteriously he asked me to come with him to the café on the corner, where he said a friend was waiting for me. I took my hat and went with him. In a far away corner was sitting—Jack Newcombe.

He was so sorry, he said; the money he had stolen from me had not brought him any luck; he had lost it all; he had been very ill; he certainly looked old and ill. Now things were looking up, his friend here and he had a little business in view and he promised that as soon as he was on his feet, he would pay back every penny of the £500. There was one little matter; I surely did not want to kick a man when he was down, an Englishman didn't do it. That business in view was in London, and he had heard that in London there was a warrant for his arrest. If he could not go to London in safety, the business would not materialize, and I should not get my £500. There was just a little formality for me to fulfil, and all would go well. We went to lunch; over the coffee Jack asked for pen and ink; would I just sign a note saying that in consideration of a promise to repay the money "owing", I would undertake not to proceed with a certain matter in which I had taken polic court proceedings. "There," said Newcombe, as he blotted the note, "that's all right now."

The two men said my hotel looked a nice little hotel;

they might stay there the night and continue to London the next day. Stay they did. In the morning they asked for the bill, and as they needed a little money for the journey, could they cash a cheque? Just £10. If I guaranteed the cheque, the hotel proprietor said he would cash it. The two accepted the notes with a nod and said they would be back the next week for a stay.

The cheque was back before they were. They never came back, and I had to restitute the amount of the cheque, which was "no good". Apparently I am one of those people who allow the same bee to sting them twice. I never saw Jack Newcombe again, but I know that within a year he died in London, in a back room in a slum street off the Edgware Road.

Our skating rink was the last to open in Paris and the first to close. It was a beautiful place, but the Parisians did not want a beautiful skating rink; they would not come. We seemed to have collected around us all the riff-raff of the roller skating world. Lonely ladies whose husbands or lovers were men of wealth and apparently engaged in pursuits of their own, came to the rink, and some of the instructors reaped a good material and emotional harvest. I saw one man steal a gold mesh bag from a woman and tried to stop him. He made a swing at me with a pair of roller skates, and departed—with the gold bag. Saved from the earlier wreck of my life was a fur coat, my one worldly possession which may have had some value. This coat was envied by one of the English instructors. Between the afternoon and evening sessions in the rink, there used to be a game of *chemin de fer* played in one of the instructors' bedroom. I played and lost, more than I could afford. Then the instructor who wanted the coat offered to play me for that. He got the coat.

We were in quite a mess. Boss never told me the exact position; when pressed for details he would invent some comic story and make an exit under a roar of laughter; but I was existing on a handful of francs. Fortunately, in those days one could eat well enough for less than a shilling, and that was all right, so long as one had the equivalent of a shilling. Then the authorities cut off the electric light because our company had not paid and could not pay the bill; we suspended the night sessions, and had morning and afternoon sessions only. Fortunately we had a glass roof.

We were approaching the summer when all the rinks were closing, but I knew that once we closed we should never open again. My last £500 had melted away and I had no money and no job in prospect. I was often hungry now; what money Boss allowed me to have I used to pay my room rent. The dreaded moment came when there was no more money at all. I paid my rent for the last time and moved my trunk into the room of the rink Floor Manager, who offered to share his room with me.

One of our most assiduous customers at the rink was a middle-aged woman who lived with a woman friend in a furnished flat opposite the rink. She appeared to like me and was always asking me to go and see her. Her chief claim to fame it seemed was that she happened to be the ex-mistress of an ex-Khedive of Egypt. One afternoon as I was lounging disconsolately through the rue d'Edimbourg, I met the lady just as she was going indoors; she invited me in for a dish of tea. She drifted into another room, leaving me with her friend who was sewing. The friend looked up after a minute and said she thought that X wanted to speak to me in her bedroom. X made me a direct offer. Would I go out with her every evening, to the smart restaurants in the Bois; she would pay all expenses; in the restaurants, I was to get into conversation with rich looking English or American men and introduce them to her. She would attend to the rest. The offer was declined with thanks and I went away, without any tea. Any free meal was welcome, because I was terribly hungry. Sam, my room mate, had no money either, and we wondered how we were going to pay the rent of the room at the end of the month. The bailiffs seized the skating rink on behalf of the creditors; I was a creditor too, I obtained a few francs, but I had to live on fifty centimes a day, a cup of black coffee and a *croissant* at a Café Biard.

Then the blow fell. Sam and I were told that unless we paid the rent we should have to go; the hotel people told him he was not allowed to share his room with me. It was June now; the nights were warm and fine. I did not want to embarrass Sam, so for two nights I slept out on a bench in the Champs-Elysées; I did not mind it a bit, but I was so hungry. I thought I would try and be a guide to English-speaking people, one of those men who accost you in the neighbourhood of the Paris Opera, but they only guide men to brothels, and when they saw me hanging about outside the Café de la Paix, they hustled me away, but not before one shabby little man accosted *me* and asked if I did not remember him? I had some vague memory of having seen him before but could not place him. He was, it appeared, a former school boy from the school I had attended in Ramsgate.

M. was also down on his luck, but I soon gathered that gambling was the cause of his downfall; he was crazy about it. We talked for a while; the next day being Sunday, M. suggested that he and I should go to Longchamps where he knew one of the men who sold those pink slips telling punters the approximate odds. M. thought he and I would be able to earn a few francs helping his friend sell the pink slips. We walked all the way to Longchamps from Paris, and as we lost the few francs we made, we walked all the way back. On the following Thursday I went again, and kept enough from what I made to buy a meal, get a shave and write to my mother. I wanted to go home and eat humble pie. My mother sent me my fare to London, but I had to abandon my clothes; these however I obtained some long time afterwards.

I was now completely crushed. I had not a penny in the world, and I had to live in a house which in those Edwardian days was passing luxurious. Business had prospered with my stepfather. He had four maid servants, a motor car and a chauffeur. How pleased he was to be able to say to my mother and I: "I told you so." All that he had foretold had come true. I had lost everything and was quite unable to earn my own living. The fact that I had spent over five hundred pounds because he did not provide my mother with sufficient money, did not occur to him, I suppose, and he bullied me so unmercifully that I could never bring myself to remind him of this, to me, essential fact. In the meantime, I was the poor relation who slunk down side-streets in case he should run into anybody he knew. When my mother was able to give me half a crown, I accepted it humbly and with gratitude. My stepfather never ceased to hurl sarcastic remarks after me. I was twenty-five and fit for nothing but the rubbish heap. I knew it; I never attempted to hide my failure from myself. I used to go up to my room early and sit there or lie on the bed and think; my thoughts went round and round in a circle. My future? What a silly word! I had no future, of course. I wanted to work, but I had no idea of how and where to start. I saw that a firm in Regent Street wanted a salesman who could talk French. I applied for the job, giving a false name. I was told to call. I got that job, at thirty shillings a week, a little more than my stepfather paid the cook in the basement. I used to get up in the morning before my stepfather was about and sneak out of the house and walk to Regent Street, and at night I would go up to bed saying I did not want any dinner, just so that I could avoid him. Then I lost that job, I was not good enough to hold it, but the real truth was that the manager would keep remembering he had not taken a reference, and I, of course, having given a false name could not give him a reference. Stalemate. I left. Another failure, celebrated in Maida Vale with a string of sarcasm.

On the rocks again, I had to accept stray shillings from my mother, who was sorry for me but could not do anything; her husband did not want me to do anything. He was, as my mother told me, "getting his own back." It seemed that long before she married my father, my stepfather proposed to her, but my grandfather, who was riding high in those days, did not think he was good enough and did not hide that from him. He went to South Africa and she married my father. As soon as he heard of my father's death, my future stepfather returned. The way was smoothed for him. My mother's family was ruined. Now here was I, the third generation, grandson of "that old bankrupt", a pauper and brother to a beggar.

When I was working in Regent Street, I got to know a French girl, Marie-Louise, who worked in a near-by dressmaker's shop; she lived over on the south side of the river. Neither of us had any money, but Marie-Louise had a job; while I had mine I used to take her to dinner sometimes, in Soho; Paris was calling me again, and I wanted to talk French. Then I had no job and no money, except for an occasional shilling, and I could not take Marie-Louise out any more, so I used to go and sit with her in her room, while she sewed and talked to me about Paris. About eleven o'clock I would say good night and start my long walk back to Maida Vale: across Westminster Bridge, along Whitehall to Trafalgar Square, up the Charing Cross Road, or along Regent Street to Oxford Street, the long stretch to Marble Arch, then the final and longest stretch along the Edgware Road and Maida Vale. It did not do the heels of my shoes any good. I was down at heel and must have looked a tramp. One night when Marie-Louise said good night I felt something in my hand; it was a shilling which she begged me to take and spend on omnibus fares so that I did not have to walk. Nothing had ever touched me as much as that gesture. I could have wept. Soon I was able to pay back that shilling; I had cascades of shillings.

A man I knew was trying to do something about cinemas; they were just beginning in London; one had opened near the Marble Arch. In this fellow's office I met a young man named Cecil Kent who since he came down from Cambridge had earned a living finding sites for Charles Urban's cinema cameras, the earliest of the news reels were Urban's. Kent was related to "everybody"; one cousin was the head-master of Eton; an uncle was Editor of the *Sporting Chronicle*; he could pull strings everywhere. He had coxed the Cambridge crew; he knew people all over London, but, like me, he was broke. One day we sat in a then famous "pub" near Piccadilly Circus and discussed ways and means of making money. In those spacious days there was money everywhere, although we had none. There were no night clubs, but people had money to spend, if there was anywhere they could spend it. Take this one instance: A man came to London from New York; he said he was a pianist who could play this new ragtime that was all the rage. He went to Oddenino and asked "Oddy" if he could play during supper time. "Oddy" said no. The young man said could he play for no salary; all he wanted was a shilling per head on everybody supping in the restaurant. "Oddy" was a sportsman and took the young American up on his offer. In less than a fort-night "Oddy" was turning people away; with tears in his eyes he was begging the young American to name his own price. I forgot to say that the name of the young American pianist was Melville Gideon.

I thought in terms of entertainment; what could we do. Suddenly a thought hit me: a series of dances which would begin at midnight! There were the Covent Garden Balls, given every other Friday night during the winter season; they seemed to make money. Excitedly Cecil Kent and I discussed the proposition. We would send invitations to all the ladies of the chorus in every London musical-comedy show; we would sell tickets, including supper, for one guinea. In a flash a title struck me: Sporting and Dramatic

Balls. Then Kent and I examined our finances; our joint capital was four shillings.

Although we had no money, we had the pioneering spirit. Kent knew an artist in Chelsea who would, he thought, do us a poster, on credit. That was arranged. Then we went to see the manager of Prince's, in Piccadilly, then very swagger, and arranged with him to provide a ball room and supper. George Edwardes was the musical-comedy "king"; he had shows running all over London. Kent knew somebody who knew Pat Malone, one of Edwardes' stage managers; we approached Edwardes for permission to call Sporting and Dramatic Ball No. 1: "The Girl in the Train" Ball (that was a show running at the Vaudeville). Edwardes gave us permission, so we had a red and green poster prepared, adding, after the name of the show ("By kind permission of George Edwardes, Esq."). We obtained the printing on credit. Then we had to find an office. At No. 3 Stafford Street, one door off Bond Street, we found a tiny office run as a theatre ticket office by an old, old man named Johnson. We explained our scheme and offered him a commission on sales of tickets, provided he let us have the use of the telephone and the office and did some clerical work himself. We sent out the invitations, and bundles of tickets to every Navy wardroom and Army mess within fifty miles of London. Then I went into the publicity business for the first time in my life. I wrote newspaper paragraphs and sent them to the more "sporty" weeklies; then we had some cards, gilt edged and very well printed, made; they were in a set of three. The first card announced a Sporting and Dramatic Ball for a date which was three nights away; we hired all the District Messenger Boys we could and told them to give the cards away to every man they saw wearing evening dress. We hired the boys for the next night and gave them the same instructions, but the cards announced: "To-morrow Night". The third night we mobilised a whole army corps of District Messenger Boys and posted them after the theatres were "out" at the corner of every street leading into Piccadilly. The cards they gave away announced "To-night's the Night". Then Kent and I repaired to Prince's and drank brandies and sodas to keep up our courage. There was a near riot; people actually fought to give us money. We cleared £63 net.

We gave another ball a fortnight later and cleared over £80 profit between us. I took my mother to Covent Garden to hear "La Bohème" with Melba and MacCormick in the cast. I wanted to give her everything I could. I was rolling in money.

Then Prince's objected to our selling tickets at the doors, we had to make other arrangements; we moved to the Connaught Rooms and had even greater success. We hired the best band there was in London in those days; Archibald Joyce's band; we gave the best suppers; we had the prettiest girls at our dances. We were IT.

The little office was next door to the first floor lounge of the "Goat", a public house much frequented then by Naval officers on leave. The lounge had nothing "public house" about it, it might have been a club lounge. The hostess was a Miss Abel, called "Bobby", because there was a famous Surrey cricketer named Bobby Abel. As I had reason to remark elsewhere in this book, we were simple folks in those days. Every day when tea was ready,

"Bobby" would knock on the wall, and I would trot down the stairs and up the flight next door. When the World War came along, the Admiralty was afraid that enemy spies might drop into the "Goat" and pick up naval secrets, so the "Goat" was put out of bounds, but you cannot beat the Navy. A Goat Club was organized, for British Naval officers only . . . and the manageress was "Bobby".

Kent and I prospered exceedingly. We gave a Boatrace Ball, and when Sunstar won the Derby of this particular year, we cleared about £150.

We started on our second season not so well, but not too badly. People copied us in a cheaper way, and let down the tone. Then we became careless and ran a ball on the same night as a Covent Garden Ball, and for the first time we showed a loss. Then we came up against disaster. We lost our nerve and tried to run things in a cheaper manner; we lost more heavily. Johnson made us a small offer for the goodwill and we sold out to him. I was just where I started: flat broke.

I used to wonder sometimes what the chauffeur thought of me while he stood on the kerb next to the shining motor car and looked at me slinking out of the gate and down the road. I never rode in that car but once. The servants looked at me curiously; they must have thought there was a mystery about me, slipping out of the house early in the morning, and creeping back at night when everybody had gone to bed. I was back to the shilling standard again; no job, no hope. Just a failure.

Marie-Louise had moved into a better job. She knew all about my affairs; she said why did I not go back to Paris. Why did not we both go to Paris? I said it was a good idea, but what about a job for me? She knew she could get a job, but I was not sure at all. Then out of the blue a job came my way.

A Frenchman named Ernest May used to be a diamond broker in Paris; he did jobs occasionally for my stepfather. He told me that a friend of his was opening a very swell hosiery business in the Avenue de l'Opéra and wanted an Englishman on his staff, would I like that? May said he could fix it and would let me know. Marie-Louise went to Paris and I said I would be there myself in a fortnight. The proprietor of the shop wrote me and said he would pay me one hundred francs (four pounds a month) and my board and lodging. I did not expect to "live in", but the call of Paris was loud in my ears, and once again I set out for the city I loved. Honesty compels me to admit, however, that I had been back once since I crept back to London from the skating rink crash. The manager of the West End branch of a travel agency told me that a minor Indian rajah who had been in England for the coronation of King George V wished to spend a few days in Paris *en route* to Bombay and wanted a temporary secretary; would I like to undertake the job? The rajah introduced me to a very beautiful Englishwoman, also a well-dressed Englishman, and said they were all three going to Paris. I was to go at once and book rooms for them and for an Indian servant and hire a car for a week. I was given some money and went to Paris and waited. I did as I was instructed, but the party did not arrive at the stated time. I went to London, called on the rajah who gave me more money and sent me back at once. This time the party did arrive. I took them to Fontainebleau but they seemed to have something on their minds. That night I was asked if I knew any of the Rue de la Paix jewellers. I said I knew several. I was instructed to go the next morning to one of the jewellers and instruct them to send a collection of jewels for the rajah's inspection; he wished to make presents to the English lady. I followed my instructions and went to a jewellers. They seemed very glad to have the instructions but they did not keep the appointment. I was sent to another jewellers. I made another appointment; but before returning to the rajah's hotel, I called at the first jewellers to ask why the appointment had not been kept. They told me that they had inquired at the British Embassy, and as a result of what they had been told, they did not intend to proceed with the matter. I rushed to the second jewellers and begged them not to keep the appointment. Then I went to the rajah's hotel and told him what I had done. I was pushed out of the room. I went to the garage where I had hired the car and told them they had better get their money at once. Then I took the train that very night to London. The Englishman and the woman were on the train. The following evening the London newspapers carried a story about the rajah who had been detained by the police at Marseilles. He was a huge man, weighing I should say twenty stone; of his morals I should not be allowed to write. After the India Office had intervened, the rajah was allowed to sail for India. I was beginning to have a slightly superstitious fear of Paris.

Nevertheless, the call of the queen among cities was insistent, and although I was offered a humble and lowly job, it *was* in Paris. I went to a small hotel; in the morning I called to see my boss. He looked puzzled. "You are not the man I engaged," he said. I explained I had never seen him before but that his friend, Monsieur May, had mentioned me, and that I had had a letter. The boss waved me away; he was busy, he said. Puzzled and worried I went to call on Monsieur May at his home in the rue Chateaudun. A woman with red rimmed eyes opened the door. Monsieur May? *Comment?* Did I not know that Monsieur May had committed suicide?

And my poor job was gone.

# CHAPTER VI

## PARIS AGAIN

"A FRENCHMAN," wrote Seton Merriman, "loves his mother—in the abstract." I, an Englishman, loved my mother completely and concretely, and until the moment when circumstances in the shape of my stepfather made me cease to see her or write to her, she was as much a part of my life as my very limbs. I want to explain how conscious I was of her, so that I can explain how I knew every knock down blow I received would affect her, not only because of the hurt done to me, but because the news of it would be twisted so that it appeared to her that her family, hence herself, was at fault, and that we, for I belonged to her, were a worthless, shiftless crew.

I was in Paris again, and once more without a job or a means of earning a living. The eternal struggle of my life went on, a continuous struggle broken up by occasional purple patches of plenitude and riotous living. Now I was plunged again into a mess; what should I do: return to London like a whipped cur, or stick it out? I decided to stick it out, hoping like Wilkins Micawber and Alec Boss that something would turn up.

I began to hunt for jobs, looking every day in the *Continental Daily Mail*, which I could not afford to buy, but I discovered that there was a copy to be seen in the lobby of a bank at the corner of the Avenue de l'Opéra and the rue du Quatre Septembre, and there I used to go every morning. Marie-Louise and I rented a room and kitchen in the rue des Martyrs; it was a dreary room looking on to a smelly courtyard; the landladies were both elderly and had dyed golden hair. We noticed that they were always peering out of the window which looked on to the rue des Martyrs. In our innocence we did not know we had gone to live in a brothel, small but particularly notorious. We knew it when the aged President of the Senate died in the place and his body was smuggled out. Then we moved, two doors higher up, but we were still unlucky. My mother sent me a clipping from the *Daily Telegraph* telling how a young Englishman had been arrested in the house. He was extradited on a charge of having murdered a harlot in London. Naturally, I followed the developments of the case with interest, which reached fever heat when the man was acquitted of the murder charge; it was the first criminal case in which medical evidence was called to prove that the dead woman had rare glands in her throat, glands which cause death on the slightest pressure.

I had not told my mother all the truth; I just said that I had not been able to secure the job which I had come to take over, but I was on the verge of finding another (heavens knows where). My mother replied that I would be sent a pound a week. Every week a postal order for a pound arrived, but as soon as I found a job, I wrote and asked that the dole should cease. It did. I found a job as an outside salesman for the Remington Typewriter Company. I was paid thirty-three francs per week. I never sold a type-writer, but my, how I clung to those thirty-three francs. I was assiduous in turning in daily reports, and I made them as hopeful as I could. I was put in charge of a Frenchman at first, a man who had the territory in the neighbourhood of the Gare du Nord. He taught me my patter; how curious it must have sounded, delivered with my atrocious English accent. Then I was turned loose in the same district. A few months ago I went to the Remington shop to purchase a typewriter; my mentor was a sort of shop-walker— fifteen years later.

I read in the paper that a job was vacant to sell a gadget to be affixed to telephones for the purpose of taking messages. I took that job and did well out of it; I sold a lot, too many, I suppose, because my English boss wanted to cut down my commission. Then I heard of a job in the American Express Company. I took it and nearly went to jail as a result of it.

The job was in the mail department of the famous American bank and travel agency, in the rue Scribe, the same place which had been robbed so dramatically a few years previously, when an Englishman was sent to Devil's Island, but escaped. The Negro nightwatch-man, Bailey, who was trussed up by the thieves, was the man who took me in to see the boss when I went after the job. What an extraordinary crowd we were in that office. There was the son of a once famous English bookmaker; there was a mysterious ex-grocer, a hard-bitten elderly man who had once owned his own business in Paris. There was a half-witted Scotchman who had secured a job through influence (he died of alcoholic poisoning); there was a French ex-cavalry officer, and there was me. We were a sort of Foreign Legion, men with mysterious pasts, all gathered together in a large room on the first floor. I was a junior in the service and had to be in the office at eight-thirty, to begin to help sort the letters in big laundry baskets. Then we sorted them again according to names and put them in the appropriate pigeon-holes; then we stuck forwarding labels on the letters for clients who had left addresses. I used to look with envious eyes at those addresses: Florence, Cairo, Monte Carlo, Berlin, Washington D.C., Rome, Biarritz, Vienna; and I swore to myself a desperate oath that one day I would go to all those places, and thank God, I did, to every one of them, and many times.

The swells were the fellows who had *guichets* allotted to them; they sat like bank clerks behind brass railings and had contact with the outer world, with the travellers who came to fetch their mail, the lucky rich. How I envied them. One morning I was promoted; I was given a *guichet*; I talked to the lucky rich and passed the time of day while I handed out mail. I was a swell. Then a cigar-chewing American pushed a golden louis under the rail and said thanks for your trouble, and I pushed it back and said there was no charge. The bookmaker's son who had heard the conversation kicked me hard on the calf; he was livid when I turned round. What the hell was the good of being "on the desk" if I behaved like a sanguinary fool? I apologized and accepted and pocketed a five franc piece that very afternoon. I was a swell.

Well, all good things come to an end, and, after all, I might have been there still if it had not happened that among the letters I was putting into the pigeon-hole behind me was a long envelope addressed to me. The name was spelt correctly, and the initial was my

99

first one: H. I turned the letter over; the flap was unstuck. I looked inside and took out a cheque for $100, the cheque was made out to H. Greenwall, but there was a letter which I read, and the letter made it clear that the cheque was not for me. Nevertheless, the coincidence so impressed me, the chump, that I showed the cheque to a colleague, an American named Charlie Brazil. Yes, I can recall his name all right, after all these years, and for a good reason.

The boss of the mail department said that the Big Boss wanted to see me. I was escorted to his office. The Big Boss said: "Hand me that cheque for one hundred dollars which you have in your pocket." I replied that I did not have a cheque in my pocket. The Big Boss said: "There is a policeman waiting downstairs for you; you had better surrender the cheque." I replied that the cheque was where it should be, in the pigeon-hole waiting to be called for. The Big Boss told the boss of the mail department to take me to the police station and charge me with having stolen the cheque. I protested that no cheque had been stolen. The man who was to take me to the police station fetched the cheque on the way. We walked to the station in the rue de la Chaussée d'Antin, where the inspector refused to take the charge, pointing out with true French logic that as the man who was making the charge held the cheque in his hand, there could be no question of stealing. Nevertheless, I was drummed out, and once again faced a dreary world in which there were no jobs for such as me.

We had moved to a tiny little room on the sixth floor of a house in the rue Joubert, and our luck did not desert us, for there was a *maison de rendez-vous* in the house, and a very swagger one opposite, but we did not move out; in order to supplement our slender income we even had a paying guest, an Englishman who took two meals a day with us, meals cooked on a tiny oil stove. Our guest enjoyed his food, but he decamped owing us money, the brute.

Then I found a school of languages advertising for a teacher of English. I already had one pupil, a mannequin who roomed next door to us and who insisted on taking her lesson in the most passionate underwear. The head of the school had no premises; he lived in a small hotel in the rue St. Honoré. Every evening he would give me the names and addresses of the pupils on whom I had to call the following day; they were strenuous days, for sometimes I found myself giving a lesson in the neighbourhood of the Place de la République at seven-thirty in the morning, and quite often I would give my last hour at ten o'clock at night. I asked the chief, a Mr. Bicknel, who was killed in the Mespot Campaign, if he had any other tutors working for him; he said he had one other, but he discouraged my meeting him. Eventually we did meet, and I discovered that my unseen colleague was a free-lance journalist, now a very famous writer in London.

L. and I, once we found one another, became fast friends. I confided to him a dreadful secret: I had tried to write. He asked me to show him something I had written. One day walking up the Champs-Elysées I produced my attempt at a short story, the one thing I had saved from my destroyed writings. L. read it as we walked slowly along. He stopped still and said: "Do you realize how good this is?" It seemed that some hitherto invisible orchestra suddenly burst into a hymn of praise. I had been praised! Me, me, ME. It was incredible. I, the blockhead, the failure, I had produced something, created something which a professional writer thought good. Incredible. L. made me promise there and then that I would start writing; he had come from Belgium to write in Paris, and he had just taken on this teaching job while he found his feet; he said that as soon as possible he was going to start to write, and I said I would, too. Without either of us being aware of it, circumstances were marching to force us both to write or starve.

Our salaries stopped, just like that; they stopped. We could not see our Chief; he was never "in". We decided to lay siege and we did; we said we would not go on teaching unless we were paid; we struck, but we did not get our money. Then we received a small hand out. Then the Chief vanished and we were stranded. I bought a twenty-second hand typewriter and started to write, anything, everything. I wrote to *Modern Society* which was edited by Frank Harris, and suggested doing a weekly Paris Gossip page. Harris knew my Vanity Fair column, so gave me the page, and what is more, he actually paid me for quite a long time, certainly until he went to prison for criminal libel; then when he came out he paid me with promises, and also with marvellous conversation. He came to Paris and stayed at the Ritz. We sat up all hours of the night talking, mostly in the winter garden of the Grand Hotel. One night Bottomley came up to Harris and said he had just arrived from Switzerland where he had been running his Derby Sweep and had made sixty thousand pounds. "A lot of money," commented Harris, "but think how much more you could have made if you ran it on the level: after all, you know, Bottomley, honesty is the best policy" (like a sheep praising vegetarianism.) "Yes," said Bottomley dryly, "so it is, Frank, if you can afford it."

I started writing articles for the *Theatre* a magazine in New York, which did me very well. When Lee Shubert came to Paris and stayed at the Astoria I went to see him. Shubert told me he had a paper of his own in New York, a theatrical paper published every Saturday; he wanted me to write for it and to sign my articles: Raoul Duval. Shubert wanted me to see Sacha Guitry to get an option on one of his plays; he was going to put up money for me in a Paris bank so that I could buy plays for him. That night Shubert took me to dinner in a Champs-Elysées restaurant. We sat outside, and from where we were sitting I could see the bench on which I had slept. I thought the story would amuse the impressario. He listened and he answered: "Do you think there are enough mussels in this sauce?" I was to go and see him the next morning, but he had left for London. I wrote innumerable articles; they appeared, but . . .

An English weekly was started in Paris, and I did the racing articles; I was tackling everything: international politics, the theatre, racing, everything was fish which came to my net. I called on John Raphael, then Paris correspondent of the *Daily Express*. He said his assistant was off that evening; there had been a slight case of double murder in the Hotel Meurice, would I like to cover it? Before the words were out of his mouth I was downstairs and jumping into a passing horse cab I was off to cover my very first news story.

An English army officer had shot a German woman and then turned the revolver on himself. Having obtained the story, I rushed back to Raphael's flat. How much? he asked. I shuffled my feet and coughed; I really did not know. Raphael settled the matter by opening a drawer and taking from it a five franc piece. He handed it to me with the remark that had his assistant been there it would have cost him nothing. Five francs, three and ninepence—not very much for a good story, plus two cab fares; but what neither the buyer nor the seller knew that night was, that within a little more than two years, the modest little fool who accepted the five francs had been given the job of the man who handed him the silver cartwheel.

I started calling on all the Paris correspondents, English and American; one man, an Englishman named Frank Grundy, who represented the New York *Sun*, in the days when it was a great and influential newspaper, became my best friend and from time to time gave me nice little jobs to do. It was Grundy who told me that Hulme Beaman, correspondent of the *Standard*, wanted an assistant. I was after that job like a flash of lightning. I secured the job and was told to start on the following Sunday, New Year's Day.

When I went into the flat I found it was empty; I walked all over the place; then I discovered a scrap of paper, a torn envelope. On it was written; "I have gone fishing and shall be back Friday; if anything happens, send it to the *Standard*." What happened was that the telephone bell rang and a Voice said it was the Editor who wanted to speak to Beaman. I said Beaman was out. Who was I, asked the Voice. I said I was the new assistant. The Voice told me not to be a fool, because there was no assistant; it added as an afterthought that the French battleship *Liberté* had blown up in Toulon harbour and I was to send five hundred words. Yes, sir, I said, and wondered how the devil one found out about battleships which blew themselves up in Toulon. I went out and bought an afternoon paper, went back and read it; while I was doing so the front door bell rang. It was a small angel disguised as a telegraph boy; he handed me a blue piece of paper which when unfolded we found to contain approximately a hundred words from the Toulon correspondent. When Beaman came back, he looked through the file and said I had done very well. To appease the gods of fortune, Marie-Louise and I had taken a small flat in the Avenue Trudaine. The afternoon following Beaman's return from his fishing trip, he called me into his office; he held a letter in his hand. "I am very sorry," he began gently, "but White (the Editor) writes to say that if I require an assistant I must pay him myself, and I cannot afford to pay one. I am afraid we must part company at the end of the week. I am very sorry."

I was terribly sorry, too. When Marie-Louise came to meet me that night, I drank three strong absinthes before I broke the news. In the courtyard in the Avenue Trudaine were two doves in a cage, and while I sat day after day and brooded, the cooing of those doves nearly drove me mad. In the depth of my despair a messenger boy delivered an express letter. It was from Beaman. I tore it open. The note told me to keep in touch with the writer, because he might need me again. I kept in touch all right, but my services were not needed. One of the bitterest moments of my life occurred some twelve years later, when I was *Daily Express* Chief Correspondent. A boy brought me in a card on which I saw the name: Hulme Beaman. I saw him at once. Humbly he asked me if I could give him a job.

Well, out we went from the Avenue Trudaine. I had
met a man with whom I was at school, Sinclair Rogers,
who was the Racing Correspondent of the Continental *Daily Mail*. He lived on the top floor of a small
hotel, and like every member of the editorial staff,
he had a copy of the paper delivered to him every
morning early, but he never rose until very late. The
paper I used to see in the bank was no longer available,
and I still could not afford to buy the paper, so I used
to go to Rogers's hotel and sit and wait for him to
come down, to see his paper. Once I broke the
wrapper while I was waiting, and he was terribly
angry. Once I went up to his room, and he was
furious. So I had to sit and wait. From Rogers I
learned the name of the editor of the Continental
*Daily Mail*: Sommerville Story. I called on him and
asked for a job. He took my name and address and
said he would write me when there was a vacancy. I
asked Rogers to let me know if he heard of a vacancy,
but I heard nothing. Then I found out what time
Story went to the office in the afternoon and took to
haunting the strip of boulevard near the top of the
rue du Sentier; I wanted to meet Story "acciden-
tally"; one day I did and he said there would be a
vacancy almost immediately. The pavement seemed
to have vanished when I went out: I walked on air
only. It was not much of a job really; but as I went
through the door to take up my job, I said a little
prayer: that I might keep the job, and I did, from
October 1911 until August 1914.

I was the only reporter on the paper; I had to go
round the hotels and find out who was staying there
and take the names; if there was anybody interesting,
I had to interview them; the real news came over the

direct telegraph from Carmelite House, in London.
Valentine Williams was the Paris correspondent; well
do I remember the first time I saw him: he had just
come from the races, in a top hat, morning coat; race
glasses slung across his shoulder. Williams was succeeded by G. Ward Price, monocled and bored looking. Gosh, I used to think, if only I could have a job
like that!

I had my fun, though. We had a nice amusing
crowd, and Story was kind to me. Soon after I left,
he was sacked : "Like a drunken butler," he wrote me.
It seemed he had fallen foul of Lord Northcliffe about
the opening of the St. Cloud Country Club, which
the Lord had thought was not covered properly.
Story engaged an assistant editor, a bald-headed man
who looked older than his years; the new assistant
editor had been the correspondent of a New York
newspaper in Berlin. He had come to Paris on a
holiday, gone to the Folies Bergères where he met and
married a harlot who spent all his money. After Blank
had been working for a few days, Northcliffe arrived
unexpectedly from London. He did not enter the
editorial room, but peeped through the open door.
"Who's that bald-headed man?" he inquired. "That's
the new assistant editor," he was told. "He is, eh?
Well, tell him he is leaving on Saturday."

At the end of 1913 there was a blight over Paris;
the talk was all about war. There will be no business
doing until after the war, people said. War . . . war
. . . war . . . Then one evening Ward Price rushed
through the office and dashed to the London telephone. "Give me the box, quickly," he said.
"Madame Caillaux has shot and killed Gaston Calmette, editor of *Le Figaro*."

The shooting of Gaston Calmette was the climax of a cavalcade of events which rocked Europe and passed like a panorama before my eyes during the two years I spent with the Continental *Daily Mail*. Paris, editors said, was an important place where unimportant things happened. But the money they spent trying to collect and tabulate those unimportant things! Both the London and New York *Times* were paying me a retainer to give them facts concerning society people; my social notes about pink teas and dinner parties attended by Americans in Paris formed the background of a long cable sent to New York on Thursdays for publication on Sundays. I was earning seven pounds a week now, and the editor of the *Daily Mail* was only paid ten pounds a week! Then a crazy man shot an Austrian Archduke in far away Serbia, and the world exploded.

That Sunday afternoon when the Archduke was shot, I was tramping Paris, mopping my brow and collecting names. The Grand Prix was being run at Longchamps, and I had backed the winner. Going into a hotel to wade through the visitors' list, a reception clerk told me the news of the shooting; it did not seem to matter much, but with the end of the trial of Madame Caillaux we realized the significance. It was stifling hot, all the windows were shut tight. The Press benches were tightly packed, but one more man, a fat and pale-faced Frenchman was trying to wedge himself in. He was all hot and bothered and cursed because criminal trials were not his business; he was a financial writer, yet he had come to help a colleague, just when there was an uproar on the Bourse, he grumbled.

Uproar? What uproar, and why? It seemed that

an Austrian brokerage house, the same one which had caused a panic of selling a couple of years ago when the Agadir incident occurred, was now staging a selling orgy and prices were tumbling down. War?

Yes, war. The most exciting month I have ever known began and continued throughout July. If this was war, it was just a glorious picnic. I happened to be passing a then post-office in the rue Boissy d'Anglas when a clerk came out and stuck up a notice: it was the Mobilization notice. A woman in black passed, read the notice and burst into tears. Friends appeared almost magically, and a little self-conscious, in uniform. Regiments marched away with flowers and green boughs stuck in their rifles. Civilians of all nations marched up and down the boulevards shouting the "Marseillaise" and revolutionary songs which had not been sung in years, and they shouted a shout which Paris had not heard since the Franco-Prussian War: "à Berlin, huh, huh; à Berlin, huh, huh." Staccato and frightening. I went and joined the British Volunteers and expected to find myself in the Foreign Legion very soon.

When France and Germany were definitely at war, we English were not too popular; the French thought we would not fight. I remember a small procession headed by a young Roman Catholic priest marching up the rue du Sentier and demonstrating outside the *Daily Mail* office; the priest kept shouting: "Hurrah for England (in English) hurrah for England," but there was a note of interrogation in his voice.

The era of smashing and bashing had died away. I saw two Germans killed during mobilization. One had disguised himself as a porter at the Gare du Nord, and had his skull battered in with wooden sabots.

The other, a brave fool, was a tailor living and working in a small flat in a building above the Café Napolitain. He shouted "*Vive l'Allemagne.*" A crowd battered in the street door, then avengingly marched up the stone staircase to the top floor, smashed their way in, beat the German to death and then tossed his body out like a dead rabbit to a pack of dogs. Later that evening I saw a broken body lying across the saddle of a *cuirassier*.

German shops and cafés had been smashed, but when Appenrodt's windows were broken, no food-stuffs were looted because a rumour ran through the crowd that the food had been poisoned.

I worked about eighteen hours a day. I did my usual job in the daytime, but instead of picking out the names of visitors, I picked up war stories, and also managed to find time to drill. In the late afternoon I went back to the office and worked there throughout the night, leaving in the dawn. We used to go to a café opposite the Folies Bergères and eat bacon and eggs and talk to the Tiller Girls who were working at the music-hall opposite. Then I snatched a few hours sleep and began all over again. What a picnic.

One of the *Mail* directors came over and after he had consulted with the advertising manager I was given an extra job. That advertising man and his assistant need a paragraph all to themselves. The manager was a former waiter, a Swiss, whom North-cliffe had picked up during a visit to Switzerland, and with his Puck-like humour had made him advertising manager in Paris. The assistant called himself Sullivan. The War disclosed that the name was Solomon.

I was asked to canvass the hotels to advertise in a

special column which was to be devoted to the names of HOTELS WHICH WILL KEEP OPEN DURING THE WAR. The first day I brought back £10 worth of business, and the second day I brought back £15 worth. I had been offered fifty per cent of the value of the orders obtained, but when they found I was doing so well, the director from London left for me a nice little note of thanks which enclosed a golden louis, sixteen shillings, in full settlement. I wrapped up the golden louis in a nice little rude note and sent it back to the director. Then I went off to do my evening job: to call at the War Office for the night *communiqué*. I had to wait some time. When I returned late to the office I found the staff in the corridor and one of the workmen taking down the *Daily Mail* electric sign. The Germans were coming. The French Government was going to Bordeaux; the *Daily Mail* was going after it, with two members of the staff only, of whom I was not one.

It was like the breaking up of a little world; we all went our divers ways. I had become acquainted with a young man who used to come round every evening on a bicycle to fetch dispatches for the New York *Times*. Like me he had been teaching. Like me, he had known hard times. His name is Walter Duranty, and to-day he is one of the most famous journalists in the world. Two of my colleagues, an Irishman who was intended for the Indian Police, and a young man from Hull, went to the army and were dead quite soon. I shook hands all round and thought that before going to bed I would pass by the window of the New York *Sun* and see if there was a light in Frank Grundy's window. There was, and once again the drift of my life changed.

Grundy told me that Alphonse Courlander, the "morose pianist" of an earlier chapter, now Paris correspondent of the *Daily Express*, was looking for an assistant because the Rumanian who had been helping him had joined the Foreign Legion. I went to Courlander's flat in the rue de Rivoli, where the *concierge* told me Courlander had left for London. Five minutes later I met him sitting outside the Café Napolitain, his nerves completely shattered. Ward Price came along shouting: "Hullo, Alphonse, what are you doing?" Courlander replied he was going home because Paris was not safe. Ward Price roared with laughter. "Greenwall and I are going to be shot against the same wall, aren't we, Greenwall?" Courlander shuddered. I saw curious scratches on his wrists. Later I learned that he had made a futile attempt to commit suicide.

Courlander told me he had moved from his flat to the Terminus Hotel, Gare St. Lazare. I went there with him and tried to make him eat some lunch. He asked me to do his work; I agreed; he asked me to come and stay with him in his flat. I demurred, and then he confessed that he had put his luggage into the train that was leaving for the coast that morning, but he had changed his mind at the last moment. We tried to find his luggage; it had gone. During the afternoon Courlander broke down completely and kept saying he wanted to go home and see his father; his wife and small daughter had been staying at a French seaside resort when war broke out. I made Courlander promise that if he went home he would go immediately to the *Daily Express* office. I promised I would look after his job until I heard what the *Daily Express* intended to do. Then I saw Courlander off for Hâvre;

he was so broken down that I put him in charge of the head printer of the *Daily Mail* who was taking his family to England.

The next morning I received a telegram from Hâvre, signed Courlander, saying: "Don't stay in Paris because it is not safe."

The French Government had gone. Paris ranked as a provincial city now, and the Germans were approaching it, faster and faster, but I had given a promise to look after the job of a man who had collapsed from shock. I was going to hang on.

# BOOK II

# CHAPTER I

## PRISONER OF WAR

ONCE WHEN I was very young, I saw Forbes Robertson in Kipling's play "The Light That Failed." The hero is a war-correspondent. Secretly, in my bedroom in Maida Vale, with the word "blockhead" ringing in my ears, when I knew I was doomed to failure, I still thought sometimes that one day I might somehow be a war-correspondent. When I was a little boy I used to read in the *Daily Mail* the despatches of G. W. Stevens, and other correspondents. How I would have loved to become one of them! The wars of my early youth had been a long way away. I was just as far away from journalism. Now, as I have related in the last chapter, now here was war on my doorstep. Somehow I was going to be a war-correspondent.

## A FOOL THERE WAS

Nominally, or legally, or whatever the correct expression is, I was still a member of the staff of the *Continental Daily Mail*. In my pocket-book was a photograph of myself on my official card of credentials, a photograph of myself with an incipient moustache, which I had long-since cast into the limbo. This, as will be seen later, turned partly to my undoing.

Also in my pocket-book was a letter appointing me Paris correspondent of the *Daily Express*, and still more damning, also in my pocket-book was a large sum of money. In fact, I had sufficient circumstantial evidence in my pocket to get me shot, and very nearly executed I was, as a spy! I escaped death, but with a threat to be kept in prison until the end of the war. This was in September, 1914, and we all knew very well that the war was going to be over by Christmas!

I was absolutely determined to be a hero. Circumstances had prevented me from fighting, but I was going to get to the field of action, even if I had to walk to it. Thoughts of marriage were in my mind, and I had talked them over with Marie-Louise and we had come to an amicable decision to part. Despite this very imminent parting, I made up my mind I would leave Paris just for a day to try and find out what was happening to the British Army. In those days in Paris news was scarce. There were British stragglers to be seen about the city. One evening, I met an English soldier leading his horse. I met him just at the corner of the Boulevard des Capucines and the rue Scribe. According to his story, he was the only survivor of the B.E.F. Vaguely, in the *Daily Mail* office, we had known that the British Army was in full retreat from Mons, but how far from Paris, or how near it, either the British or the Germans were, nobody knew, and when the *Daily Mail* packed up and went to Bordeaux, there was still the same lack of news.

Reading the official *communiqués*, meagre as they were, and looking at the map as one read them, it was possible to make a fairly intelligent guess as to where parts of the British Army might be found.

Early on a Sunday morning, I went to the Gare de l'Est and booked a ticket to Lagny, in the Marne department. There was a military picket at the station and I was not allowed to go outside. The train was going back to Le Raincy and I went back with it, and leaving Le Raincy station, I walked into the market place and there met a carter who was taking vegetables to Chelles. I went with him.

Outside Chelles I left the carter and walked along the river and went and had a drink in a little inn. There for the first time I heard artillery fire and was told that there was an action going on at Chaye. The report was that the Germans had been pushed back ten miles.

Leaving the *auberge*, I walked towards Lagny, and was held up several times by French pickets. Among the other papers in my pocket-book was what is known as a "*coupe-file*", which is a small card issued by the Préfecture of Police to journalists. This little card is most important in Paris, but is not of the slightest use outside the city gates. Nevertheless, this little piece of pasteboard was a magic pass those days along the Marne. Every time I showed it, the French soldiers stood back and saluted and allowed me to walk on.

When I reached Gournay, however, there was some real trouble in store for me. A French officer would not take any notice of my police pass, nor of my meant-to-be honeyed words. He consented, however, as it was a very hot day, that we should drink a mug of cider. We sat down and talked, and when we had finished our drink, I got up and shook hands and strolled onwards.

I began to meet wounded Colonial troops, some

walking wounded, and others being taken to hospital in country carts. The weather was absolutely glorious, the sun was hot; church bells were ringing, and along the banks of the Marne civilians were fishing, although very near, not more than a few hundred yards away, were the ruins of a bridge which had been blown up by a British engineering unit only at daybreak that very morning. As I walked, I heard the boom of guns, echoing through the valleys. Pigeons and other birds started up in alarm, but I lit my pipe and walked on. I was determined to be a hero.

### Late for Dinner

I forgot all about my promise to Marie-Louise that I would be home for dinner. I went on and reached Lagny just as dusk had fallen. I realized that it was impossible to get back to Paris that night, I thought that I might push on as far as Jossigny and there get myself put up. It was dark when I left Lagny and first realized how close I might be to the Germans. I was told that a patrol of Uhlans had been seen in the neighbourhood. During the daylight hours, that did not seem to matter so much, but now it was dark, I began to feel fear, fear of the unknown, fear of being afraid. So that my shoes should not make too much noise treading along the dusty road, I began to walk on the grass at the roadside. Suddenly, just ahead of me, I saw a flash of light through the trees. I stopped. Nothing happened. I started forward again, but then there came through the night a shout: *"Halte-là!"* I stopped and waited. Nothing happened. Again I moved forward, then suddenly the trees above my head appeared to have been lashed with a whip, fragments of leaves fell at my feet. There was another whistle through the air, and again the bough was hit as if a whip had cut across it. I shouted out in French: "*Je suis Anglais.*" In a few moments six elderly French territorials came towards me, their rifles levelled and bayonets fixed. They were harmless gentlemen. After looking at my "*coupe-file*" and my papers, but luckily not understanding anything, they allowed me to go on.

## I Meet The British Army

Very soon after I had been shot at, I was glad to meet a man riding a bicycle. He was going to Jossigny; he dismounted and we walked along the road together. When we reached Jossigny, I began to knock at doors, seeking a lodging for the night; the doors were all locked, the inhabitants all had left. It was so dark that one could see absolutely nothing; then I heard the steady tramp, tramp, tramp of soldiers. The man with the bicycle said they were French troops. We stood together, the Frenchman and I, at the crossroads, where the troops would have to pass. It was so dark that although the men were quite close, I could not distinguish their uniform. Then out of the night came this sentence: "Good night, old sport." It was the British Army, in full retreat from Mons.

## Night-time on the Marne

I asked one of the passing men what regiment he belonged to, and he said the Essex Regiment. Then came the Connaught Rangers, then the Inniskillin

Fusiliers. It was the 4th Division, commanded by Brigadier-General Snow.

When I looked round, the Frenchman with the bicycle had disappeared. But in a moment I had another companion, a young despatch rider, an Englishman on a motor bicycle, who like me was hungry. We found a jovial baker, who invited us to sit down with his family. He was one of the few people left in Jossigny. He provided us with food and would take no payment. He gave us all he had: sardines, pears and bread and milk and wine, and handed out litres and litres and litres of red wine to any soldiers who cared to dash out of the ranks and seize a bottle and run back again.

The despatch rider said that he thought he would find the Essex lines and sleep there, and I was alone again. A detachment of the Army Service Corps then arrived and turned into a field behind the baker's house. I asked the officer in charge of the unit if I could stay with them. He told me they had just come from Brie-Conte-Robert, and he and his men were in a pessimistic mood. I was given a blanket, and before turning in for the night, I partook of cheese and biscuits and rum and water; then I fell asleep. I was tired out, but very soon, it seemed only a matter of seconds, I was prodded in the ribs by a booted foot. The unit had to be on the move again.

I walked as fast as I could, tired and footsore, but I could not keep up with the mounted unit. I was not far from a rear wagon, however, when I heard wild screams of terror; scream upon scream, rising crescendo to hysteria, and then out of a cottage by the side of the road came running a woman carrying a small child in her arms and with two tiny children plucking at her skirts. They were all crying and screaming. Just as I reached them, there was a sound of galloping horses and up came two mounted military policemen. The woman was now perfectly frantic with terror, she threw herself upon her knees and begged for mercy. She thought we were Germans.

One of the policemen asked me to interpret. The woman's story was that there was a German soldier prowling round the house, trying to break in. The policemen jumped from their horses, drew their revolvers from their holsters and asked me to hold the horses. The woman and the children remained with me. The two policemen entered the garden together and went round the house. Presently there was the sound of a struggle, loud curses and finally a ringing laugh. One of the policemen called out: "Here is your German," and came out of the garden dragging with him a Dublin Fusilier. The soldier, one who had drunk of the baker's wine, had been overcome; he had been marching and fighting on an empty stomach; he had broken ranks and wanted to get a rest for the night. The police took him away.

## PRISONER OF WAR

Again I was alone and very tired, very scared. I hurried on as quickly as I could, intending to catch up with the convoy. From behind came sounds of a humming motor, and out of the dark came a little grey army car. In it were two British officers. They pulled up alongside of me and asked in very bad French if they were on the right road to Villeneuve-St. Georges. Alas, if only I had answered in French.

I replied in English that I had not the faintest idea. The two officers conversed together in whispers. Then I was invited to get into the car. Full of joy and gratitude I got in and was most profuse in my thanks. I looked round and found myself in the company of three men who said they were French cavalry who had been captured by the Germans and who had managed to escape, with the help of a village schoolmaster who had provided them with civilian clothes. Not for one moment did I doubt their story.

On we went through the night, and then pulled up with a jerk at the gates of a *château*. The gates were opened and we drove along the carriage way, passing many military cars parked to the right and left. The three Frenchmen were told to get out. I was left alone for a few moments and then was told to come along.

When it came to my turn to be cross-examined, I must have made an utter fool of myself. My pocket-book was removed, examined and there spread out in front of me were my credentials from the *Daily Mail* and the *Daily Express* and the whole sum of money I was carrying on me. I was pressed and pressed and pressed to answer questions. I was told most politely that I was a liar. I was unable to say exactly at what time I reached Jossigny. There was a crowd of men all looking at me with great disapproval. Nearly all were British officers, but there were a few French *liaison* officers. Suddenly, to my astonishment, I saw a face I knew. He was a French journalist, a man who knew me quite well, who had spoken to me only about a week before in Paris. Now he was mobilised and, on account of his extremely good knowledge of English, he was attached to the British Army. I smiled:

"Hello de C——." I exclaimed, "how are you?" He stared at me coldly and answered: "I don't know you."

That seemed to be the end. An officer in the middle of the group who, I afterwards learned, was General Snow, said to me: "You are a prisoner of war." A guard composed of men of the King's Royal Rifles was turned out and I was marched away to a stable. Humbly I craved permission not to sleep in the stable and I was accorded this gratification. I was given a few handfulls of straw and made to lie down on the cobbles in company with the French cavalry soldiers. We were all suspected spies. The Provost Marshal, Captain James, came along and I talked to him. I asked him to send a message for me to the *Daily Express*. He said he could not do this, but he was good enough to send a message for me to Marie-Louise, and a very cryptic message it was. I did not sleep very much, but I talked to the men who were guarding me. They were changed every hour. They were very good-humoured despite all they had suffered since Mons. The principal topic of discussion was whether the Prince of Wales was coming out to France or not. Everybody was sure that the war was going to be over by Christmas.

In the morning, I washed at the pump, and as a suspected spy, politely stepped back, when Major Poore, of the Hampshire Regiment and a pre-war famous amateur cricketer, came along to perform his morning ablutions. My guards and I robbed the *château* henroost, and stole peaches and pears from its sunny walls. We breakfasted on biscuits and jam and tea, and then hell broke loose. I did not know it at the moment, I did not know anything very much, but

the noise I heard was the beginning of the Battle of
the Marne.

Captain James came along and told me that a wire
had been sent to G.H.Q. asking what should be done
with me. In the meantime, I was placed under an
armed guard, and as the army had to be on the move,
I went along with it, a prisoner of war. I was warned
that I was not to speak to anybody and anybody who
tried to speak to me was immediately removed. All
day long, I was marched, hearing the sound of the
fighting, but actually seeing nothing at all. That
night, we reached Villeneuve-le-Comte. Once again
a *château* was headquarters. In the fading sunlight,
the French interpreter, the former journalist, de
C—— came up to me and whispered: "I knew you all
right last night, but I'm going to write a book about
this war myself. So long." And that, as they say, was
that.

## To be Shot or——?

I was conducted to the top floor of the *château* and
there pushed into a room where I found numerous
civilian prisoners; there were the three suspected
cavalrymen, several civilians, two of them who claimed
to be Belgian refugees; two British soldiers, one of
whom was the Dublin Fusilier. We sat all together,
talking in whispers. At dawn, the two British soldiers
were taken out and shot.

Next morning, I was marched away again, still
under guard, and that night reached Montmirail.
The Germans had been in occupation of this *château*
only a few hours before we reached it. Half-eaten

food was scattered about the brocade sofas and chairs, and in a laurel-bush, three German prisoners were hiding. That night, I slept in a cellar with the three Germans. They all belonged to the 5th Company of the 36th Regiment of Infantry and came from Magdeburg. I bought a belt from one of them for a franc.

The next morning I was put in a motor lorry with the three Germans and sent to Tournon.

At Tournon I was held under a guard and was then about to be put in a cattle-truck and sent to Limoges, which was a three-day journey. I happened to be sitting on thê embankment at the side of the railway, waiting for the cattle truck to be ready, when a British officer passed by in a motor car. He came over and talked to me and I told him my story, which he checked up with some other officers. He came back to me and said that if I would give him my word of honour that I would not try to escape, he would take a chance and let me go with him to Melun, where he was to proceed on a special mission to General French. Naturally I gave my word of honour, and very soon I was driving through the pouring rain. The officer who was in charge of me handed me back my papers and also my money.

## In Handcuffs

As soon as I got to Melun, I was taken before General Sir Neville Macready, who had recently come to France from Ireland. The first question the General asked me, when he heard I was a reporter, was: "Do you know ——?" he named one of the most famous *Daily Mail* correspondents who, as compared to me, was as a giant alongside a pigmy. I shook my head. The General burst out: "He used to come and mess with us in Ireland and then go home and write scurrilous articles about us." I was glad that I shook my head. General Macready then turned me over to Colonel Bunbury, who was Provost Marshal at G.H.Q.

The General was perfectly sure that even if I were a journalist, as I said I was, I was also a spy, and after arguing out loud with himself, he came to the conclusion that it was almost worse to be a journalist than a spy.

Colonel Bunbury took away all my papers, and confiscated my money. Then he ordered me to be taken away. Before I left his presence, I said: "What are you going to do with me, Colonel?" He mused for a moment and then he said slowly: "I don't know, but I don't think we'll shoot you."

That night I ate dinner in the mess of the officers of the Irish Light Horse, who had just come out from Ireland and had been aeroplane guard at Le Cateau after the retreat. I was sent to bed in a dormitory of a Melun girl's school. Just before I went to sleep, I heard that General French was moving his headquarters the next morning at nine o'clock to Coulomiers.

At four o'clock in the morning I was awakened and found three khaki figures standing at the foot of my bed. I was perfectly certain that this was the end and that I was going to be shot. I was told to dress quickly and then I was handcuffed between two French gendarmes. I was taken out of the courtyard, General French in a motor car went past me, only separated by a pane of glass in the window of his car. He glanced at me, a dusty, dishevelled, unshaven ragamuffin as I must have looked.

G.H.Q. was moved away, and all that remained were two plain-clothes detectives, who removed my handcuffs and then took me into a room and cross-examined me. They showed me a letter signed by Colonel Bunbury saying: "This man should be kept in the Cherche-Midi Prison until the end of the War." Cherche-Midi was used as a military prison in Paris. I was put in the motor car with the detectives and driven towards the French capital.

I was taken to the Préfecture and there once again cross-examined. I gave the names of people who knew me very well indeed, who had known me for years. The detectives filled up many sheets of paper with my information. Then suddenly I remembered that I knew a French detective and asked if he was anywhere about. This man, Inspector Paris, happened to be in the next room. He came in and identified me, and I was turned out into the sunny street, free to do what I liked. I bought a paper and read that the Battle of the Marne was over and that Paris was saved.

# CHAPTER II

AFTER THE Marne was over, I settled down to learn my job. My experience of journalism was really very limited. I had joined the *Daily Mail* staff in Paris at the end of 1911, but it was a very small office and my job as the one reporter the paper owned did not give me very much experience of the wider world, so, as I say, I had to learn. The offer the *Daily Express* made me was this: they would pay me £5 a week more than the Continental *Daily Mail* had paid me. The *Daily Mail* had paid me the magnificent salary of £12 per month, so I started work with the *Daily Express* for the sum of £7 per week, and, on September 30th, 1914, I got married. The ceremony was performed in the *Mairie* of the first *arrondissement*, in the room in which Napoleon Bonaparte was married to Josephine.

The Government had gone to Bordeaux. Paris was a provincial city, but had prepared in a way for a siege, and the masses of dried vegetables, tinned sardines, tinned meats and other things were all apparently wasted. There was nothing much to write about; as there were no telephones and no cables working between Paris and London, it was just as well that there was not much news. Nevertheless, a steady stream of articles had to be kept up; the *Daily Express* and myself organized a service of couriers who came over one a day by the night boat between Southampton and Hâvre. They called for the articles about six-thirty every morning. What fights there were over these couriers. I had been told to go and live in the flat which had been rented by Alphonse Courlander. It was situated in the rue de Rivoli, overlooking two tiny courtyards; it was a most depressing place. I had to live there and to work there. My few sticks of furniture did not matter; I was living like a cuckoo in somebody else's nest. I had heard nothing from or of Courlander since the telegram which I mentioned and which he sent me when he was leaving France. Then I did hear, indirectly, what had happened to him. He did not keep his promise to me to go immediately to the *Daily Express* and tell the editor how he felt about matters. What he did was to go to a police station in Bloomsbury and there give himself up. The kindly police inspector saw that Courlander had had a bad nervous breakdown, so after noting his name and a few particulars about him, the inspector telephoned to the editor of the *Daily Express*, who himself told me this story. One morning the police rang him up and asked if they had a member of the staff named Courlander. The editor replied that Courlander was their Paris correspondent. Maybe, replied the police, but at the moment he is in bed at our police station. You had better send and fetch him. Courlander went from the police station to a nursing home in the country; a few months later I had the distressing news that he had committed suicide.

When the Germans retreated from the Marne to the Aisne, the Government returned from Bordeaux; so did the *Daily Mail*. The editor, Sommerville Story, sent

me an express letter asking me to return for duty that
night. That made matters rather difficult. The *Daily
Mail* had abandoned me in Paris. The editor of the
*Daily Express* had insisted that I should be released
from active service; I had accepted the offer made me.
I went back to the editor of the *Daily Mail* and explained the situation to him. He shrugged his
shoulders as though to say: "Well, you young fool, I
suppose you know what you are doing." I returned
to my miserable flat more miserable than ever.

The *concierges*, husband and wife, of the rue de
Rivoli building, did not like me or my wife. Firstly,
they were in great terror of the Germans and, secondly,
they thought that having a journalist in the house
would be an added danger when the Germans in-
vaded Paris and began to shoot people. Every night
I had to go down and fight for the admittance of that
day's courier from London. The *concierges* refused to
allow the courier to pass; I had to insist that pass he
should. In the end, he always did, but every night
there was a fight, and again most mornings, when the
courier came to fetch the mail.

## A Mystery of Paris

Passing Ian Malcolm's Red Cross office in the rue
de la Paix one morning, a friend introduced me to a
young man in a blue suit and a straw hat. Mr. Blank
said he was a naval officer. We crossed the road and
sat on the terrace of the Café de la Paix, where the
young man told me he was a god-son of Admiral
Beresford on his way to London on a secret mission.

He told me how his ship had been chasing the German raider *Emden*; he told me how he had been in a submarine fight with a German cruiser and how he had bombed the German concessions in China. In my pocket note-book he drew a map of the area where he had had all these exploits; he described to me the German wireless he had found in the coconut trees in Ceylon. That day, the Anglo-American Press Association was holding its weekly lunch, and I asked Mr. Blank to be my guest. He accepted; off we went. In the crowded room, Blank and I came face to face with a wizened little lame man who hailed Blank as Doc and expressed surprise that they should meet like this. Blank drew me on one side and said he would prefer not to sit at table with the little man, because he was such a common little fellow; but as it happened, when we came to sit down to lunch, the little fellow sat opposite Blank and chattered about the club, without saying what club he meant, but there were frequent references to what the little man called the "Islands". After the meal, I managed to have a word with the little man apart and asked him how he fared and from whence he had come. He told me unhesitatingly that he had been the steward of a club in Manila where Blank had been a doctor. There had been some little unpleasantness because when war was declared there was excitement in the club and Blank had refused to drink confusion to the Germans. Subsequently, said the little man, Doc and he had sailed together for Europe; they were staying at the Hotel X in Paris. I had previously invited Blank to dine with me at my rue de Rivoli flat, but I felt in something of a quandary. Blank had lied heavily, maybe it was nothing more than stupid boastfulness

133

. . . but it was wartime, and you never know, I told myself. I consulted a friend who advised me to inform the police. I did so. What happened to him I was never able to discover.

In the spring of 1918, I went into the Café Napolitain, where the journalists used to meet, always at the same table, and there sitting with them was Blank, now Captain Blank, wearing the uniform of an officer of the Royal Army Medical Corps. We recognized each other. Blank followed me out of the café and said he remembered me denouncing him to the police; he said that of course he could have had me punished very severely and even now, because of his highly placed friends, he could have me expelled from France. I invited him to do whatever he thought he should do, but he did nothing. I saw Blank several times, still in uniform; he said he was stationed in Paris. He was something of a mystery to several of the newspaper men; one had the curiosity to look Blank up in the Medical Directory but could not find the name.

After the War, Captain Blank stayed on, in uniform. One day when Mr. Lloyd George was at the Hotel Crillon, I went to call on my friend, Sir John Davies, who was the Premier's secretary. Davies came downstairs and said: "Greenwall, we have come away without any cards, here is L.G.'s plate, can you get some engraved quickly?" Before I could even answer, Blank had the plate and said he would order the cards. He went off. Two days later, Davies called me up and asked for my friend's address, because the Premier still had no cards. The thought of Blank going around Paris with the Premier's engraving plate gave me furiously to think, as the French are supposed to say, but seldom do.

Then Blank appeared without uniform. He was going to practice in Paris, he said. There was an English chemist named G. with whom I was one day when Blank appeared. I introduced the two. Some days later, G. said to me: "I like your friend, but I find he has no degree to practice medicine in Paris, so I am arranging for him to go to Lyons to get a degree." Sometime later, G. who supposedly had a very good business in the centre of the city, was charged with trafficking in cocaine; he was sentenced and appealed and was given a *sursis*, a suspended sentence. Within a very short time he died. Not very long after this tragedy, Blank was giving his friends visiting cards on which was inscribed the information that he was Doctor to the British Embassy. Blank, who seemed to have forgotten his grievance against me, offered to have brought over from England in the diplomatic valise anything I wanted, such as tobacco, etc. I declined. Later Blank seemed to have abandoned his post as Embassy Doctor, but carried on a private practice near the Eiffel Tower. It is a long time since I have seen Blank. I wonder where he is now. I have called my little story A Mystery of Paris and I would like someone to solve the mystery for me; I cannot.

## A Child is Born

With the beginning of trench warfare, news became more stabilized. We finished with the *courier* service; it was now possible to telegraph despatches to London after they had been submitted to the military censor. Messages, however, took many many hours to cross

from Paris to London. Paris newspapers consisted
for the most part of one sheet only, so I was able to
read through the whole Press very quickly. The
bombing of Paris had not yet begun and life continued
to be quiet and peaceful. The *Daily Express* arranged
with Courlander's widow to remove or sell her furniture; so, without a pennyworth of capital, I was
faced with the necessity of purchasing furniture. I
borrowed £70 from the *Daily Express*—what a fortune to me in those days—and arranged to pay them
back at the rate of £2 weekly out of my salary;
all I had was five pounds a week; then I heard
that a child was to be born. I could not visualize
the birth of a child in my miserable apartment, so
as most French doctors were mobilized, I found an
old English doctor and consulted him. He told me
that in a turning off the avenue du Bois de Boulogne
was an English nursing home. I went to see the
matron and arranged that my wife should go there
and that I should pay one guinea per day, more
than I was earning in cash, but it had to be done,
somehow. I went back to the rue de Rivoli to explain
the arrangements I had made. The doorbell rang, I
opened the door myself and there, on the mat, stood
a stranger, obviously an Englishman, who handed me
a letter from the editor of the *Daily Express*. The
letter said that the bearer of the note, Mr. Alfred
Stead, was empowered to dismiss any person he found
in charge of the *Daily Express* office and to make any
arrangement he thought desirable. I invited Mr. Stead
to step inside.

As matters turned out, I was not dismissed, Stead
and I worked together for some long time and then
Stead departed. I was left in charge again. I had not

informed my mother of my secret marriage, but when I knew a child was to be born, I told her. She promised to come over and stay with us. Out of the few pounds I had managed to save, I furnished a room in my miserable flat. Then once again, my stepfather intervened and forbade my mother to come. The week my baby was born, my mother wrote and asked me to lend her £30. For the first time in my life, I had to refuse.

On Saturday morning, July 31st, 1915, I called a horse-cab early in the morning and drove my wife to the nursing home. The matron assured me that everything was all right and that I was not to worry. I arranged that I would telephone about ten o'clock. I did so, but the matron was out. At ten-thirty, at eleven o'clock and at eleven-thirty, I telephoned again. The matron was still out. Then I went to the nursing-home myself and found that the brokers were in possession. I waited until the matron returned. She had been to consult an English lawyer down town. One of this lawyer's sons became, in later years, my chief assistant.

When the matron arrived she told me that there was nothing whatsoever to worry about because the child would not be born for many hours yet. Back I went to the rue de Rivoli. I found some bread and some jam, and that was my meal that day. About four o'clock in the afternoon I returned to the nursing-home and eventually saw the matron. She tripped gaily down the stairs and said: "Oh, didn't you know, you had a daughter born at two o'clock this afternoon." It was not until my wife was stronger that I heard the real story of the birth of my daughter. Arrangements had been made for the attendance of a French doctor, one of the few who were not mobilized for active service. The doctor's name was Pottet and I particularly call attention to his name in the light of subsequent developments. The doctor happened to call in to see another patient. The matron was out, the nursing-home was in the charge of a young Irish nurse who could not speak a word of French. The doctor on the other hand could not speak a word of English. The young nurse called the doctor in to see my wife, and throughout the birth of the child, my wife had to act as interpreter between the doctor and the nurse. The doctor behaved somewhat strangely, but this was not surprising, because within a fortnight Dr. Pottet was removed to a mental asylum.


## ON WITH THE JOB

I was correspondent of the *Daily Express* in Paris from the late summer of 1914 until 1932 when I asked to be relieved of my job, to become a reporter at large.

For eighteen years I made Paris my Press G.H.Q.— Paris was my date-line. During those eighteen years, I made incursions into every European country; but I always came back to Paris. I interviewed King Albert in Brussels, King Alphonso in Madrid, King Constantine in Lucerne, Queen Marie of Rumania in many places, and King George in Athens; but I always returned to my first love: Paris.

I interviewed *chefs* about their latest dishes, actresses about their latest failures, financiers about their latest loans; I saw potentates in large and small ways of business. I interviewed every Prime Minister of

France in every Government that rose and fell, and I liked it very much.

Eventually, I managed to leave the rue de Rivoli misery, and took a small flat, "a small thing but mine own", on the top floor of a building in the rue de Grammont, just one step away from the boulevards. In those days we had to have our workshop close to the *Bourse*, because the *Bourse* is the central filing office for Press despatches, and all despatches to London, when the telephone was not working, had to be sent from the *Bourse*. I was up and down those five flights of stairs twenty and thirty times a day. I had no one to help me, and I took all my own despatches and did everything myself. I wanted to be a success, God, how I wanted to be a success!

Then the air-raids began. I had paid back my £70 debt and my salary had been increased gradually and it now stood at £12 per week. In addition, the *Daily Express* allowed me two pounds a week towards the rent of my flat, as office-rent. I was passing rich. One night my wife and I went to the Opéra Comique, and during the first interval we heard there were Zeppelins over Paris. Fortunately, the theatre was only just round the corner from the rue de Grammont and in a minute or two we were back. The Zeppelin did no more harm to Paris than did the earlier Taube raids, but then the real raids began, and how I remember the first big one. Sirens announcing the approach of enemy aircraft had brought us always out into the street at night, but we never saw anything. One night in January, a very cold night, my wife was making hot drinks. It was a bright moonlight night, when the sirens announced about eleven o'clock the approach of German aeroplanes. I went out on to the balcony.

It was so clear that I could see an air fight in progress over Montmartre. I kept up a running commentary to my wife in the kitchen. Then I heard a plane approaching the house. The fight seemed broken off and I thought it was one of the French planes returning. I called out that a plane was coming our way. Then I called: "Come quickly, come and look, it is almost over the house." Just at that moment, there was a noise which I can compare only to an express train rushing through a station. Then there was a dull boom and the noise of falling stones and broken glass. It was a German plane and it had dropped a bomb just on the other side of the Crédit Lyonnais Bank, which is exactly opposite where I lived. It is thanks to the huge bulk of the bank on this island site that I am writing these lines. The bomb fell on to a house and killed people in bed and wrecked part of one street and did considerable damage to one section of the rue du Quatre-Septembre. It was the first big bomb which ever fell in the centre of Paris.

## BIG BERTHA

At seven-thirty in the morning of March 21st, 1918, there was a sound of a bomb bursting. It seemed to be the announcement of a daylight air-raid. There were several explosions during the morning—people were mystified. In an early edition of the paper *Liberté*, the late Paul Painlevé, a noted scientist and future Prime Minister wrote an article explaining that the bombs were probably dropped from German planes which were flying so high over Paris that they were invisible. At 5 p.m., the *Temps* appeared with an official *communiqué* that the bombs were not bombs but shells and they had been fired by long distance guns placed somewhere in the neighbourhood of Soissons. Very few people believed that *communiqué*. They thought the Government had issued it to calm the nerves of Parisians. I saw a man buy up all the copies of the *Temps* he could find; he said that one of these days they would be worth £1 apiece.

Nevertheless, the *communiqué* was absolutely correct. Every day the guns started to fire at seven-thirty in the morning. They continued throughout the day, at regular intervals. *Excelsior* published on its front page a map of Paris showing how the shells always fell within the same line. It showed that the guns were merely moved a fraction every day. One of the first shells struck a baker's shop just off the Grands Boulevards; a young girl had her leg blown off; she later and for some time achieved fame as a harlot along the boulevards, plying her trade hobbling along on crutches.

Life went on more and more hectically. With the Big Bertha shells mingled the bombs dropped during daylight raids, and then later we had night raids as well. The nerves of the Parisians were not shaken. People used to go down to the cellars at night and take food with them. Then they had to go down to the cellars during the daytime, also taking their food with them. I heard my three-year-old daughter say to her mother who was putting her to bed: "Don't take my socks off, it's not worth while, we shall only have to go down to the cellar." Then I arranged to send my wife and baby out of Paris. When I was living alone, I did not think it worth while to go down to the cellars at night. I became a fatalist and stayed up on my fifth floor, sometimes when the whole house shook like a jelly. Bombs were dropping and anti-aircraft guns were firing from a nearby street. It did not seem to matter.

## THE BATTLE OF PARIS

The United States were now in the war and for some time I became an accredited correspondent to the American Army. Crowds of American officers and soldiers were in Paris. Never, I suppose, has the gay city been as gay as it was in 1918. The casualties during the Battle of Paris, as the Americans called the events and doings of those days were heavy. One man, a member of the American Red Cross, who had been well-known as a writer in the United States in pre-war days, committed suicide by throwing himself into the Seine. Another American officer, son of the founder of a famous weekly publication in New York, was summoned back to the U.S.A. and committed suicide by jumping overboard, just as the ship entered the harbour.

In a little narrow street, just off the Place de l'-Etoile, was a *maison de rendez-vous* known as Madame Hélène's. This house was the meeting place of hundreds of American officers—and others—on leave. Famous French aviators also used to drop in. Sometimes at night, the steps were littered with American officers who had overstayed their leave and who feared that if they went out they might be rounded up by the military police and taken to the Hotel St. Anne, which the Americans were using as a military jail.

One night I was at Madame Hélène's when an air-raid occurred. I will not attempt to describe the scene, because it would take the pen of a Zola or the brush of a Corregio to picture it in all its realism.

## MURDER AT MAXIM'S

The story told during those hectic days of a shooting at Maxim's remains until this day much of a mystery, although it was said that the only mystery was caused by a fear of international complications. In any case, the censors refused to allow the story to leave France by cable. The American Army expression for officers absent without leave is A.W.O.L. Many of these officers did their drinking at Maxim's. The story is that a drunken American officer had his attention attracted by a pretty French girl who was supping with a Frenchman. The Frenchman also happened to be an officer, and he was not drunk. The American went over and tried to strike up an acquaintance with the girl and the Frenchman. The Frenchman tried to keep his head, but the behaviour of the American was so bad that the Frenchman lost his temper. Over went the table. There was a fight and the French officer shot the American officer. Another American officer, so goes the story, then shot the French officer.

## THE BATTLE OF PARIS (CONTINUED)

Once again the German Army was approaching Paris and once again there was talk of the Government leaving. An American colleague, Whythe Williams, and myself were out together one night in a little theatre in the rue Caumartin, where there was more drinking and dancing during the *entr'actes* than there was actual theatre. We looked down on the amazingly drunken scene, and Williams said to me: "Is this hope or is this dope?"

There was plenty of dope in Paris, I am writing of the period when cocaine arrived in Paris in quantities; there was some hope too and hope rose higher when the Americans attacked in the Argonne, and turned the tide towards victory.

I was shot off towards the east, as I have related elsewhere, but I never went east, I went to Berlin. I was absent from Paris for a long long time and did not return until June, 1919, when I reported the signing of Peace at Versailles. I wrote the stories of the signing of various other Peace Treaties, and then I was snatched away to be made an editor in London.

## London Again

When I returned to Paris in June, 1919, and after having "scooped" the world on stories from the German capital, I was still getting my old salary of £12 a week, and I found that my assistant had during my absence managed to obtain such increases in salary that he was being paid more than I. I went to London still with £12 a week, and it was on this rather meagre salary that I was appointed Acting Editor of the *Sunday Express*. I had to leave my furniture behind me in Paris, transport my family to London, and live in a furnished flat in Hampstead. I was broke, flat broke, and broke or not I did not want to be an editor; but I still wanted success. I did not want money particularly, but I looked upon money as counters which represented success. My mother who had throughout my youth been told by her second husband that I was an utter fool who would never achieve anything was very proud of what I had achieved, but my stepfather who was now unable to refer to me, either in my presence or behind my back, as a damned fool and a blockhead, had to take other steps to make me as unhappy as he possibly could. His favourite method was to attack, in a would-be sarcastic manner, the authenticity of the stories I had written from Germany and which had been published all over the world. I suppose what I should have done would have been to have gone to him and said to him now are you going to pay me all the money I have advanced on your behalf. You are supposed to be a rich man, you like to be called a rich man, why don't you pay me back? but I never did. I made up my mind that so long as my mother lived, I would not; then everything changed.

My mother had to undergo an operation on her eye, it was the second operation she had had and it was not successful. Another operation had to be performed to remove the right eye. The operation was to be performed on a Sunday morning. Sundays were my days "off". As editor I had to stay in the office until the early hours of the Sunday morning. Then I went back to my flat in Hampstead and stayed in bed until late. One Saturday night we were burgled. In the afternoon of that particular Sunday, I went to my mother's flat in Maida Vale for news of the operation. I went into the dining-room where my stepfather lay back in a state of real or well-simulated drowsiness. He sat in one chair with his feet on another chair and his waistcoat undone. I asked him how my mother was: "I don't know," he replied. To every question he made the same reply. I left the dining-room and found the maid and asked if I could see my mother. I went into my mother's bedroom and saw her, she said she was quite all right, the operation had been entirely successful. She said she had expected me to be present in the morning while the operation was being performed. I said, perfectly honestly, that I thought that when an operation was being performed, the fewer people there were in the flat the better. My stepfather of course had seized upon my absence as an excuse to attack me. In my mother's state of health, his attitude had the effect he desired. When my mother had fully recovered, she was egged on by my stepfather to make a real attack upon me, and the basis of the attack was that I had been absent on that Sunday morning. From that day and for a period of twelve years, I never spoke to my mother, nor did she make any attempt to try and see me. From that day and until the present moment, I have never spoken to my stepfather, although he is still alive somewhere or other.

## BACK TO PARIS

As I have related, I threw up my editorship and begged to return to Paris where I plunged into the world of work. The telephone was now functioning, but it was quite a job to obtain a connection with London. There was plenty to do: there was news in

Deauville and Cannes and Le Touquet, and more and more news in Paris. First I had a staff of one, but within a year or two I had a staff of four. Then the telephone service improved, it improved so much that it became a nuisance. Instead of taking two or three hours to get on to London, London was able to get on to me in three or four minutes. I had slept for years and years with a telephone beside my bed. When I went out to dine, I had to leave the telephone number of my host; when I went to a theatre, I had to leave the number of my seat, and time and time again I was called away, back to the office. It was a hectic time, a good time; Paris was the centre of everything for which the city has been renowned for years. There was wine, women and song in super-abundance, but my voice was never good. I enjoyed everything else, however, except the singing. I had the best of good times, but how hard I worked. I was at the office from early morning until the early hours of the next morning, and I was always in constant touch either with the Paris office or with London. Then I thought I had had enough. In 1932, I made up my mind that I would be a reporter at large, I would continue to live in Paris, my favourite among cities, but I would not be tied to an office, I would not be tied to one job, so for the last time I wrote my name over the dateline Paris.

# CHAPTER III

IN SEPTEMBER, 1918, I paid my first visit to London in a period of a year and nine months. It was the first real glimpse I had had of war-time London. Except for a brief visit in 1915, I had not been in London for a very long time. The contrast between London and Paris was striking. If there was less gaiety in Paris than there was in London, there was certainly much more food in Paris than in the English capital. Food was not strictly rationed anywhere in France, and most certainly not in Paris. I stayed for a few days at the Waldorf Hotel and my mother came to stay with me. She was frantically anti-German. When I said good-bye to her to return to the Continent, she asked me to promise that never in my life would I ever shake hands again with a German. I am afraid I did make a light-hearted promise, yet, two months later, I was in Berlin.

As soon as the Armistice with Austria was signed the editor of the *Daily Express* sent me a cable asking me if I was prepared to go to Constantinople and then travel further east as the special correspondent of that newspaper. Joyfully I cabled back that I was all ready to go. My enthusiasm was slightly damped, when I was told to go to Berne and there await further instructions. It was my first time in Switzerland and I found the capital of that neutral country in a far worse plight than either London or Paris.

148

# A STROKE OF LUCK

There were no fewer than nineteen ration cards. The scourge of what was known as Spanish flu' was cutting people down in swathes. In one week in the Bellevue Hotel in Berne, three members of the staff serving on the floor on which I was living, died. There were no theatres, no cinemas, and the cafés closed at nine o'clock. It was like a city with the plague within its walls.

## ARMISTICE NIGHT

The British Legation in Berne was full of news. I was told a great exclusive story which has never yet appeared in any paper. The story told to me by a Secretary of the British Legation was that the Deputies representing the French-speaking cantons of Switzerland had served notice on the Swiss Government that unless the Bolshevik strike in Zurich was settled immediately, the deputies would request the French Government to incorporate the French-speaking cantons of Switzerland in France. I was warned there was no way to get that story past the Swiss censor, so I tried to communicate with the *Daily Express* correspondent in Geneva, a man who died some years back. He was an excitable little Irishman, extremely loyal, but he also liked looking on the wine with a very benevolent eye. Owing to transport difficulties, it was a very precarious journey that I made from Berne to Geneva. To telephone the special story was dangerous, so I had to take it in person. There was only one train that day and the train consisted of a locomotive and one coach in which the only other passengers besides myself were two members of the Japanese Legation. My colleague in

Geneva said that he had a special pass which allowed
him to cross over the frontier into France and back
and he could send despatches from Annemasse. I
handed him my despatch and asked him to take it as
quickly as possible to Annemasse. He promised to do
so, and I returned to Geneva. What actually happened
was this: my colleague, after seeing me off at the
station, went in to a nearby café and when he came
out he crossed over the rue Mont Blanc and filed my
despatch in the Swiss post office. The censor several
months afterwards was good enough to refund me the
cost of the cable.

Almost as soon as I returned to Berne the Armistice
with Germany was signed. There were reports of
wild scenes in Paris, London and New York, but in
Berne people were dropping dead, and the only sign
of gaiety was a roulette party in the hotel. While we
were playing I heard coming down the street a small
band of French interned soldiers. They were singing
the "Marseillaise".

### THE HUNT IS UP

There were enough spy and counter-spy stories in
Berne to keep novelists busy for a lifetime, but I was
more interested in other things. I wanted to get out
of Switzerland and see some action. No instructions
came from London, so I asked if I might go to Vienna.
I received permission from Mr. Blumenfeld the editor,
to go to Vienna if I could do so with safety. I had not
the faintest idea whether it was safe or not, but go I
did and the story of my journey to the Austrian
capital I have dealt with elsewhere in this book.

Vienna seemed small fry; I wanted to get to Berlin,

and to Berlin I went. My travelling companion, an American newspaper man named Edward Thierry, and myself, literally had to fight our way to the German capital; we were flung off trains; everything possible was done by the German authorities to prevent our reaching the heart of the country; but get there we did. I was still full of keenness and enthusiasm, and when I discovered I was the first English newspaper man to reach Berlin from the outside world, I do not think I would have exchanged my job for anything that anybody could have offered to me. I was present at the liquidation of the mighty German Empire. There had been a small revolution which brought about the Armistice, but that was nothing in importance compared with the revolution which swept Germany, and principally round Berlin, in the winter of 1918-1919.

When I listen to Hitler's speeches and read the German newspapers, I am forced to wonder whether Germany has really forgotten how she stood during that black winter. I was staying at the Hotel Adlon, and in the Hotel Adlon one had the best of everything, but the food was only just eatable. Had it not been for the Danish Red Cross, which had its headquarters in the nearby British Embassy, I really do not know how I should have managed to exist. The Danish Red Cross allowed me to buy canned supplies from them. Germany was beaten flat, make no mistake about that. It may not have been a defeat of the German Army, but it was an overwhelming defeat for the German people. When one is very hungry, one is apt to say that one is starving, but here I saw not one or two or three, but hundreds and hundreds of people who were starving. I have walked about the poorer districts of Berlin, and I have seen women who carried babies in their arms. The babies were like small monkeys, nothing but skin and bone. They were wrapped in pieces of canvas sacking. The complexions of the women were like light ash. Their cheek-bones seemed to be about to protrude through their flesh. Their eyes appeared to be sunken in their sockets. Their hands resembled claws. During the war years and the post-war years, I have seen hundreds and thousands of refugees of all nationalities, but never in my life have I seen such scenes as I saw in Berlin in the "Black Winter". I hope never to see such scenes again. Some of the war profiteers had *caches* of food, but the poor people walked through the streets in the early morning, picking through the dust-bins and retrieving scraps of food and potato peelings.

## Hell Breaks Loose

Then the fighting started. About 800 sailors marched in from Kiel and entrenched themselves in the Kaiser's palace. They brought their women with them. They claimed to have found in the palace stocks of food and wine. The Government troops tried to drive them out and for days a pitched battle raged. Heavy artillery battered the palace; the sailors were driven out and took up a new position in the Royal Stables. Finally, a handful surrendered. The rest were killed. All over the city there was battle. An American newspaper correspondent who was living in another hotel came to see me. Fighting broke out around my hotel and the American had to stay with me for three days and three nights. There was fighting up and down Unter den Linden. The Govern-

ment put machine-guns on top of the Brandenburger
Gate and layed a barrage along the Linden. There
was nothing to eat but plenty to drink. Life was cheap.
Nobody cared. Women of all classes were willing to
barter their virtue for a slab of chocolate. I have seen
time and time again in the arcade which links Unter
den Linden with the Friedrichstrasse, mothers hawk-
ing the bodies of their young daughters, girls between
twelve and fifteen years of age. I have called this
chapter "A Stroke of Luck", and it was a stroke of
luck to me. Opportunity came my way and I seized
it. I lived twenty-four hours a day. I slaved for
£12 a week. I wanted so desperately to be a success.
There were no direct communications between Berlin
and London, so I had to send my despatches to Copenhagen to a correspondent there, to send them to
London, and when Copenhagen broke down, as it did
sometimes, I sent the despatches to Geneva, where
my colleague functioned very well indeed. He had
been badly shaken up as a result of that moment of
forgetfulness in Geneva.

During those first months of living in Berlin, I had
almost every possible thing happen to me that could
happen to a man bent on reporting the German scene
as it was. I had two soldiers come into my bedroom
in the middle of the night and ask permission to put a
machine-gun in the window. I was warned that I
was going to be arrested by a group of officers
who were plotting a counter-revolution and who
wanted to create an international incident which
would bring the Allies to Berlin. For days I had an
armed guard outside my bedroom door.

One night when I came from my bathroom to my
bedroom, I found a woman with a dressing-gown over

her nightdress standing near the door; she had got in with a pass key. She said that unless I gave her money, she would scream. I did not give her money and she did not scream.

The Hotel Adlon was a centre of gaiety. Correspondents flocked in from all over the world. A number of Belgian girls who had become the mistresses of German officers stationed in Brussels, also came along to Berlin, because they thought it would be safer for the time being. There was tragedy and comedy all mixed up together. I remember meeting a Belgian officer who had been sent to Berlin on an official mission to trace down and take back with him to Belgium several thousand carrier pigeons which the Germans had taken away during the retreat. After many weeks, the officer discovered that the pigeons had been eaten. Food was the only topic of conversation. The man in the street did not care one bit what was being discussed in Paris. What he wanted to know was when food was coming to Germany. Strangers used to stop me in the street and ask that question.

After being in Berlin in a semi-starving condition for two months, I asked permission of my newspaper to go to Switzerland on a week's leave, prior to going to Weimar for the National Assembly, which was to remake the Constitution of Germany, the same Constitution which Hitler unmade. I received permission and arranged to go to Geneva, where my family was to come to see me. The train arrangements in Germany were extremely precarious, and I first of all had to go to Munich, where I knew I would have to spend the night before going on from Munich to the Swiss frontier. The only other traveller in the first-class compartment with me was a very fat German who had several cardboard boxes with him, and these he placed carefully in the rack above his head. Shortly after the train left Berlin, he introduced himself as Herr Cohn. Every time the train stopped, a number of soldiers would climb aboard and force their way into the first-class carriage. They were requested to leave, but they refused to leave. The train would wait until somebody came along and forced them to leave. Then just as the train was pulling out, three or four soldiers would jump on board again. Instead of reaching Munich at five in the afternoon, we arrived at one o'clock the following morning. But Herr Cohn made the journey very entertaining. When he was sure there was nobody else likely to look into the compartment, he took down one of the cardboard boxes and showed it to me, it was full of hard-boiled eggs. Box after box of foodstuffs he exhibited to me and asked me to help myself. I refused. He pressed me, and when he heard that I was an Englishman, although he might have guessed that from my accent, when I spoke German, he became very confidential. He told me he had a most charming daughter of marriageable age. He invited me to go and see him. I was equally candid with my companion; I told him I was married. He brushed that away as being entirely unimportant. He insisted I should come and see him and his beautiful daughter. He told me all her virtues and his personal wealth, and again and again he pressed food on me. He was a type only too typical of a certain class which made his co-religionists a byword throughout Germany. . . . A comparatively few have ruined the lives of hundreds of thousands of good upright German citizens.

The streets of Munich were in complete darkness and the snow was a foot thick on the ground. I had never been in this German city previously, and I groped my way trying to find a room. Most of the hotels refused to answer the ringing bell, and those I did manage to waken, quickly slammed the door and said they had no rooms to let.

Out of the shadows, a tall young man came up. I noticed he was wearing uniform, but it was too dark for me to distinguish what uniform it was. He asked me if I was looking for a hotel room and when I told him I was, he said that he had booked a double room for his father and mother who were supposed to arrive by the same train as I had travelled in but had not arrived. He had paid a deposit on the room and he said I could have it if I refunded the deposit. It sounded like a foolish story, but I said I would take the room if he would come with me to the hotel. He agreed. As we walked along the snowy streets of Munich side by side, I asked the young man what he was and he told me he was a second lieutenant in the Navy and he had just come back, after surrendering his torpedo-destroyer to the British in the North Sea. I said to the young man that this was a curious situation, because I was one of his nominal enemies. I told him I was an English journalist. The young man stopped dead, put his gloved hand in front of his eyes and burst into tears, and I had to stand there in the snow and pat the back of the young man and tell him to buck up and not to mind. Presently he dried his eyes and went with me to the hotel where I obtained a room.

Despite the collapse of the old German Reich, the arrangements made at Weimar were marvellous. For

instance, at the railway station, there were booths one
for German journalists and another for foreigners.
Guides to the ancient city of Weimar were distributed,
written in English, French and Italian. We were
billeted in hotels. The Assembly was held in the
Opera House, with the background of the first act of
Faust. Numerous telephone booths had been erected
at the back of the dress-circle for the convenience of
journalists. The road was so thick with snow that we
had to travel in jingling sleighs.

At Weimar I met a number of English journalists
who had been in Berlin before the war and who during the war were stationed in Holland. They made
their re-entry into Germany through the back-door
of Weimar. One journalist in pre-war days had been
a famous correspondent of English and American
newspapers in Berlin. He said that he would accompany me back to Berlin when I proposed to return,
as I had suggested doing for a matter of forty-eight
hours. When I told him I was staying at the Hotel
Adlon, he was horrified. He told me I must move
out of this hotel immediately, because during the days
of the German mobilization in 1914, the manager of
the hotel had threatened to pour burning liquid on
the group of English women and children who were
huddled for protection.

In Weimar too, I met among others Ben Hecht, who
had come to report the German scene for the *Daily
News* of Chicago, and who at that time had never
heard of Hollywood or a scenario. He had with him
his first wife, Mary Armstrong, a "sob sister", and
when we all went back to Berlin, she used to cook
breakfast for us, frying surreptitiously procured eggs
and British canteen obtained bacon on an inverted

electric iron in the Hecht bedroom. Ben and I shared confidences, hopes, ambitions and a German male secretary named Abel, who flew with Hecht to Munich to report the Communist uprising. The plane made a forced landing on the estate of ex-King Ferdinand of Bulgaria, who lent the outfit the money to continue the journey.

Among the ambitions Hecht and I shared was the praiseworthy one of making much money, and he made good and I did not; but we thought we were both about to make money, when I received a mysterious letter written in English asking me to meet the writer outside the Vaterland Café. The writer said I was to speak to a man who would be humming "Tipperary". Hecht came along with me. We met a man humming under his breath. He was an Irishman named Harry Quin, who was wearing a uniform of a Casement volunteer. He had been a private in an Irish regiment and had been taken prisoner and had "volunteered". He was an intelligent young man and I thought we could make a lot of money if we wrote the life story of a Casement soldier; but first we had to get him back to England. I got Quin back and another Casement soldier, Henry Burke. They were interviewed at Scotland Yard, and a few days after they got back to Dublin, their bodies were found tied to lamp posts. They had been shot dead, and on each body was pinned a scrap of paper with the word "Traitor" on it.

## AFTER THE ARMISTICE

What hectic days those were in 1919. There was murder in the hotel room next door to mine, and two or three sensational robberies, but robbery and murder were not out of the way specialities in those days. Food came, and with the coming of food, gaiety returned, but it was a forced gaiety. Nobody knew what was going to happen on the morrow. What did happen, of course, was the collapse of the German mark.

I stayed in Germany until June 1919 and then went to Versailles to cover the signing of the Treaty of Peace. From then onwards, for a number of years, I spent several parts of each year in Germany. When I wrote despatches which were detrimental to the country, they were given great prominence in the papers, but when I tried to be constructive, my articles were not published. I knew very little about national economy or finance, but I did have the sense to see that our old standards of economy and finance had gone wrong. Germany had no gold, but she was double-tracking her railway lines, building new machinery right and left, and every railway official had a new uniform. I went to London and I beseeched the editor to listen to me, but all he would say was: Did you see any gold anywhere? Of course, I had to say I had seen no gold at all. Had I been wiser, I would have pointed out that one did not see any gold in London either.

## FIASCO

I was sent to Leipzig to write about the first trial of the war prisoners' torturers, or alleged torturers. What a fiasco that was. At tremendous expense, the British Government sent a strong legal delegation to appear before the High Court at Leipzig. The prisoners who had been badly treated, instead of being allowed to appear in their old suits, were given each one of them a new blue serge suit. They had been well fed since their return to England; they looked fine. The first witness, a little cockney soldier, went into the box. He talked about the mud in the prison camp, but when the Judge, after listening to him for some little time with great patience, asked him when the bad treatment began, the witness, with great surprise, said that he had never been badly treated. Although the prisoner was given a sentence of two years, he never served it, and with one or two other trials this fiasco ended and the French withdrew their charges; all the cases built up so laboriously came tumbling down, to the great joy and delight of the Germans.

### RECOMPENSE

When I returned to England after my Berlin scoops I went down to the country to see Lord Beaverbrook at Leatherhead. I had not seen him since 1917. He congratulated me warmly on the scoops I had obtained in Germany, and he added that I had had influence with him and that he had a certain amount of influence with the Prime Minister (Mr. Lloyd George). Those words sounded very sweet to me. Then I went to the *Daily Express* and managed to get an increase of salary. Back I went to Germany, again and again, and I tried to write what I saw, although a lot of what I saw I did not understand. I saw the face of Germany changing. I saw that our old standards concerning political economy and finance were gone for ever and I tried to write these stories, but the editor would not print them. I drew

attention to the work Germany was doing—work paid
for in paper marks. So long as I wrote stories about the
collapse of the mark, so long did I remain on the front
page, but when I wanted to be serious, when I wanted
to draw the attention of the public to what was
happening in Germany, nobody paid any attention to
me. My editor wanted me to accept the post of
Berlin correspondent, but I refused and went back
to my first love, Paris; but from Paris I was called
upon to go to Germany, several times a year. I was
there during all the changing phases, and I saw the
coming of Hitler. I did manage to get a story published and I should like to quote it, because I want to
go on record as having given notice of what the coming
of Hitler meant to the Jews of Germany. It was Louis
Golding, the novelist, who put me in the way of
getting this story. Late one night, in the Savoy Grill,
he told Mr. and Mrs. Baxter and myself his adventures
in Berlin, when he and a Cambridge friend had been
beaten up in the streets. My daughter was then at
school in Dresden, and I went to see her, but on the
way I visited Hanover, where I had been to school,
and two or three other German cities, and this is what
I wrote: (the story was published on April 8th, 1932)
I said: ". . . the sinister shadow of Adolf Hitler lies
across German Jewry. Already millions of marks have
been changed into sterling. Fear seems to be the
driving force behind this selling. People are fearful
of talking politics to each other. The very café walls
have ears to-day. I noticed a group of Jews sitting in
a café; their coffee had grown cold, their cigars had
gone out, tragic groups, but typical of the tragedy
through which Germany is passing. The victory of
Hindenburg next Sunday—I firmly believe that the

grand old man will achieve his last victory—will be a mere palliative (he was elected as I predicted). The President is eighty-four. His days are numbered; but the real tragedy of Germany is that it lacks men of the Stresseman calibre. Hitler, the ex-house-painter from Austria, promises 'freedom and bread', and the workmen rub their eyes confusedly. The anti-Hitlerites speak of 'Hitler's dictatorship'. The result is confusion. Rumours of another invasion of the Ruhr if Hitler wins, rumours of civil war in six months if Hindenberg wins and then dies. Rumours . . . and fear.

"A motor tyre bursts and people jump because they fear a bomb—Jews who fear pogroms and Gentiles who fear the 'Jewish revenge'. . . . Rumours and lies —and a terrible fear that makes women stay in their houses and men walk abroad with pale faces. Poor, tragic Germany!"

The day after the despatch appeared, the Foreign Editor of the newspaper telephoned me to Dresden to say that the Berlin correspondent—a Berlin-born Englishman—had telephoned to say that Hitler had protested against my despatch and said it was not true. According to the correspondent, the same man who obtained such a graphic story of the Reichstag fire, Hitler invited me to go to Brunsweig, where the Nazis had control of the Municipal Council, and there I could see for myself that the Jews were not threatened with anything. I could not accept the invitation, because I had to go to Danzig to write about the Polish corridor, and thereby fell out with the Poles. Two days later came a cable "Rush Paris Doumer Assassinated".

# CHAPTER IV

## CONSTANTINOPLE

IN SEPTEMBER, 1922, the headlines on the front pages said that Smyrna was in flames, so I was sent chasing off to Greece to see what I could write about it. The Greeks had been defeated by the Turks and Mr. Lloyd George was very angry. He had backed the wrong horse. I went to Athens where in the Hotel Grande Bretagne I made the acquaintance of Max McCartney who was a correspondent at large for the *Times*. We discussed the situation and decided we were a long way away from the news. It is true that a number of wealthy refugees of Greek nationality had arrived in Athens, but the bulk of the poor ones were being driven out of Macedonia, back to Greece. We decided to go to Salonica to be nearer the scene of action. We took ship at Athens and when we arrived in Salonica we found that we were still quite a long way from where things were happening. We were cut off; of course, there were no trains which were available to civilians. The retreat of the Greek Army and the migration of masses of refugees had disorganized all traffic. We set about finding ways and means and eventually we discovered that if we went by goods train, we would make our way to Adrianople. We inspected the cattle trucks, found them exceedingly dirty, but finally decided they were the best thing available. Behold then handsome Max McCartney, former barrister, and the present writer, sitting in the truck dangling our feet and waiting for the train to start. We had been told it would start at four, but at eight we were still waiting. He had bought in the town a couple of blankets; fortunately it was very hot, and we had also collected a number of tins of salmon and other foods, most of which later turned out to be rank bad. Hundreds of refugees were arriving in carts drawn by bullocks, and others footsore and weary had tramped hundreds of miles. The old people who had known previous wars in the Balkans looked at us with piteous eyes, but the young ones were still gay enough, despite their troubles. Two buxom Greek girls, aged perhaps fifteen or sixteen came and tried to persuade us to take them with us in the cattle-truck to wherever we were going.

## MADAME MARIE'S

When we reached Adrianople, we found the town deserted because the Greeks were running from the invasion of the "Infidels". We heard of a hotel in Adrianople, but the word hotel should be written between inverted commas. Madame Marie's was the mess of the French Officers who for some reason or other were quartered in Adrianople. McCartney and I were given the only available bedroom. It had two beds and I should imagine that the sheets had been changed on the previous occasion during the first Balkan war. The bed-linen was brown, not that brown was its natural colour; the sheets had just turned brown; also the pillow cases. In the morning McCartney and I found our shoes full of lice.

And there in Adrianople, at Madame Marie's we lived, if lived be the right word, and worked. There were excellent stories, picturesque, descriptive stories, of this great migration of a population. Nevertheless, despite the hard work which we did, McCartney and I became very depressed. Everything was depressing: the food, the bedroom, the people, everything. Then there arrived from Constantinople a gay Italian reporter. He brought with him stories of beautiful women, gay music, sparkling life; good food, everything that appealed to the weary newspaperman. McCartney and I went into conference. We asked about trains. We were told that Constantinople was twelve hours away. Twelve hours may sound a long time to you, Readers, but to McCartney and I at Madame Marie's it was·just a space between misery and merriness. We decided to go to Constantinople.

## THE PERILS OF PERA

Our intention was to spend two or three days in Constantinople and then return to Adrianople; but fate willed otherwise. *The Times* had a distinguished correspondent in Constantinople, named Phillip Graves, but the Turkish authorities had requested that Mr. Graves be withdrawn; so Mr. McCartney, somewhat to his bewilderment, was appointed Correspondent at Constantinople. Then I inquired about the *Daily Express* correspondent; his name was William Drakeford. I wondered whether it was the same William Drakeford I had last seen in a basement in Old Burlington Street, London, where he was a tailor's cutter and trimmer. I found that Mr. Drakeford had resigned, but it was the same Mr. Drakeford, and after all these years I met the girl from Ashford who had become the first Mrs. Drakeford. What a tragic story his was. After he had left Old Burlington Street, he went to Constantinople to be a tailor's cutter. He became a member of the British Secret Service and remained in Constantinople throughout the War. He became a journalist directly the War was over, and a most excellent journalist he was. Then he had to leave Constantinople, also by the desire of the Turkish officials. He went to Cairo, where he was divorced and remarried and there, in Cairo, he died on a Christmas Eve.

## MORE PERILS

The British, the French, the Americans and the Italians were all in occupation of Constantinople. I imagine that Paris, after the Battle of Waterloo, might have been a little like Constantinople was when I first saw the then capital of Turkey.

General Wrangel's army and government in the Crimea had been defeated by the Bolsheviks and evacuated by the British and Americans to Turkey. Russian Princes were driving taxi-cabs; their wives and mistresses were running night clubs. The best restaurants in Pera, the European quarter of Constantinople, were Russian. Paris after the World War may have been gay, but Constantinople was, I believe, much gayer. Everybody seemed to have money to spend, and the Chanak Crisis merely added a little more emotion to the Turkish scene. The defeat of the Greeks by the Kemalist Turks brought

Great Britain to the verge of another war. Constantinople was a city of rumours and no rumour was too fantastic to be believed. Every night brought a new story and every dawn a new denial. There was at this time a very strong British military censorship on all outgoing despatches. Chanak was the focal spot, because at Chanak Turks and British troops faced one another across a No Man's Land that was narrowed every day by the Turks. A Canadian newspaper man wanted to go to Chanak and called on Captain Slade, the Director of Naval Intelligence. Captain Slade, a most helpful man, said to the Canadian: "All right, I have a tug going down the Dardanelles this afternoon."

"I don't want to go to the goddamned Dardanelles," said the Canadian, "I want to go to Chanak."

"There is a map on the wall behind you, Mr. X," replied the naval officer, good-temperedly. The Canadian looked round and saw the map and saw Chanak and saw his mistake. Then he switched the conversation.

"Is this tug of yours clean?" he asked.

"If you're not in a hurry," answered Captain Slade, "I'll get *Thunderer* to get up steam for you."

Nominally, all the Allies were supposed to be on the verge of another war with the Turks, but actually within the Allied lines there was a private war going on. M. Poincaré was carrying on a secret intrigue with Mustapha Kemal. The Italians politely stood on one side and said to the English, in effect: "After you, *Signori*." The British Government, Army and Navy, had to stand the whole brunt of the aftermath of Smyrna. The gaiety continued as usual.

# I HATE TO-MORROW

## The Little Fields

Next door to the Pera Palace Hotel where I was living, was a night establishment called the Petits-Champs. Neither McCartney nor I ever thought of visiting these premises, although we merely had to walk a matter of perhaps twenty yards. We visited some of the Russian night clubs and approved of them, and got tired of them; and then we used to spend our evenings sipping whisky and soda and telling one another of our adventures in London when we were young. The only distractions we ever had were fire-alarms. These were a nightly as well as a daily occurrence in Constantinople. Many of the buildings were just wooden structures and went up in flames in a few moments. There was a British fire brigade, but the Turks were very jealous of it, because they lost their perquisites. Down in Galata was a high stone tower on which a watchman stood. When he saw a fire, he began to make a noise and the Turkish fire-brigade turned out. The first thing was to turn the men out of the drinking dens. Then they went to fetch an antiquated fire-extinguishing appliance which was hand-carried to the fire. The Turkish firemen, all ragged and bare-footed, jog-trotted along, shouting as they went, probably to keep away evil spirits who might get first to the fire. It was very important that the Turkish firemen should be there first, because the first thing they did was to loot the burning premises; then they let the fire have its way.

Late one night, when I was sound asleep on the top floor of the Pera Palace Hotel, there was a loud banging at my door. I awoke and unlocked it. A friendly harlot who lived further along the corridor told me to hurry and get dressed, because the building opposite had caught fire.

But to return, or rather to go to the Petits-Champs. I think it was Ernest Hemingway, who first called our attention to the Petits-Champs. Hemingway was then a young newspaper man representing one of the Hearst agencies. He was carrying on a small private war of his own with the correspondent in Paris, one Frank Mason. Mason and Hemingway were really quite good friends, and they had a way of cabling each other beginning each message with the name Frank and Ernest. There had been in pre-war days a famous black-faced vaudeville act—played by a man named Frank Tinney, who carried on a conversation with a *chef d'orchestre* whom he addressed always as Ernest. Frank Mason would cable to Ernest Hemingway in Constantinople: "Hello Ernest, please send expense account." To which Hemingway would reply: "Hello Frank please cable 90 dollars." Then came a message: "Hello Ernest unable send 90 dollars before receiving expense account." Hemingway returned with this: "Please upstick accounts backwards." Not to be outdone in politeness, Mason replied: "Hello Ernest please be reasonable."

But I am keeping you away from the Petits-Champs. In one of his early novels, Robert Hitchins mentions the establishment as a sort of open-air music-hall, I think. When I first met it, it was the most marvellous night club I had ever seen, or for the matter of that have ever seen. The members of Wrangel's army and their wives had formed a Russian ballet. They had painted their own scenery and made their own costumes. The first ballet I saw at the Petits-Champs was Coppelia, and after having seen it once, I went back night after night; but I must confess that the ballet was not the only attraction. One could eat and drink and watch the ballet, but it was the female adornment of the audience that formed one of the chief attractions. Women seemed to have come from all over the world to assemble at the Petits-Champs. There were French women and Italian women, Greeks and Armenians and Montenegrins, and Germans and Russians. They spoke all languages. They dressed magnificently; they were most entertaining company. What a weeping and a wailing there must have been when the Army of Occupation was withdrawn from Constantinople. Fortunately, I was not there to see it.

I was having the very best of good times. There were plenty of good stories to cable every day, plenty of excitement to keep one on tip-toe, threats and rumours and denials and always the Petits-Champs in the evening. In this cavalcade of harlotry and licentiousness, it was pleasant to come across one woman who was untouched by the exotic excitement which went on all around. She was a Frenchwoman, young and dark and intelligent. She was employed in a shop in Pera. I used to walk with her very often up the Grande Rue and leave her outside the premises where she worked. She was a married woman, so she told me, and she had a child. I had never seen her anywhere but in the Grande Rue; but one day, I asked her if she would come to tea with me at my hotel. She agreed to come on the following Saturday. I have never seen her again, and here is the reason.

# CONSTANTINOPLE

## SMALLPOX

On the Friday night, my friend, W. G. Massey, of
the *Daily Telegraph*, and myself went out to dinner at
the Cercle de Constantinople, next door to the hotel.
We went back to the hotel for a night-cap. I began to
shiver, my teeth began to chatter. Massey counselled
a hot drink and bed. I took his advice but spent an
awful night with feverish dreams. I was horribly sick.
As soon as I drank my early morning cup of tea, I was
sick again. All day long, I lay in a fever and I could
not remember the name of the girl who was coming to
tea. That worried me fearfully. I did not know her
address. She must have thought that I was just one
of those people who make appointments and who
don't keep them. I had not given her my name, but I
had said I would meet her in the tea-room of the hotel.
I lay there half-conscious and then I noticed to my
horror that on my left wrist were two greyish spots. I
asked for the hotel doctor. He came; he was a Greek.
He said I had some stomach ailment and prescribed—
Epsom salts. I was sick, and how sick, and there I lay
being sick, with a fever that seemed to get worse and
worse.

Drakeford and his Turkish assistant came to ask
whether they could use my portable typewriter and
work in my room. I nodded my head. They came in
and out and I lay there, sometimes conscious and
sometimes not. Other spots appeared on me and the
Greek doctor prescribed some other medicine, and I
was sick. I saw Drakeford and his Turkish friend like
strange figures in a nightmare. On my bedrail I saw
little goblins and gnomes sitting. They were sitting,

too, on the curtain rail above the window. Of course, I knew they were not there, but they were there. They never spoke aloud, but they seemed to be able to talk to each other by signs and by moving their mouths. They kept on pointing at me and calling one another's attention to me as I lay there tossing in a fever. Of course, they were not there, but there they were all the time, never speaking but always keeping up a mute chatter. I used to pray that if only they would go, I would try to be a better man. It sounds foolish, doesn't it? but I did. I became worse. Newspaper friends put their heads into my room and made cheery remarks. Then came Massey who looked worried. He suggested that he should find a mutual friend of ours, an Army doctor. The next morning he came. He examined me and said that he wasn't sure, but he thought that it was smallpox. He suggested I should be moved from the hotel to the German Hospital which had been taken over by the British as a military hospital. The hotel management was scared out of its wits. A case of smallpox in the hotel! Ruination! So I was smuggled out wrapped in blankets and taken downstairs in the luggage-lift and then placed in a military ambulance and removed to the British hospital. There I was examined most carefully; smallpox was the verdict.

I was one of the first cases which fell to that epidemic. Within a few days, people, Europeans, civilians and military, were being picked up all over Constantinople and brought to the same hospital. A soldier put into a bed next to mine died within a few hours. Then they re-opened the 20th Stationary Hospital at Mashlak, opposite the Constantinople Golf Club. I was put into a hut by myself.

## NICE TREATMENT IF YOU CAN GET IT

Austrian doctors captured by the British had given our people a new treatment for smallpox. In lay terms, it is very simple. Each individual spot has to be painted with a strong solution of permanganate of potash. The patient must be kept in bed and given as much alcohol as he can possibly consume. Several times a day my spots were painted by orderlies. So within forty-eight hours I looked like a Red Indian. All this time, I was kept full of alcohol; I was pickled in it. Port, brandy, champagne, something of everything was kept continuously on the move downwards. It was a strenuous battle. Smallpox v. Myself. The struggle was to keep the smallpox from getting inside, reaching the lungs, because once it does that, it is all over. Never can I say too much about my gratefulness to the devoted medical officers and the three nurses who helped me win the battle for life. When I came out of the worst of the fever, I lay in the hut alone and weak and depressed. At night I used to hear the hyenas round the dust destructors. Sometimes at night, Gladys, a Welsh nurse, the only young one of the three nurses, would come and talk to me. The orderlies were also most devoted young men. One of my doctors, Captain Foley-Green, used to tell me wonderful stories of the evacuation of the Russians from the Crimea. No wonder the Bolsheviks won. The old regular army officers, when their alcohol ran out, used even to drink the petrol out of the British supplied tanks, but I could not criticize anyone who took to drink in those days, because I suppose for a fortnight at least I never drew a sober breath day or night.

My most devoted friend at that time was W. C. Massey. He used to drive all the way out from Constantinople, and when I was allowed to smoke again, would bring me fine cigars. Never did he come without something to read, and though he was not allowed to see me, he would stand outside my hut and wave to me through the window. Simple things, but marvellous things if one is all alone hundreds and hundreds of miles from home, out in the Turkish wilderness.

There came a time when in hospital "blues" I was able to walk a few paces, and I was asked if I would go and cheer up a young naval officer who had just been brought in with smallpox. His name was Rich, and he was the son of Colonel Rich, who was the Governor of Maidstone Jail. We became great friends, and he made a fast recovery. We lost sight of each other. Many years afterwards, in London, I was about to publish a book and a man rang me up and said he was the managing director of the firm of publishers. He said he would like to meet me. I asked him to come to my club for a cocktail. I asked him his name, but he would not give it to me, he insisted he would know me when he saw me. No doubt you have guessed who it was. It was the former naval officer, who is now a well-known publisher on his own account.

## CONSTANTINOPLE AGAIN

After my escape from death, I made a vow to myself that never again would I return to Turkey. But sure enough, within two years, I was back again, writing stories about the breaking up of the Turkish harems. Then again I went back, and for the second time in my life, how glad I was to see the gleaming white minarets of Stamboul. I had come out of Russia, from Odessa, across the Black Sea and I was shivering with cold. For weeks and weeks, I had not seen the sun, when early one morning I awoke and found the ship was at a standstill. We were at the entrance to the Bosphorus. It was a spring morning and the hills were covered with green; everything, the whole landscape looked marvellous. It was like walking out of hell into paradise. An English girl who was on the ship, and myself, wandered about during the early hours, watching it get lighter and lighter, and we beheld one of the most glorious sights either of us, we agreed, had ever seen. Gone were my nightmares of Constantinople. I was happy to see the Turkish city again.

## ALADDIN'S TREASURE

That visit was memorable to me because I was taken to the Palace of the Osmans overlooking the Golden Gate, and shown all the wealth of bygone sultans. Golden thrones studded with precious stones, and sacks full of rubies, pearls and diamonds. It was a dream such as one never expects to come true.

# CHAPTER V

IN MAY 1926 when I went to Russia for the first time
circumstances and Nature seemed to combine to make
my entry as dramatic and awe-inspiring as possible.
From Berlin I ambled eastwards across Poland, breaking the journey in Warsaw and then travelling through
limitless pine forests seemingly uninhabited except for
an occasional stork. The real journey started in Manchester, because it was there I heard that Arcos House,
the Russian headquarters in London, had been raided,
and I said casually to the editor that I would like to
go to Moscow to see what it was all about. It is
dangerous to speak thus to editors because they sometimes take you at your word and then you have to go.

I went to Paris to apply for a Russian visa, Great
Britain having severed diplomatic relations with
Russia. I paid £2 for an application to be sent
to Moscow in the diplomatic valise and for a reply
to come by telegram; a friendly fellow in the Russian Consulate told me that if I asked for the reply
to be sent to the Russian Embassy in Berlin I should
get it all the quicker. I went to Berlin and from there I
started off on a journey which was a jump into the
dark. I had never been to Russia and had chosen a
bad moment to make the first trip; there was no
diplomatic protection and the English were most un-
popular, as I was to discover. The visa came in good

176

time, so hating to-morrow, as much as ever, off I
went.

When my train reached Niegoreloye, the frontier
town, the scene was like something they do so well at
Drury Lane. What a thrill was there! All evening a
storm had been brewing; there was an angry red sun-
set, and as we drifted away from Poland, leaving
behind masses of barbed wire and red and white
striped poles like one sees outside barbers' shops, the
storm burst. Lightning played over the tops of the
fir trees; rain lashed the windows of the carriages;
thunder smote the ears like the rumbling of distant
artillery fire. The train moved on. The storm died
away. In a wooden shanty beside the railway a number of Russian soldiers with their tunics unbuttoned
began to sing, singing like a professional choir, and
just ahead, forming an arch beneath which the train
had to pass was a sort of banner stating "Soviet
Russia abolishes frontiers". No barbed wire. I know
just as well as anybody that it is all nonsense, maybe
it is just good clean fun, but anyhow it was an impres-
sive moment and I have never forgotten it.

Since that time I have been twice to Russia; on one
trip I travelled two thousand miles all over European
Russia. I never talk to people about Russia unless I
have to because people are too annoying; either they
are so pro-Russian, particularly those who have never
been there, that one must not criticize either the people
or the Government, or else they are so anti-Russian,
and this applies most certainly to the people who
have never been there, that they say, oh of course
you only saw what they allowed you to see. To which
the best answer I find is sure, and of course the English
always invite visiting foreigners to go and see the

delightful distressed areas. The fact of the matter is that everything you say about Russia is true. It is dirty, it is delightful, it is beautiful, it is wretched; it is boring, it is most exciting. It is Russia. Time and time again I have stood in Red Square wishing I could paint. I would want to paint the crowd waiting to be admitted to Lenin's Tomb. No place of entertainment in the world has ever had a crowd queueing up like this. Lenin, that sandy-haired little man who stood Russia on its left ear, is not a dead statesman, but a latter day saint and that queue is as pious as any pilgrimage. And then, not a hundred yards from the Square, you will find beggars with verminous rags barely covering their filthy flesh, lying dead drunk in the gutters; and just outside the Square you will find the Iberian Shrine where despite what you read you will find women kneeling on the pavement praying, and almost over their heads is that famous inscription "Religion is the Opiate of the People". That is Russia.

## THE MAN WHO KNOWS

Walter Duranty, the Boy with the Bicycle of an earlier chapter, is the uncrowned king of Moscow. Go and stay with Duranty and you will be able to write a book about Russia. I know because I did just that. Duranty whose father was Chief Constable of Liverpool went to Russia to look it over and has stayed there more or less ever since. Walter is the true *raisonneur* of the Shakespearian plays. He lost a leg in a French railroad accident and so walks with a stick which adds much to the force of his arguments; how

he does love an argument; I think that if Duranty
convinces you too easily he is liable to start all over
again and argue the same question from a different
angle. And he will be just as convincing. In the same
evening I have heard him prove that in the event of
war with the U.S.A. Japan would immediately capture the Philippine Islands, and that never in a thousand years could Japan ever capture the Philippine
Islands. That was a particularly good evening. One
afternoon, Duranty came to see me at the Savoy
Hotel in Moscow and said he could only stop for a
few minutes. We drank some vodka. About two the
following morning I remembered to ask Walter what
he had come to see me about. It is no good going to
stay in Russia unless you like conversation. Duranty
is a grand master of conversation and that is one of
the reasons why the Russians like him so much and
because they like him so much they trust him and
because they trust him they tell him things and because
they tell him things Duranty is the best informed man
alive about Russia. Sometimes the things people
tell him or ask him must be most embarrassing, and
the people who ask are not invariably Russian. Once
there were two sisters, American girls, in Russia,
studying the country, and they went to Duranty one
day and told him they wanted to have an illegal
operation performed. Duranty said that of course that
was possible, but one musin't believe all one read
about Russia. He asked when they wanted the
operation and they said at once, and then Duranty
cleared his throat and asked which one it was who
wanted the operation performed and they said that
both of them wanted it. Duranty then discovered that
the illegal operation about which they were seeking

information consisted of changing dollars into roubles. The girls wanted their money changed on the Black Bourse, that was all.

## *Bist Du Da*, STALIN?

This money changing question is all important in Russia.  In the ordinary way, the Russian banks exchange one pound for twenty roubles, but on my last trip I was able to obtain two hundred roubles on the Black Bourse.  I met a young German who had been several times to Russia, in connection with a side show he was running in the Moscow Amusement Park.  He was doing a little smuggling on the side; dresses which he bought in London for three and six-pence and for which he obtained the equivalent of five pounds in Moscow.  He used to go round the ship and seductively ask young women to take the dresses in their luggage going into Russia; then he got them back; he was lucky enough to meet a party of English tourists who obliged him, but they believed he was taking the dresses to help poor starving Russians! This young man was what they used to call a "card". He seemed to fear nothing, and not even the Secret Police frightened him.  While most of us discussed Russia in whispers, the German would work his favourite joke, going to a ventilator in the bedroom and pretending it was a telephone and calling out *bist du da*, Stalin?  He sold his dresses all right.  He would accost a girl and offer a dress, pointing out that it was specially imported from England and say, calling attention to the tab inside, *Sehen Sie, nichts* Marks *allein aber* Marks UND Spencer!  It was this young German who obtained the two hundred rate on the Black Bourse, and goodness knows how he did; I have often wondered what commission he took for himself.

## FEAR

Life, however, is not all comedy in Russia. A new Terror had started the first time I went to Russia and many people were fearing either for their liberty or their lives. I listened to one of the Countess Tolstis telling how she and her mother would tremble every night in their flat, dying a thousand deaths every time a vehicle was heard coming along their street. I had an interpreter, the wife of an engineer, she would call on me every morning and translate the newspapers to me, her English and French and German were fluent. One morning she came with her face as white as chalk; while she had been making some small purchases for me she had lost her note book containing notes of matters into which I had asked her to inquire, and also the addresses of her friends; she could not remember, poor soul, whether by any chance she had left her own name and address in the book. If she had, she would have been surely arrested. Fortunately she had not left her name and address, but imagine the agonies she suffered for at least twenty-four hours.

A Russian barber in Paris used to cut my hair. When I told him I was going to Moscow he asked me if I would take a case of razors and scissors to his brother who was a barber in Moscow. I took the case but instead of taking it to the man's address, the shop, myself, I asked the hotel interpreter to go and tell the

man to come and see me in the evening. He came.
His brother in Paris never heard from him again.
When I told Duranty, he said that the interpreter was
well known as a secret police spy. That is Russia.

## NITCHEVO

The only way to understand Russia is to learn the
many inflections and meanings of Nitchevo, which
can mean I don't know, I don't care, who knows?
who cares? or just plain what the hell? It all depends
on what you want it to mean. When you can understand Nitchevo you can quite understand Russia,
because by then you will have become a fatalist.
Once Duranty happened during the time of the afore-
mentioned Terror to tell me that the prisons were so
full that cells held fifty prisoners and they had to sleep
in relays. I put this in a cable to my paper. The
censor shook his head and said that was not true.
Without divulging the source of my information I
insisted it was true. The censor said wait a minute
and he would go and ask Mr. Rothstein. He returned
and said I was both right and wrong because there
were not fifty prisoners in the overcrowded cells, but
sixty, and very politely he corrected the figure for me
and passed the cable.

## ROAMING RUSSIA

I packed up my things in Kharkoff to go to Kieff
but when I went to the station they would not allow
me to get on the train because all the seats had been

taken by government officials. I was already angry enough with Kharkoff because I had been charged ninepence for an orange, so I went back to the hotel, furious because I had to spend another night in the dreadful place, and at the top of the staircase I shouted down with Russia, hoping that I should provide a little excitement but nobody took the slightest notice. And yet when one is trying to be inconspicuous, that is just the moment when attentions become unwelcome. I was chased the whole time I was in Kieff by a sort of stage American who pretended he was an American pianist on a concert tour. He was a Russian Secret Police spy, he never let me out of his sight for more than an hour; he was waiting when I arrived and saw me off for Odessa. One of his favourite tricks was to dash into my room and ask me to give him dollars or pounds or francs for some roubles, and always I blandly replied I had no currency but roubles, all foreign currencies being forbidden. He was an insistent devil and never gave up hope of catching me out. Of course, I had both pounds and dollars in my wallet and he knew it just as well as I did.

When the train rattles through the night, that is the time for conversation and when you really hear what is going on. The majority of the young folk believe all the Russian papers tell them. I have been asked in Moscow when England will have underground railways like they have there; theirs is about three years old; I have been asked if the "new King" in England is a good dictator, and by children whether the people in England live in caves or in houses, "like we do". Nearly everybody asks how the Revolution is going in England. In the night time people

7

edge up to you and feel the stuff of which your suit is made and ask how much it costs; their shoddy suits cost the equivalent in English money of ten pounds. They peer at your wrist watch and ask the price of that and when you tell them they look at you with shrewd cunning eyes and seem to be calling you a liar, deep down inside them. You cannot convince the young people, and don't forget it Soviet Russia is twenty-one years of age, that outside of Russia things are different, that there are cheap clothes and amusements and that when a man leaves work he goes home or does what he likes. When a man leaves work in a Russian factory, he has to go and listen to a lecture in the factory or else put in some practice in the factory rifle range; his actual working time may not be more than five hours, but at least three more hours have to be given to what he is forced to do, whether he likes it or not. Do you care, Ivan Ivanovitch? Nitchevo, shrugs Ivan Ivanovitch.

Once for a whole week in Odessa we lived on caviare. This was not an orgy, but the food at the Londonskaya became too monotonous, twice a day there was bortch and boiled chicken. I was waiting for a ship to go to Constantinople, and there was nothing to do but eat and sleep and take a bath. Fortunately it took a long time to take a bath. Four hours was the average time it took to reach the bath from the first time of asking Comrade Chambermaid to get one ready. Comrade Chambermaid had to find Comrade Woodchopper and he had to talk the matter over with another Comrade, during which time one called Comrade Chambermaid again and several other things she fortunately did not understand. When the wood was chopped, another unseen Comrade lit the fire, and then one took a nap or went out for a walk while the fire heated the water. Then, if nothing else happened, such as Comrade Chambermaid having completed her three day tour of duty and being replaced by Comrade Chambermaid II who knew nothing of the bath, one had a bath. The general condition of the hotel made baths extremely necessary. There were six Turks . . . but that is an entirely different story.

The caviare *fest* took place in the bedroom. First of all I used to go to a Co-operative store and buy the caviare and take it back in a sheet of newspaper, rather like fried fish and chips, and then use all my wiles to get some toast made, the butter I also bought at the Co-operative store. Then there was no more to be done than to get a waiter to bring the samovar containing the hot water, for which he expected sixpence; then we had tea and caviare and toast. Twice a day.

The first time I went to Russia I telegraphed Duranty to know what I could bring him; he wanted some American coffee and some silk stockings for Katcha. On subsequent trips to Russia I never asked friends what I should bring. I knew. I took toilet paper, and, my, was I the popular young man!

# CHAPTER VI

## INTERLUDES IN SPAIN

A FEW days before I began to write this book, the *Daily Mail* called up from London. I was sitting in my Paris flat, facing the Seine. While waiting for the call to be put through, a clear young girlish voice said: "Is that Mr. Greenwall himself? Do you remember Albert Dawson in Spain?" Did I remember Albert Dawson? Of course I remembered him; memory will fade completely before I have forgotten him. The young girl said: "He is my father." She was speaking from the International Telephone Exchange. Passing boats on the river were blotted out by another memory. It was one summer's day in 1917, and I was in a garden in Vaucresson, playing with a baby. A maid handed me a cable. It said "Go Spain immediately cover revolution." It was my first assignment outside of France, and I was thrilled. The Franco-Spanish frontier was closed and it was very difficult to obtain a visa. I went to see Will Irwin, who had just returned from Spain. He said there was no revolution, but because no news was coming out of Spain, newspaper editors thought there must be a revolution. All that was happening was some unrest among army officers because promotion was delayed. He spoke a word of warning about passports. He told me to sleep with my passport pinned inside my pyjama pocket, because English and American passports were very valuable and as Spain was honeycombed with German spies, it was easy to have one's passport stolen. I much appreciated that warning within a week of its being spoken, because while travelling between Paris and the Spanish frontier, a dear old gentleman who said he was a Russian and who was going to Spain on business made several semi-plausible efforts to handle my passport. I kept it safely hidden away.

## The Spain That Was

I can realize now in 1939 that in the summer of 1917 I saw the first scene of the first act of the Spanish tragedy. Spain was nominally neutral. The people were mostly pro-ally; the clergy, the aristocracy and the Queen-Mother were pro-German, or perhaps it would be more correct in the case of the late Queen Mother to say she was pro-Austrian. She was an Austrian princess. The King himself was quite frankly pro-British and pro-French. He made no attempt to conceal that fact in private conversation.

The Spanish parliamentary machine was worn out and the King did nothing to renew the machinery. He was content to let things be; his close personal advisors, principally Count Romanones, who had known him since birth, encouraged him not to do anything at all. There was an unimportant Republican party headed by a man named Alexandre Lerroux, but he used to dine at the Palace with the King and his Party never meant to take any political action whatsoever. The Socialist party existed but had it not been for later developments, when the Socialists and the Republicans joined forces, the King would have been on his throne to-day.

The story I had gone to cover was quite unimportant, but Spain thrilled me, after three years of living in a country of war, it was like going into a new world to see bright lights, plenty of sugar and plenty of butter and bread that was snow white. I was in no great hurry to leave Spain, but I had no good reason for remaining there, so I had to find a reason and I made up my mind I would interview the King. I had never interviewed a king. The King of Spain had never been interviewed. Something ought to be done, I thought, to change this. The first step I took was to go and see Senor Merry del Val, the Spanish Ambassador to London, who was spending a short holiday in Madrid. He gave me an anonymous interview, expressing the point of view of the average Spaniard towards the world war. He also, kindly gentleman that he is, promised to do anything he could to facilitate my self-imposed task. Every foreigner going to Madrid in those days was the object of close inspection, not only by the Spaniards, but by the British and the French and the Germans as well. Spies of all nations had their headquarters in Madrid. The woman at the top of the British black list was a brunette, not very young and not particularly attractive, but very vivacious. She, I was told, was particularly dangerous, a notorious German agent, in the pay of the German Embassy, and looked upon by them as one of their ace spies. She was Mata Hari, afterwards shot at Vincennes by the French. A secretary of the British Embassy said one night: "See that fair girl over there (to-day, no doubt, he would have called her a blonde). She is an Austrian married to an English officer, and she calls herself a Dane. She is a spy, but not dangerous." I found her very nice indeed. Another woman, not on the British black list, was a girl who was appearing at a Madrid theatre. She was a French spy employed by the French Naval Intelligence. Her previous exploit had been remarkable. She had been sent to Salonica to watch M. Venizelos when he was working out the revolution paid for by the British and French Governments. On her way back from Salonica, the ship in which she was travelling was torpedoed in the Mediterranean. Another French spy was a very attractive ex-mannequin from the rue de la Paix.

The story that I was trying to interview the King got about the hotel, and I had all sorts of kind and willing helpers. Among those who offered assistance was the King's Belgian trainer, M. de Neuter, and the King's American jockey, Lynes. An American confidence trickster also tried to do something about the matter, but what he wanted to do was not very clear, and still another confidence man offered help. He was an Australian who had been turned off most of the English race courses and had gone to Spain. A few months after I first met him, he was conducted to the frontier and there handed over to English detectives and extradited to England; but there is one thing the King did not know, and that is that when I did get my interview, I was wearing the Australian crook's cashmere trousers. I did struggle hard to get this interview, but when everything was fixed and I was summoned to the Palace, I had no clothes. I mean I had no official clothes. I had to wear a top hat and a morning coat and trousers, and I had none of these things. One man lent me a top hat, and the head of the reception office, a Swiss, who happened to be in the employ of the British Intelligence Service, lent me his morning coat and waistcoat, I had the Australian crook's trousers, and as a kindly gesture he also lent me his silver-topped malacca cane. The shoes were my own. Just as I was setting out for the Palace, Mr. Baring, one of the British Embassy attachés, telephoned me and seemed very agitated. He told me not to forget that I was to kiss the King's hand.

## I Meet The King

Outside the Palace Hotel, I picked up a horse cab and drove away in a state of great exultation. It was a very hot day and I told the driver to wait for me in the shade. I anticipated a wait of perhaps half an hour. I entered the Palace in my borrowed clothes, showed my letter and I was conducted through long corridors where at every turn was a halberdier, who as I passed banged his halberd on the floor and startled me completely, so that when I arrived at the door of the King's study, my nerves were frayed. His Naval Attaché, in a white drill suit, knocked at the door and in a couple of seconds I stood in the presence of King Alphonso the XIII of Spain. He was wearing a brown suit and looked very jolly. I suppose I ought to say that he looked every inch a king, but I prefer to tell the truth and say that he looked every bit like a very nice fellow. He held out his hand and I tried to kiss it, and the King prevented me from kissing it, because the more I pulled it towards me, the more he pulled it back. And then he closed the door, pointed to a sofa and asked me to sit down and he sat down beside me. In a second or two he jumped up and walked over to the mantelpiece where there was an enormous cocktail shaker. He lifted it up and asked me if I would have a cocktail. It was eleven-thirty in the morning and I said thank you very much but I would rather not have a cocktail. The King put the shaker back and it appeared to me he was rather relieved and he said: "I won't have one either." Then he came back and sat down beside me and he talked for nearly two hours. At the end of the conversation, he said: "Mr. Greenwall, you have interviewed me and now I want to interview you." I replied: "What can I tell you, Sire?" The King smiled quizzically and said: "They tell me that your King was hooted in Manchester last May." I was astonished, because I had not heard of such an incident and I told the King I knew nothing about it. He answered: "Oh yes, they tell me the people were shouting 'go on you old German'," and the way the King said this was most comical. I again told His Majesty that I had never heard anything whatsoever, but as I was dining that night with an Ambassador, I would ask him, and I would let the King know through his Secretary. I asked the Ambassador, who told me it was quite true, and I saw the King's Secretary the next day and the message was conveyed to the King, who sent me a signed photograph of himself as a token of appreciation. I was so thrilled with my interview, that when I left the Palace, I waved my borrowed cane in the direction of the horse cab which was waiting in the shade, jumped in and drove back to the hotel, considerably overpaid the driver and went upstairs and sat in front of my typewriter, also borrowed, and wrote the interview. Then I had some lunch, and then I went out and enjoyed myself. That night, I went to bed about ten o'clock. About eleven o'clock, the telephone in my bedroom rang, the night porter said that there was a cab-driver downstairs who had waited in front of the Palace since ten-thirty that morning and now he thought he ought to be paid off. Well, they say that all coons look alike and all I can add to that is that all Madrid cab-drivers look alike to me, particularly when I am excited.

## THRILLS IN PLENTY

In October, 1917, I was heading for Spain again, but this time my mission was not entirely journalistic. The British Government was not quite satisfied with its propaganda in Spain and I was asked to advise. Furthermore, there was another Service which thought I might be useful to it. I went first of all to St. Jean de Luz, not far from the frontier, and here I met Albert Dawson, who had become, for wartime purposes only, Commander Dawson. Dawson had been in the coal business in Spain and spoke the language fluently. He was the man who made Spain safe for the Allies to operate in during the World War. A high official of our espionage service was a very amusing regular officer about whom the British Ambassador once made a very cryptic remark. The regular officer was friendly with a lady who had come from America to play in musical comedy in London. Her nickname was the "Darling of the Guards". Because this young person showed too great an interest in Zeppelin raids, she was after one warning from Scotland Yard, asked to return to America. She went back to the States, but sailed almost immediately for Spain where she met the officer, and then she went to Paris.

Another friend of this particular officer was a German Princess of English origin, who had lived in France for so long that she was allowed to remain during the war. She did not go to Spain herself, as the young actress did, but she went and stayed very close to the frontier, at Biarritz, and our friend, the officer, used to take frequent trips across the Pyrenees to visit her. One night at dinner at the Embassy, the officer's name came up, and the Ambassador said: "Yes, yes, such a nice man, his job is in Spain but his morals are in France."

While waiting in St. Jean de Luz for instructions, a large Rolls Royce car stopped in front of my door. Two officers belonging to the R.N.V.R. got out and fetched me and told me to get my bags at once and jump in. One of the two officers was Albert Dawson, and a finer man I never hope to meet. His courage and intelligence are equally matched. On this occasion we dashed over the frontier to San Sebastian and there again I was told to wait. Then things began to happen, and for weeks I thought I was living in the pages of the most sensational spy novel I had ever come across. Backwards and forwards I dashed in the Admiralty-owned Rolls Royce car. I had to go over to the French side of the frontier to fetch T.N.T. and bring it into Spain. German submarines had bases all round the North and the South of Spain, as well as on the Catalonian coast. There were some ten thousand known German and Austrian agents. The Official Secrets Act prevents me from telling a full story of the things, the most amazing things that used to happen, but there is no reason at all why I should not tell what the Germans did, and how we were able in most instances to checkmate what they did. Daw-

son was responsible for the sinking of most of the
German submarines, which met their end in Spanish
waters. It was he who had photographs taken of the
German Morse signals. For propaganda purposes, the
Germans had a line of commercial submarines running between Kiel, San Sebastian and Bilbao. These
submarines brought letters and newspapers from Germany which were used by the German Propaganda
Service in Spain. It was intended to show they did not
care anything about the British blockade. Those submarines were not dangerous, but the others which
were sinking food-carrying ships bound northwards
were dangerous, and they could not have operated
unless they had had bases in Spain where they could
obtain petrol and food. The only way to get rid of the
submarines was to get rid of the bases, but as there
was so much pro-German feeling in high places, it was
extremely difficult to do anything, and indeed nothing
could be done unless it was done by a direct action,
though this was a violation of neutrality, but it had to
be done; anyhow, the Germans were also violating
Spanish neutrality. There was a certain ship in San
Sebastian which used to go out regularly to revictual
a large submarine which signalled its approach in
Morse. Having learned the signal, Dawson tried for
weeks to buy off the skipper of the boat which was
carrying victuals to the submarine. On one occasion,
he had anonymous letters written to all members of
the crew, saying that the most unfortunate things
would happen to them if they went on with their
work. Some of the crew struck, but the skipper obtained others. Eventually, a way was found to sub-
stitute one of the packs containing turnips which were
to be carried to the submarine. The actual pack which

was substituted contained turnips filled with T.N.T., and a time-fuse. The submarine did not appear again. One night I was dragged out of my bed, pushed into the car and driven miles to a lonely spot on the coast and then handed a woman's silk stocking filled with sand. Another man and I had to go and pay an unexpected call on a German wireless operator. The apparatus was somehow smashed. The operator must have had a headache in the morning.

All exploits did not end with success. A Spanish priest who was taking a wireless emitting post which it was known he was going to put up on his church spire had to be followed. The priest must have known he was being followed because when the train arrived at its destination, although at every stopping place one had made sure that the priest was still in his compartment, there was no priest.

The Germans were very keen on running the blockade with cargoes of wolfram, which they obtained from mines in Spain and which they used for hardening steel. The Germans purchased two Spanish schooners and named each of them the *Berri-Berri*. One schooner carried an innocuous cargo and the other carried a mixture of glass and wolfram. When it became difficult for one schooner to run the blockade, it was arranged that the other schooner should carry the wolfram out to sea and then transfer it to a submarine. The puzzle was to know which of the two schooners carried the wolfram. The only thing to do was to try and stop both schooners. There was an old British cruiser called *Duke of Clarence*, which was stationed at Biarritz to take charge of northbound convoys from the Mediterranean. One *Berri-Berri* put out to sea from San Sebastian and proceeded northwards within the three-mile limit. Of course, a ship cannot be searched within the three-mile limit, but can be outside. *Duke of Clarence* met the *Berri-Berri* within the three-mile limit. International regulations make plain that warning must be given by firing a blank round so that a ship knows it is a signal for her to stand to. The *Duke of Clarence* complied with the law, but unfortunately the gunners made a mistake. Instead of firing blank they fired a real round, and the mast and rigging of the *Berri-Berri* came crashing down. Drifting outside the three-mile limit, she was searched and found to be carrying wolfram to Germany. She was towed to San-Jean-de-Luz.

Several times I was sent dashing back to Spain and then I received orders which sent me back to my work of reporting. I never went to Spain again before the Throne began to totter.

My last trip during the War years ended on a note of comedy. The King's Messenger working between Paris and Madrid, Parkington-Goff, fell ill, and I was pressed into service as temporary King's Messenger. An officer in charge of our espionage service, to whom I have already alluded, rang me up and said: "I hear you are taking the bag (the diplomatic valise) to Paris to-night. I want you to take something for me. Give me the number of your sleeping berth and I will have what I want taken sent to the train." I saw a servant from the British Embassy staggering towards the train, carrying, with the aid of a porter, a suit-case which appeared to be extraordinarily heavy; it was difficult to lift it into my compartment. I was handed a letter from the officer. The letter enclosed the key of the locked suit-case, which I was told to take to Miss X at the Hotel Crillon, before taking the diplomatic bag to the British Embassy. Miss X was the musical-comedy actress from America who had been requested to leave England. Instructions were instructions, so I carried them out. Two porters carried the locked suit-case from the train to my taxi and when I stopped in front of the Crillon, two hotel attendants had to carry the suit-case in. I telephoned to the lady's apartment and said I had something for her. The lady asked me to come upstairs. Two attendants followed me with the mysterious suit-case. I gave the lady a letter from her friend. She began to read it while I looked at the photographs scattered all over the grand piano. There was reason to call her the "Darling of the Guards". Suddenly there was a ripple of girlish laughter. "Oh, what a dear man he is to send me all this sugar," she giggled, "he must have heard that there is a shortage of sugar in Paris."

It had nothing at all to do with my visit, but six weeks later, the lady was requested to leave French territory.

## HUMPTY-DUMPTY

It was inevitable that with all the friends I had made in Spain during the war, I should be well-placed for information of importance in post-war developments. Slowly, but surely and relentlessly, the Spanish tragedy moved on towards the Abdication of the King. It is easy to be wise after an event, but in the case of the Spanish bloodless revolution, I can say that I did foresee it and foretold it. No correspondent is a hero in his own newspaper office, or if he is a hero, he is a sort of a wonder hero whose fame endures no longer than a night and a day. It was reported to me that when I sent my message from Madrid on the night the King left, the editor exclaimed "Greenwall was right for once."

One of the men who brought about the fusion of the Spanish Republican and Socialist parties, was Alvarez del Vayo, whom I had known personally in Berlin, when he was the correspondent of a Buenos Aires newspaper. Later he became the Madrid correspondent of the *Manchester Guardian*. I knew all the moves that were being made about twenty-four hours before the public knew. When the Spaniards were defeated by the Riffs, it was apparent to all who knew what was going on behind the scene that the scandals which implicated the King's friends could not be kept much longer from the public. I was present when the Queen and her children left Spain, twenty-four hours after, the King went away. In another work, I have expressed my considered opinion that if the King had not left Madrid on that fateful Sunday night, he would still be at the Royal Palace. The greatest mistake he made was when he decided to go. He said, or it was said for him, that the only reason he went was to avoid bloodshed. Now look back at what has happened in Spain since 1936 and think of the blood that has been shed—blood that might not have been spilt if the King had decided to stay where he was. The night the King went there was high carnival in Madrid; there was singing and dancing in the streets, but there was not a drop of blood spilt. Those who desired the overthrow of the Monarchy were astonished at the ease with which their desires were fulfilled.

# CHAPTER VII

## THE CITY OF ILLUSION

ONE OF my enemies' favourites jibes is that I helped to destroy the League of Nations. I should like to give you a picture of myself sitting in a hot bath late one night in the Hotel Adlon in Berlin. It was not quite a month after the Armistice was signed, and here was I in the capital of our chief enemy, reading the Paris edition of the New York *Herald*, and, as I read, tears streamed out of my eyes. I was reading President Wilson's plan for the foundation of the League of Nations, and I said to myself here at long last is a new Messiah.

The first time I was assigned to Geneva, I was greatly honoured. I believed firmly and hopefully in the future of the League; but gradually and then finally, I was bitterly disillusioned. I became one of Geneva's most caustic critics, because I was disillusioned and because I hate hypocrisy, particularly in high places. It is not so much a question of fighting a principle, but of combating those who pretend to defend not so much a principle as well-paid jobs. I pay tribute to those members of the Secretariat of the League of Nations, the members of the staff of the International Labour Bureau, who would work for far less than they are paid if they thought that by doing so they would be able to make the League of Nations a living League. My attacks are not directed against those people, but against others who are so cynical in their references to the organization which for so long has provided them with such excellent positions.

When I began to criticize the League I took care that my facts should be correct; but once when I slipped and instead of telephoning the word Council, I said Assembly, Sir Eric Drummond (now Earl of Perth), then Secretary-General of the League of Nations, sent for Mr. Vernon Bartlett, who was in charge of publicity, and told him to draft a letter to Lord Beaverbrook. Bartlett sagely told Sir Eric to forget it.

## DRAMA AT GENEVA

The League of Nations, as it was constructed, was destroyed by its best friends. Perhaps one day, the Covenant of the League will be rewritten, and out of the ashes will arise a new and stronger organization. Most sincerely do I hope so, but I hope with equal sincerity that if such a thing comes to pass, efforts will be made to avoid the mistakes which were made when the League was founded.

The moments of emotional drama which I and hundreds of my colleagues have witnessed in Geneva pay eloquent tribute to the agonizing anxiety with which millions of people spread over the world regarded what was taking place in this city on Lake Leman. While Germany was still a member of the League, but when relations between Austria and Germany were becoming more strained, Baron von Neurath, the German Foreign Secretary, led a Delegation to Geneva. Little Dr. Dollfuss mounted the rostrum and addressed the Assembly. So moving was his speech that the German Delegation forgot its manufactured hatred of Austria, and every member, including the leader of the delegation, applauded frantically.

The greatest drama in the history of the League of Nations I should say occurred on March 8th, 1926, when Germany was to enter the League, and to take the seat on the Council which had been reserved for her. The Berlin Foreign Office had sent formal letters to every member of the Council saying that Germany consented to put forward her candidature as a member. Every member of the Council except Brazil sent a favourable reply. Brazil answered that until she was granted a permanent seat on the Council, she would not vote in favour of any other country taking a permanent seat. It is important to remember this point, because it helps to understand why the League gradually faded out of the picture of international affairs.

Instead of negotiating with Brazil *before* summoning the Council and the special Assembly to admit Germany, the Secretariat of the League put the cart in front of the horse and brought the German Chancellor, Herr Gustav Stresseman, and Dr. Luther, and the German Delegation to Geneva, and showed the world one of the greatest diplomatic fiascos ever staged. The late Sir Austen Chamberlain and the late Aristide Briand worked hard to persuade Brazil to withdraw her opposition, but Brazil remained calmly adamant. There was nothing to be done, but Sir Austen tried to do it, and in the trying he made himself wretchedly ill, and made the League the laughing stock of the world for weeks.

# I HATE TO-MORROW

A Mr. George Stewart, a former reporter in Manchester, was in charge of the London Foreign Office press relations with the international correspondents in Geneva. Mr. Stewart appeared to be inspired by the "leaders" in the *Times*, and the "leaders" in the *Times* several days old, incidentally, were ponderously repeated to members of the World's Press who were seeking real information. Mr. Stewart was a keen golfer; but during acute crises he soothed his nerves by walking in the older parts of Geneva with paper and crayons and made the most excellent sketches. Meanwhile other sketches were being made by diplomats who had come at great inconvenience thousands of miles to be present at a historical moment. Germany was to become a member of the League of Nations. Mr. Stewart no doubt inspired by Sir Austen Chamberlain, refused categorically to admit that all was not for the best in the best of all possible Genevas. In vain correspondents tried to elucidate the question: was Germany coming in or was she not? The excitement in London and New York was immense. All night long I was on the telephone and on three occasions during this historic week in March, 1926, the *Daily Express* brought out special editions in the early hours of the morning. I went from the French Delegation to the British Delegation and then to the German Delegation and then back again and up and down I ran and rode and raced. The conclusion I reached was that Germany was not coming in because she could not obtain a seat on the Council. Up to the very last moment, when members of the Assembly were pressing for a yes or no, saying that they had to return to their capitals, Sir Austen was still trying to smile heroically, and he wished us

all to believe that Germany would come in. Maybe
Sir Austen believed that the age of miracles was not
past.

All kinds of political manœuvres were tried.
Sweden offered to resign her seat on the Council.
This was not acceptable. Germany was bullied, then
cajoled, then bullied again, all to no purpose. Stresseman and Luther smiled and shook their heads. A seat on
the Council after election by the Assembly, or nothing.

When all hope was over, Sir Austen Chamberlain
asked the English correspondents to come and see him.
We trooped through the pouring rain to the Hotel Beau
Rivage, and there in Sir Austen's sitting-room we sat
and listened to him. There were tears in his eyes and
tears in his voice when he told us that the Assembly
had been convoked for the morrow, but Germany
would not be present. When the Assembly met and
Sir Austen and Aristide Briand expressed their
regrets, Stresseman and Luther sat in their sitting-
room, in their hotel, and through ear-phones listened
to the speeches. Finally, of course, Germany did
come in and did take a seat on the Council, but that
was not until very much later.

## COMEDY

Mysterious movements of certain European Foreign
Ministers used to keep the Foreign Offices of Europe
busy guessing what they meant and what "sinister"
motives lay behind their travels. Once Geneva
laughed loudly when one of these "sinister plots" was
exposed. The late M. Venizelos went travelling
round Europe and visited, amongst other capitals,

Rome and Warsaw. The French Foreign Office was most intrigued. Cypher messages passed backwards and forwards between Paris and French Ambassadors stationed abroad. What was M. Venizelos doing? What was he plotting? Was the man who formed the famous Balkan *bloc* which led to the Balkan war between the *bloc* and Turkey, planning another war-like move? France communicated with her Allies. Ambassadors were told to obtain the truth at any cost. John Gunther and myself discovered the truth. The World Economic Crisis made salesmen out of states-men, and M. Venizelos had been selling Greek wine, and it is said had been extremely successful.

Then Count Bethlen, who was Prime Minister of Hungary, went travelling. He went to Rome and saw Mussolini. "Ah ha," murmured the Foreign Offices. This means that Hungary is planning a revision of the Treaty of Trianon. Wants her pre-war frontiers restored. Of course she did, but Count Bethlen at that moment was busy selling Hungarian wine. Then came Dr. Edouard Benès, who was at this time Foreign Minister of Czechoslovakia. He was busy going from Prague to various European capitals. Dr. Benès was selling boots. Then there was Herr Marinkovitch, the dark little Foreign Minister of Yugo-Slavia. He too went travelling, and he was selling hides, and it is on record that Dr. Benès' boots were largely made from Herr Marinkovitch's hides.

## DRAMA AGAIN

In June, 1932, while the Disarmament Conference was still sitting in Geneva, there was an International

Conference held in Lausanne. The late Mr. Ramsay MacDonald was Prime Minister of Great Britain. President Hoover was still in the White House, and M. Edouard Herriot was Prime Minister of France. Although the United States had a delegation headed by Mr. Hugh Gibson in Geneva, it had been announced to the whole world that the Americans would not travel forty miles away to Lausanne where there were not only the Prime Ministers of Great Britain and France, but other important diplomats as well. Then there was a sudden change. On the night of Monday, June 20th, there was a secret meeting at the little village of Morges, six miles from Geneva. The meeting was attended by Mr. Hugh Gibson and Mr. Norman Davis and M. Paul-Boncour, Minister of War, who had come from Geneva, and by M. Herriot and M. Germain-Martin, the French Minister of Finance. The meeting place was a little inn beside the stormy lake where the statesmen sat in a small sitting-room on the first floor. The innkeeper was so pleased to receive such guests of mark, that he presented them with a bottle of the local champagne. The meeting began at half-past nine at night and finished at ten minutes to twelve. The purpose of the meeting was to try and get the French to reduce the sums they were spending on armaments. How foolish all this sounds to-day—just seven years ago.

The morning after the meeting the French Delegation was furious because the spokesman of the American Delegation had announced why the Americans and the French had met. The spokesman said categorically that France was spending more money than she could afford on her armaments, in view of the size of her war debts, yet France expected America to cancel the French debt to the United States. The spokesman went on: "So long as France continues to spend as much money as she is doing at present on her Army and her Navy and her Air Force, it is quite useless to expect the United States to take any steps towards the cancellation of War Debts."

M. Herriot spent three hours in private conversation with Mr. Ramsay MacDonald, and then made another appointment to meet him again in the afternoon. Then a surprising thing happened: M. Herriot arrived at Mr. MacDonald's hotel and heard from me, incidentally, that upstairs with Mr. MacDonald were Mr. Gibson and Mr. Davis. The French Prime Minister was amazed. He asked me if I were quite sure. Then he went upstairs looking very bewildered indeed. As soon as he reached the floor on which Mr. Ramsay MacDonald was living, the French Prime Minister was requested to wait until the other conversations had come to an end. He sat down looking very worried.

In the end it all came to nothing. That is just Geneva all over. The City of Illusion.

## More Comedy

The International Club in Geneva was a great place once upon a time for international discussions between journalists from all over the world. Sometimes Mr. Anthony Eden would come in and talk confidentially. But the Restaurant Globe, in the upper town, was the place where all the foreign diplomats used to meet and talk. Sometimes very remarkable indiscretions were to be heard in this little restaurant. M. Nikolas

Titulescu, who has been Rumania's Ambassador to London, its Prime Minister and for years its Foreign Secretary, used to like to sit and talk at the Globe. I remember one time an American newspaperman asked M. Titulescu where Madame Lupescu was. Titulescu waved his cigarette impatiently. "That's the King's business," he said. "What do I care where she is. She might be here for all I know."

Another time, M. Titulescu told several newspapermen of a party he had attended at Lady Astor's in London. They played musical chairs, and he gave a graphic description of himself trailing along just ahead of Mr. Maisky, the Soviet Ambassador. It must have been quite a nice party.

The eclipse of M. Titulescu coincided with the crumbling of the League. During the heyday of Geneva, it was impossible to imagine the Swiss city without such faces as those of the cheerful Rumanian and the very nervous little Dr. Benès. I can see in my mind's eye gaunt Sir John Simon, smiling Austen Chamberlain, vain and rather pompous Mr. Ramsay MacDonald; portly M. Herriot; several laughing, smiling little Japanese and solemn looking Chinamen; what a procession has passed through Geneva. What secrets have been whispered behind bedroom doors. And now one may well say: all that for nothing.

## TAIL-PIECE

Reporting Geneva was a strenuous job but often good fun. I drove there one week-end with an American reporter who represented a New York evening paper. We arrived there on a Sunday and he had nothing to do.  I almost forgot that I had to prepare a preliminary story for the next morning's paper.  We went to lunch at the Globe.  The food, as usual, was excellent, so was the conversation, so was the port.  We sat sipping port until teatime.  Then I suddenly remembered I had to write a story.  I had collected quite a good one, so I went back to my hotel, took off my wrist watch, put it beside the telephone, rang London and said: "Now listen, here is a story, I am dictating it without notes, but I want you not to ask me to repeat it because I have got it all in my head."  Then I started.  When I saw I had been talking for twenty minutes I said: "That's all.  Good-bye."  And rang off.  I had not the faintest recollection what I had said.

The next morning I received a cable worded as follows: "Thanks excellent story Editor."

# BOOK III

# CHAPTER I

## MAX AND BAX

A LITTLE man stood in front of the lift-shaft in the Hotel Crillon, Paris. He wore a fur coat and a silk hat, tilted at the back of his head. Beside him stood a tall, cadaverous looking man, who was later known to me as Captain "Freddie" Guest.

The little man pressed the button impatiently; he wanted the lift, as he wanted everything else in life, quickly.

## I MEET MAX

It was one morning late in 1917. I was about thirty years old and I still believed in Journalism. I had just returned from one of my interludes in Spain. Mr. Bonar Law, then Chancellor of the Exchequer, was in Paris at the Hotel Crillon, but who was the little man with the silk hat tilted at the back of his head? He looked intriguing.

"Who is he?" I nodded towards the little figure, and asked M. Dequis, manager of the hotel.

"That is Lord Beaverbrook," whispered the manager. "He has come to see Mr. Bonar Law, but I have told him that Mr. Bonar Law is out, but he insists on going upstairs." That was all I wanted to know.

I walked up to the little man and said: "My name is Greenwall; I am Paris correspondent of the *Daily Express*."

"You are the very man I want to see. Come on up," said the Lord. The lift having arrived, we three: Beaverbrook, Guest and myself, stepped in together.

I followed Lord Beaverbrook into Mr. Bonar Law's apartment. There was not a secretary, there was not anybody in the suite, but Lord Beaverbrook just kept on walking and then he came out into the corridor again. "Come on over to the Ritz and have lunch."

At that time I had heard of Lord Beaverbrook as a man who had more than one finger in the *Daily Express* pie. I wanted to see this figure who was reputed to be cutting a swathe across the sky of England. He had come from Canada alone and unknown. I have good reason to remember that lunch, because from that moment onwards and for the next eighteen years, I had Beaverbrook roast, boiled, fried and fricasseed.

### THE LORD SPEAKS

Within two hours of meeting Beaverbrook, he had got me into a fight with the Provost Marshal of Paris. Lord Beaverbrook asked me to get a special visa for him on his passport. I took the passport to the Provost Marshal's Office in the rue du Marché St. Honoré, and there the Provost Marshal threw the passport on the table, and told me to tell Lord Beaverbrook to come and get it himself. About two hours previously, Lord Beaverbrook had said these words to me: "You are a moral policeman in France." I suppose in those days I thought those words full of meaning, but I still am thinking what they did mean, if anything. Anyway, I stood up and had a verbal tussle with the Provost Marshal. In the end I obtained the visa and went back to the Ritz, full of glee and triumph. Then the fun really started.

Shakespeare's Puck said he would put a girdle round the earth in forty minutes. Our Puck from Canada would try and improve on that record. In those days of 1917 Lord Beaverbrook was running a little private war of his own, and he ran it from a small suite in the Ritz Hotel in Paris. I was caught up in a whirlwind of military and political intrigue. One minute I would be calling up Haig's headquarters, and the next I would be undergoing a cross-examination of relations between the British Embassy and the French Cabinet.

## WHAT SORT OF A MAN IS MAX?

Spread over the years, my association with Lord Beaverbrook has dotted the landscape of England and France. I have sat up at nights talking to him at Monte Carlo; I have walked with him in the early morning at Deauville. For hours and hours and hours we tramped Paris, talking, talking, talking. What sort of a man is he, the strange little figure who for ever walks the backstreets of English political life?

I remember when we started in the film business. He knew nothing whatsoever about it. He got everybody connected with the business to come and talk to him. Within three months, he knew as much, or more about the film business than all the people with whom he had talked. In those days Lord Beaverbrook's health was extremely precarious. He imagined he was suffering from an incurable disease. Then he found he was not a sufferer and he underwent a complete change, not only of character, but also of temperament. He became more intolerant than ever.

### BEAVERBROOK IN BED

One morning I went to see Beaverbrook at the Hyde Park Hotel in London. He was sitting up in bed in light-blue silk pyjamas and reading the *Daily Express*. It was the moment when the franc was beginning its slide to perdition. The pound stood around thirty-five. "Interesting thing, this drop in the franc, isn't it?" he said. "Not so interesting to me, because my francs are in Paris and I have left everything I have in France."

"I don't suppose that amounts to very much," he answered. Since that moment, numerous replies have occurred to me.

One of Beaverbrook's editors once said to me that the mistake I made with Beaverbrook was to ascribe simple motives to him, whereas, in reality he never had a simple motive in his life. This remark seems to mean that if Beaverbrook said the day was fine, he had some ulterior motive in saying so. Personally I am not sure whether the strange little man is sincerely insincere or insincerely sincere. Even after an association which lasted as long as mine did, I really do not know.

In trying to sum up the character of the man who for so long meant so much to me, and then disappeared completely out of my life, it would not be possible to forget his strange sense of humour. Once he had a small dog called Picasso. Beaverbrook was at Southampton waiting for a yacht he had chartered. He walked up and down the Hard carrying the dog. A strange man walked up to Lord Beaverbrook and said that the dog he was carrying was a nice little dog. Beaverbrook agreed that it was a nice little dog. The strange man said he would give five shillings for the nice little dog. Beaverbrook shook his head and walked on.

The strange man followed him and offered ten and then fifteen shillings for the dog. Beaverbrook said the dog was not for sale. Then he walked on. Suddenly a thought struck him, he turned back and he said to the strange man that he would sell his dog, he would sell it for fifteen thousand pounds. The strange man gave one strange look, then yelped and ran away. He found a man coming from the yacht and asked the name of the man who was carrying the little dog; he was told it was Lord Beaverbrook.

The man went back to Lord Beaverbrook and humbly apologized. Lord Beaverbrook looked at him and said: "My wife always did tell me I ought to change my tailor."

## BEAVERBROOK WRITES ME A NOTE

Like many men who are rabidly anti-French, Beaverbrook spends much of his time in France. One day in Paris he asked me to lunch on the following day. I accepted and arranged to be at the Ritz Hotel about one-fifteen. The Reparations Commission was sitting in Paris, about an hour before my lunch appointment, Lord (then Sir John) Bradbury's secretary telephoned to me to say that Bradbury wanted to see the English correspondents at one o'clock. I tried to telephone Beaverbrook to say that I could not come to lunch. My host was out and I left a message, then went on to keep my appointment at the Hotel Astoria. Living in the neighbourhood, I thought I would go home for a hasty meal. My wife said to me: "Lord Beaverbrook telephoned you this message: 'Tell your husband I am of more importance than Sir John Bradbury'."

I went back to my office and found pushed underneath the door this note: "I am leaving for London on the four o'clock train. Kindly inform my secretary what your office hours are."

## I Write to Beaverbrook

"Dear Lord Beaverbrook,

I received your message and your note. My job is Paris Correspondent, and I cannot share your view that this morning you were of greater importance than Bradbury.

I have no office hours outside those of the twenty-four.

Sincerely yours,<br>Harry J. Greenwall."

## The Human Man

Baron Beaverbrook is Max to Jimmy Maxton and to Winston Churchill alike. One might term him a righteous Bohemian. He believes in three things: Himself, the Presbyterian Church and the *Daily Express*. He once bought a house in Putney because he liked the tennis court. He had a man kept at the *Daily Express* office from midnight onwards to collect all the early editions of the London newspapers. Then at seven-thirty in the morning, this man had to ring through on a special line to Beaverbrook's London house and then read out the news from the newspapers. A special telephone line was connected with a loud-speaker in Beaverbrook's bedroom.

## BEAVERBROOK LOVES TO CREATE

He has made a large personal fortune. One would say perhaps that with his money he could do almost anything, yet, I doubt really whether he can be classified among the happy men on this earth. Time and time again, I have seen men leave him. Into some men he can instil fear, into almost any man he can instil confidence, but I know of only one man who is associated with him who is really affectionately disposed towards him. Beaverbrook, with all his money, with all his mental power, cannot find affection. In his entourage Beaverbrook is known as the "Little Man". That sounds like an affectionate term. It is not.

## MAX MEETS BAX

Arthur Beverly Baxter, M.P. like the man who made him, Beaverbrook, comes from Canada. Baxter, son of a Scotch-Canadian father and a German-Canadian mother, carries the hall-marks of both parents. He is tenacious, emotional, and possesses a certain hard brilliance. He has a somewhat hard and brittle brilliance, which does not mean that I am comparing him to a diamond; nevertheless, if I could buy him at my valuation and sell him at his own, a good stroke of business would result. Ernest Hemingway was right when he said to me that there was a novel in every family. There is certainly a grand novel in Baxter's family. Once when he was staying with me at Le Touquet, he held me enthralled for hours while he told me about his early days in Canada; he told me of his grandfather fiddling in a barn while the Great Lakes were in storm. He told me of a loved brother, who gradually wasted away. He told me of his early struggles, and how he became a piano salesman. His own account of his meeting with Beaverbrook is epic.

Beverly Baxter, "Bax" in Fleet Street, the House of Commons, at home and in the Savoy Grill, came out of the Army and wanted to meet this man Beaverbrook, who was making quite a noise in the Newspaper-Political World. He had a message sent to Beaverbrook and was told to go to the Hyde Park Hotel. Beaverbrook was in a bath when he received Baxter for the first time. The Lord asked the ex-officer what he wanted; did he want a job? Baxter shook his head. Beaverbrook fumbled for the soap. Here was something most surprising. Somebody who apparently did not want anything from him.

## Conversation Piece

The conversation between Bax and Max proceeded I understand along these lines: Beaverbrook: "Where

were you educated, young man?" Baxter: "Nordheimer's." (Nordheimer was the name of the piano
firm which had employed Baxter.)

Beaverbrook: "Not bad, but not so good as the
Insurance." (Beaverbrook had been an insurance
salesman.) Beaverbrook looked at the fresh-faced
young Canadian sceptically. What did this man want
from him? The answer was apparently still nothing,
and Baxter went on his way back, back to Canada
where he found jobs were not so plentiful. He thought
that after all there might be something in this Beaverbrook fellow who had jobs to offer. He communicated
with the man he had met in the bath and asked for a
job. Back came the reply: "Come to London at your
own expense."

The winter of 1919-20 I was the acting editor of
the *Sunday Express*, which was then a stepchild of the
*Daily Express*, and I and my staff of one was housed in
a back room in Shoe Lane. I shared this room with
Dave Blumenfeld, eldest son of R. D. Blumenfeld, then
editor of the *Daily Express*, my secretary, Kathleen
Woodward, who is now a very well-known writer,
Sydney Mosely (my staff) and a quiet young man who
sat in a corner and who was reported to be in charge
of the Literary Page of the *Daily Express*. The quiet
young man was of course Beverly Baxter.

One began to hear of Beverly Baxter, not in newspaper circles, but in fields as far off as St. John's
Wood, where he appeared as a Lesser Lion in Literary
Circles. Baxter in those days was a shy young man,
incredible as this may sound to-day. He flirted with
golf and with bridge, and no doubt being the clever
man he is, he knew the social value in London of
these accomplishments.

# I HATE TO-MORROW

After five months of misery in London, editing the *Sunday Express* with one hand, writing a whole page feature, and all the leaders, and with the other doing stories for the *Daily Express*, I asked to be relieved of my post and to be allowed to return to Paris. This seemed to me to be a very reasonable request, but Mr. Blumenfeld did not think it was, neither did Lord Beaverbrook, when he returned from Monte Carlo and cursed me roundly for leaving my post. Nevertheless, I stuck to my decision. I went back to Paris, and James Douglas was appointed in my place. James Douglas was a writer and not a real editor. Beverly Baxter was moved out of his corner and put into the *Sunday Express*; then things began to happen. Beaverbrook believed in this young Canadian and gave him a free ride. Baxter jumped on the band-wagon and kept the big drum drumming.

Just as a flower opens and blossoms forth in warmth, so did Baxter thrive in the warmer atmosphere created by Beaverbrook. Perhaps this is the only manner in which Baxter does resemble a flower, but I can think of no better simile. The voice of Baxter was now louder in the land.

## What Fun People Have

Baxter became acquainted with the late Arnold Bennett. Baxter no doubt read a book called *The Card*, and decided, though perhaps he never did read this book, to become a bit of a card himself. Baxter sings, he has a very pleasant tenor voice. He shook the dust of Shoe Lane from his feet, packed a bag and threw in a temporary lot with the Carl Rosa Opera Company.

With this Company he sang the part of Pinkerton in "Madame Butterfly", in Burnley in Lancashire and also in Brighton. Then he returned to the *Daily Express*.

Arthur Beverly Baxter was now managing editor, but he did all the work, or nearly, and had very little kudos. Then once again he was a Card, but only for a very little while.

Baxter again walked out of the *Daily Express*, walked across Fleet Street to the old *Daily Chronicle*, signed a contract said to be worth £11,000 a year, but which turned out to be unworkable. Baxter told me he could have collected £25,000 to £30,000 indemnity, but he did nothing—just a Card, and evidently one of the last of the Romantics.

Baxter crossed the "Street" again to Beaverbrook and had a really good contract handed to him. He was now editor of the *Daily Express* and sat in the chair while the circulation for the first time reached the figure of two million.

## MAX AND BAX

I have said earlier on that after I stepped out of the *Daily Express*, I never saw or heard anything more of Lord Beaverbrook. He had the faculty of making his associates really believe that the universe was bound up in Beaverbrook; but since I left the *Daily Express* I have certainly heard more of Beverly Baxter than I did when I was an associate of his, and most certainly more than I hear of Beaverbrook.

When Baxter was in the editorial chair, he used to be rung up every twenty minutes or so by Beaverbrook, who never came to the office. He had abandoned the flat he had "over the shop". On Baxter's desk, next to the special telephone line connecting him with Beaverbrook was a little red light, and when the red light lit up, it meant that a voice was speaking either from Leatherhead or from Scotland or from Paris or Le Touquet and was making derogatory remarks about the *Daily Express* of that day. The voice said that the paper was "B-a-a-d". Perhaps it was, but it was never as bad as all that. After Baxter had left the *Daily Express*, Beaverbrook said that it was impossible to praise him. I asked why, and Beaverbrook said that Baxter could not take criticism. I would say that neither could Beaverbrook.

When Baxter is speaking at any length a rapt expression comes into his eyes. He always seems to be listening to celestial music, his hands beat a *tempo* as if he were conducting an invisible orchestra. As a matter of fact, all that Bax is doing is listening to his own voice. He likes it a lot.

Baxter believes in himself, in whatever job he happens to be doing at the moment, and then in himself. A most excellent and successful combination.

# CHAPTER II

## I STRIKE COTTON

DURING THE time Mr. Ramsay MacDonald was Prime Minister of Great Britain, I had occasion to "cover" several newspaper stories which were a little bit out of my usual line. Twice I accompanied the Prime Minister to the United States. I went to London to attend the abortive Naval Conference and also the equally abortive World Economic Conference, but what interested me most was an almost accidental assignment which took me to Manchester to write about the great cotton strike, at the end of August, 1932.

I had only been to Manchester once before in my life, for though I had travelled in all parts of the world I did not know my own country.

I had myself suggested this assignment because I was particularly interested in the industrial situation in Great Britain, and I wanted to compare it at close quarters with conditions existing in other parts of the world. However, I thought that the whole story would not last longer than forty-eight hours; in point of fact, I was there for three weeks and had to purchase a complete outfit in Manchester!

After making preliminary inquiries among the strikers and among the masters, I was struck by the callousness of the Government. If Mr. Ramsay MacDonald could have seen the workers of whom he was supposed to have been so fond, perhaps he would have relented and would have helped Lancashire in the same spirit in which he tried to help so many European lame dogs. The courage of the young Lancashire girls was amazing. The strikers in the cotton trade were a part of their lives. A strike to them was as inevitable as death itself. Their wages were not high, their housing conditions appalling; yet they carried on with a smile.

## 1932

On September 1st, 1932, the cotton strike in Lancashire was ninety-five per cent operative. The Lancashire strike leaders informed their colleagues that the amounts at the disposal of the various unions for strike purposes were not sufficient to carry on any protracted struggle.

I discovered that three weeks would be the limit of the period for which a strike could be carried on. At the end of August, 700 cotton mills in Lancashire had closed down. The object was to make the strike as complete as possible, as quickly as possible. The strikers used shock troops which acted almost with military precision. The brains behind the strike movement decided that no pickets were to be used in these shock tactics. It was feared that if the pickets consisted of operatives who were half-hearted about the strike, they might want to go into the mills and work. Subsequently it was decided that pickets were to be used, but no cotton operative was to be a member of a strike picket. The pickets were given a red badge and were trained to jeer and raise sufficient noise to frighten operatives away from the mills which were being picketed. I saw hundreds of potential Gracie Fields entering the sheds and wearing goloshes instead of clogs, because the clogs were too noisy, but the goloshes enabled them to creep through the mill doors. One night, I saw about 20,000 people outside a Blackburn mill all booing and chasing the operatives who had been working there. The next morning at eight o'clock, I saw hundreds of young girls reporting for work the moment the hooter sounded. They did not want to strike. I found that the strike meant a loss of a million pounds a week in wages, several million pounds a week in lost trade; but that was merely the fringe of the loss; in addition there was the loss to tradesmen, the loss to landlords, the loss to building societies. It was just appalling, and what was more awful, nobody seemed sufficiently interested to do anything about it.

## I STRIKE COTTON

I found myself in the middle of the greatest strike the history of Lancashire had ever known. There were 232,000 operatives affected. I began to write long articles which I telephoned to London. I seemed to cease to be a reporter and I wanted to plead for the right to work. I found that in Burnley the strike had been going on for five weeks and was a real hardship. Strike pay had been paid out at the rate of £16,000 a week, and although this may sound a lot, it must be borne in mind that this sum had to be divided between about 23,000 members of the Weavers' Union. Considerable numbers of people had not contributed more than a few coppers—anything from a penny to fourpence, and consequently had only been receiving for five weeks ten shillings a week strike pay. The officials of the Northern Textile Trade Federation said to me, as I find noted in my diary: "Unless some step is taken, it simply means a fight until neither side can fight any longer. The only possible hope is Government intervention." This is what I tried to bring about, but Mr. Ramsay Mac-Donald would not intervene. He said that matters had to take their course, and this from a Socialist Prime Minister of Great Britain!

I interviewed the leaders of both sides and both sides expressed their deep regret at the situation. I reported the great loss of trade, based on facts I had collected from the Manchester Cotton Exchange. There was a cold stagnation creeping over business in Lancashire. Dealers in all the outlets abroad, in India, China, Egypt, South America, Continental Europe, as well as in the Dominions, were refusing to place orders unless manufacturers agreed delivery dates. The crisis came at a time when there had been a sharp advance in all cotton prices and buyers had not been able to place the orders which, in the ordinary way would have been placed. I managed to get the Conservative Member for Burnley to make a direct approach to the Premier, but the reply was in writing: "The Government has no power to prevent a stoppage, and its intervention can only be useful in an atmosphere of good will." The articles which I published in the *Daily Express*, in Manchester and in London, drew hundreds of letters. I was unable to cope with them. The majority of my correspondents were women who begged that the "truth should be

put before the public." One woman wrote to me from
Blackburn: "A few days ago I read in your paper
that a four-loomed weaver earned twenty-eight shillings per week. It is quite true, speaking from a
weaver's point of view, that we could earn that money
if we were kept in full work. But how often in these
days of trade depression do we get a full week's wages.
We work the same number of hours, but finish up the
week with one pound or between that and thirty
shillings, through waiting for and running two or three
looms instead of four. I do personally disagree with
a wage reduction, because I feel we deserve every
penny we get. It is impossible for anyone to realize
outside the cotton trade how much energy it does
take out of workpeople in the mills to-day. Married
men weavers cannot keep a shelter over their heads
without their wives turning out to work too. That
means in many cases that the children are put out to
nurse. I find a personal resentment against the strike.
I have watched the Lancashire Cotton Corporation
with interest and I know they try to improve things in
the Industry. They are ever ready to carry out any
suggestions which might help. In spite of all their
efforts, there is no unity. The Unions brought out
their members in sympathy with other mills. Hundreds crowded round the mill gates in the hope of
going to work, as they had no grievances, but were
advised by pickets who are being paid three pounds
per week by the unions, to keep out, as they could not
work without tacklers or overlookers who had been
brought out in sympathy with the weavers. Work
would eventually stop, and then there would be no
dole, no strike pay to those who were disloyal to their
union. Many returned to their homes disappointed,

hoping it would all come to an end soon. The only people who appear to be happy about things are the pickets, who are receiving better wages than they have ever done in their lives before." This human document urged me to continue my fight for Government intervention. This industrial war seemed to me just as futile and stupid as an international war. But if the Government had lifted its little finger then the silent mills of Lancashire would have been humming again.

## THE END

Back to Burnley where, after £72,000 had been paid out in strike pay and the receipts from tram-cars and omnibuses had decreased by nearly £4000, in the fourth week of the strike, and the co-operative societies sales showed a reduction of £3000 on the corresponding period of 1931. The Communist Party disguised as the Textile Minorities Movement sent three lorries containing six tons of food-stuffs from London. For propaganda purposes, the lorries travelled by way of Leeds and Sheffield where meetings were held and the lorries used as propaganda exhibits.

It was extremely difficult to understand the mentality of many of the Lancashire cotton operatives. At Nelson near Burnley, the Employers' Association posted notices that they were prepared to pay the old uniform list of prices. Yet when the hooters sounded the following morning, 16,000 operatives stayed away. In the Ashton-under-Lyne district roughly 10,000 operatives broke away from their leaders and refused to listen to the call to strike. And yet Mr. Ramsay

MacDonald refused to intervene. A Conservative Member for Burnley, to whom I have already referred, journeyed to Lossiemouth to try and see the Premier. He failed. The strikers' leaders began to call for mediation. In the end the strike collapsed, and as usual it was the women who suffered the most. Since 1932 there has not been any major disturbance in the Textile Trade of Lancashire: but at the moment of writing, I hear that the cotton mills are working three days a week only.

If my attempts to help settle the textile dispute in Lancashire did not meet with success, my writings did some good in other and entirely unexpected quarters. My despatches appeared to have met with the approval of Lord Beaverbrook, the principal proprietor of the *Daily Express*, and one day when I was eating my lunch in a public-house at Burnley, I was rung up by the Manchester office of the *Daily Express* and informed that Lord Beaverbrook wanted to speak to me urgently at Leatherhead. I put through a call and very soon I was asked to put some more silver into the box. I put in all the available silver and again and again was cut off, while Lord Beaverbrook fumed. I kept on dashing out to the bar and borrowing shillings against a pound note I had hurriedly thrust down on the counter. In between the breaks in the conversation, Lord Beaverbrook told me that he strongly approved of my policy and he wanted me when I had time to write him a report on the conditions then prevailing in the Manchester offices of the *Daily Express*. As a result, there was a reorganization and a new editor.

Once again, dear children, we see how good may come out of evil!

# CHAPTER III

## A GENTLEMAN FROM PERSIA

THE AGA KHAN stretched his feet on to a brocaded chair in his suite in the Ritz Hotel in London. His golf shoes carried with them some of the soil of Surrey, but the Aga Khan did not mind, and as he is such a very good customer, who is always right, I am quite sure that the Ritz Hotel did not mind, either.

My acquaintance with the Aga Khan began in a lift in the Ritz Hotel in Paris and it has continued throughout the years on a very close and intimate basis, but I am afraid our relations somewhat cooled after a meeting in his villa on the Cap d'Antibes, when he asked me to try and obtain between six and seven thousand pounds for his life story. I must say that he had already agreed to write six articles for a fee of two thousand guineas for a London Sunday newspaper, but had changed his mind at the last minute because—but I had better give the story in his own words.

"See here, Greenwall, the older I get the more I realize what my memoirs are worth. Supposing Max (Lord Beaverbrook) died, which God forbid, think of the interesting things I should have to say about Max."

"Yes," I made reply; "but supposing you died, which God forbid, think of the things which Max is sure to publish about you."

# A GENTLEMAN FROM PERSIA

We will now return to the Ritz in London. What I really wanted to do on this day, after having discussed the market in Wall Street with Michael Arlen in the lobby, was to find out what all this talk in Parliament and outside was about, these statements that the Aga Khan wanted to obtain some territorial concessions. He is a sort of Moslem Pope, he rules over roughly forty million Ismali Moslems, but although he has very wide spiritual powers, he has no temporal powers whatsoever, and it appeared that temporal power was what he wanted. I had heard reports in Paris that the Aga Khan's name had been put forward as a prospective King of Syria. In London, in the House of Commons, the Government had been asked questions. What was the truth. The Aga Khan answered my question in one sentence: "Perhaps one day the British Government will recognize the services my family has rendered to Great Britain." In point of fact, the Aga Khan himself has rendered very great services to Great Britain. To millions the Aga is a play-boy of the West. But really in the West he represents the East of legend and romance, and in the East he represents the West as seen through Eastern eyes. You may catch a glimpse of him in a grey top hat, leading in the Derby winner at Epsom, but not so many days previously he was attending a meeting in Lausanne which, for the time being, made Peace in the Moslem world. Quite likely you caught sight of him coming out of Prunier's, where he had been eating a very plentiful lunch, but he was just off to Geneva to preside at the Annual Assembly of the League of Nations.

# I HATE TO-MORROW

## WHO IS THE AGA KHAN?

The Aga Khan is, on his mother's side, a direct descendant of Allah. The title of Highness is a courtesy title, but the Aga Khan's full title is Sir Aga Sultan Mohamed Shah. He is a G.C.S.I., a G.C.V.O., and a G.C.I.E. His family comes from Persia, and his ancestors ruled in Persia, Arabia and in Egypt. Three rival factions divided the inheritance of the Prophet Allah. The Aga Khan's branch descended from the Fatimites, a section which has produced many scholars and soldiers. The followers of the Aga Khan are to be found principally in Sind, Bombay, in Zanzibar and scattered along the coast of Africa as well as in Persia, Arabia, Afghanistan and Turkestan. There are even followers in Central Africa. There are some legends which will never die. One of them is that the Aga Khan sells his bath water in which he washes. This is a pure fantasy, but the story that he is weighed once a year against gold is true. I have not the faintest idea how wealthy the Aga Khan is, but despite heavy losses which occurred during the Wall Street crash, I still estimate the Aga Khan's wealth as being high among the first ten names of wealthy persons in the world. In India the Aga Khan possesses eight or nine palaces. He has a house at Cap d' Antibes and a house in Paris. His first wife was his cousin; his second wife was an Italian lady who is buried in Monte Carlo; his third wife, his living wife, was a former dressmaker in Paris.

232

# A GENTLEMAN FROM PERSIA

## A VERY REMARKABLE MAN

I must put the Aga Khan way up ahead in the list of the most remarkable persons I have ever met. His vitality, he is moving towards the sixties, is tremendous; his shrewdness proverbial, and there are times when he has flashes of humanity such as I have never met. In Jermyn Street in London, there is a hairdresser named Jopper who cuts the hair of the Royal Princes and, among the many well-known persons upon whom Jopper waits in person, is the Aga Khan. A man who can afford to have his own personal boxing instructor, his own personal golf professional travelling with him, thinks nothing of taking a hairdresser with him when he goes to Ireland to visit his stud there. Jopper told me that when the Aga Khan took him over to Ireland and met him the morning after he had spent his first night there, his patron said to him: "Jopper, did you sleep well; have you had a good breakfast; do you feel fit?" The gentleman from Persia keeps a very good table, as the saying is. He enjoys good food well prepared. Before he was married for the third time, the Aga Khan had a house at Cimiez just above Nice. Even when I have been lunching with him alone, I remarked that the gold plate was "out", and red roses (in March) decorated the table. I remarked that the Aga had next to him a menu and he noted with pride and delight that each course was delicately served. One day in the early part of the year, I happened to say a "no" to ice pudding. The Aga Khan said: "Will you have some strawberries?" I said I would like some strawberries. The Aga Khan clapped his

233

hands, and when a maid came into the dining-room the Prince said: "Monsieur Greenwall will take strawberries," and in less than a minute strawberries appeared. The Aga Khan has one personal Indian servant, but all the domestics in his European residences are female. Naturally I exclude the corps of chauffeurs who drive his fleet of motor cars.

Buried in the family mausoleum at Monte Carlo with the Aga Khan's second wife is his first-born son. The heir, Prince Ali Khan, is the son of the same marriage. The younger son born of the French wife is a small child. His third wife was a Mademoiselle Andrée Carron, and the Prince was married to her in the town-hall at Aix-les-Bains. This marriage was a simple affair in comparison to the first wedding which took place on the plains of Poona and must have been something like an Arabian Nights spectacle, for there were no fewer than 25,000 guests present. The festivities continued for a fortnight. Many Moslem Princes attended this wedding, and jewellery worth hundreds of thousands of pounds was worn by them. The wedding cost fifty thousand pounds.

## WHEN A DRINK IS NOT A DRINK

Often I am asked how it is that a man like the Aga Khan who is the spiritual head of millions, may take alcohol when it is denied to his followers. Once I had the occasion of putting this question direct to the man most concerned. We were lunching alone in his house and he said to me: "I want you to try this little white wine," which is a literal translation of the French expression *"ce petit vin blanc"*. I tried it and found it very nice and dry. Then I said to the Aga Khan:

# A GENTLEMAN FROM PERSIA

"Tell me, how is it that you can drink this wine; I thought your religious principles prevented you drinking wine." The Aga Khan looked at me and he said: "You see, I am so holy that as soon as I drink the wine it turns to water."

## We Go Racing

One of the would-be biographers of the Aga Khan wrote, so I noticed, that the Aga Khan never bets. Well, well. We were both in Paris one time when I wanted to see him concerning some Indian matter. I rang him up at the Ritz and he asked me to meet him after the first race that Sunday afternoon at Long-champs. The Prince had a horse in the second race, and I asked him if he thought it was going to win. He said he thought it had a good chance. I backed the horse and it lost. After the race, the Aga Khan asked me if I had backed it, and when I said I had, he asked me if I had lost much, and I said I had lost more than I wanted to. Bookmaking in France is forbidden. The pari-mutuel is the only method of backing horses, if one wants to stand within the law, but like most forbidden things in France, one can have a bet if one wants to, if one knows how to go about it. In the paddock of every racecourse in France, there are clandestine bookmakers who deal with people they can trust, and mostly with owners. After the second race, the Aga Khan and I walked across the paddock and he went up to a bookmaker and he said to him very loudly put 26,000 francs for me on Jeff Cohn's horse for a place and it was second. After the race, the Aga Khan asked me if I had backed Jeff Cohn's horse for a place and I said I had. The Aga Khan answered, I hoped you would, that's why I spoke loudly, but I did not like to give you another tip. I think that is another quite good instance of the man's humanity.

## I Get Cold Feet

When racing was resumed after the war, there was a boom. At one of the first post-war Sunday meetings at Longchamps, I ran into the Aga Khan who asked me to do him a favour. He handed me fifteen one-thousand franc notes and asked me to go across the course and back his horse for him; he had a horse running in the next race. One is apt to get a slightly better price on the *pelouse* than one does in the *pesage* at a French race meeting. I stuffed the notes in my pocket and started to elbow my way through the crowd, when I ran into another friend, Carlisle MacDonald, the newspaper man who wrote Lindberg's story for him. We had not met for a long time and we started to chatter. Suddenly the saddling bell sounded and I remembered the commission I had promised to undertake. I seized MacDonald by the arm and said to him: "Come on, help me to fight my way through," meanwhile telling him what I had promised to do. We had a tremendous struggle to get to a betting booth on the *pelouse*, and I just got the money on when the "off" bell sounded. I was quite relieved I had carried out the commission, because the horse won and paid eight to one.

## A Whole-Time Job

The Aga Khan is blessed with one of the most beautiful and efficient secretaries I have ever known a man to have. Her name is Miss Florence Blain and she is almost as interested in racing as her chief is, and I would not mind wagering that she knows just as much about the game as he does himself, and that is quite a lot. Although a multi-millionaire owner, the Aga Khan runs his stud and his stables as a business concern. In fact, like the late Sir Basil Zaharoff, there are very few important industries in the world in which the Aga Khan is not interested. Whether the story is true or not about his being a sleeping partner in a famous firm of Wall Street brokers, I do not know, but I have been with the Aga Khan when he has spent the morning dictating his correspondence, and it has ranged all the way from buying an expensive three-cornered Cape of Good Hope stamp, to a Russian ikon. His average morning mail brings him about a hundred begging letters. What with his golf and his racing and his real job: being this spiritual head of forty million persons, the Aga Khan is kept pretty busy. That is what he likes. He lives every minute of his life. No matter whether he has guests to lunch or not, he gets up after the meal and says: "I'm going to bed now," and goes upstairs and takes off his clothes and gets into bed for two hours. He is a very wise man. Another wise man is Lord Rothermere, who spends one day a week in bed.

## How Many Men Is He?

You may see the Aga Khan wearing his Eastern robes going to the Coronation ceremony in Westminster Cathedral, or you may meet him all dressed-up on his way to Ascot, or in serious clothes going into the League of Nations meeting in Geneva, or once again in Eastern dress you find him in Bombay doing his job. In front of him are hundreds and hundreds of people, and hundreds of tiny little babies. Somebody calls out: "Name this child," and the Aga Khan answers: "I name him Ali," and the happy and proud father contributes a few rupees which go into the Aga Khan's coffers. He needs all the rupees he can get, because he gives away millions.

had great reason to be grateful to this strange, wandering fat man who, very soon after Hitler came to power, disappeared completely from the German scene. I have sought him everywhere except in the Concentration Camps where I am not allowed to go. His sister is dead. The house in den Zelten is closed up. Arnold von Rechberg has been "sunk without trace".

## ARISTIDE BRIAND

"Pertinax" would have it that Briand was the son of a French aristocrat and a peasant woman. Personally I could see nothing very aristocratic about the appearance of the man who has been one of the greatest outstanding figures of my lifetime. Briand's hands may have been delicately shaped and his mind was fine, but his body was gross. He never married and despite many amorous adventures, he remained true to a woman in his native village by whom he had a son who is still living.

Briand began to write for a Paris paper called *La Lanterne* and was very soon caught up in politics and while still a young man became a *député*. It is on record that no one was more surprised than the young man himself. He possessed a magnificent voice for speaking purposes, shrewdness and wit. Briand, without any political intelligence and certainly without education, was destined to go almost as far as any French politician can go. He never reached the Presidency of the Republic, but was very near, so near that a certain paper, which wished to be on the street before its rivals, published a faked photograph of Briand driving back in triumph. Maybe Briand never really wished for this honour. He was by way of being an intriguer; he was one of the people who prevented Clémenceau from becoming President. Briand liked good living; he liked good wine and he was not particular about his women friends.

Many times Premier, and Foreign Secretary times without number, Briand was always throughout his political life, in the limelight. Had he been more active both mentally and physically, he would most undoubtedly have been a man who would have made friends with Germany. He was well on the way towards this aim, when Gustav Stresseman died, and brought a dream to a rude awakening. Briand's health broke down soon after Stresseman died. He suffered terribly from insomnia during his last months of life, and used to fall asleep while he was eating or while he was talking. Not long before he died, he invited a few of us to lunch with him in Geneva. At the beginning of the meal, he was in magnificent form; he told us how one day he went with Armand Fallières to visit the sculptor Rodin. "Rodin," said Briand, "as usual had a head in one corner, a leg in another and limbs scattered all over the studio. Fallières looked around and said quite seriously to Rodin: "I am sorry to see that your stuff was broken up in transit!"

We all laughed immoderately. Two minutes later, Aristide Briand, Foreign Minister of France, was fast asleep.

# PEN AND INK PORTRAITS

## Ramsay MacDonald

If the captain hates the sea, Ramsay MacDonald certainly hated newspaper men. Whenever he lunched with them or dined with them, as their guest of course, he attacked them, and the attack was always the same words, it never changed. I have heard the same speech made at the Press Club in London that I heard in Lausanne and in Geneva, in Washington and in New York and at the Park Lane Hotel, in London.

Twice I was in the United States with Mr. Mac-Donald, "the poor boy who made good". He was the vainest man I have ever contacted. Once we were lunching at the Ritz in New York with the English Speaking Union. Mr. MacDonald was then the first Labour Prime Minister England had ever known. At the end of lunch, when cigars and cigarettes were passed round, the Prime Minister looked into the box of Coronas, looked up, snapped his fingers and said in a peremptory tone of voice: "Bring me a new box."

We, that is to say, the journalists accredited to the League of Nations, gave a lunch for Mr. MacDonald during the meetings of the Disarmament Conference. Mr. MacDonald was attending a meeting of the Council. He and Mr. Arthur Henderson, who was the Chairman of the Disarmament Conference, were not on speaking terms. Mr. Henderson's chair was empty, and Mr. MacDonald's seat was opposite the empty chair. Before he sat down, this vain and rather pompous Prime Minister objected to his seat. He thought he ought to be sitting on the other side of the table, next to where Mr. Henderson was not sitting. The question of etiquette was put to him and he sat down rudely enough and ate his lunch. Directly lunch was over and the toasts had been proposed, Mr. MacDonald made his speech. He attacked his hosts and then marched out of the room. He did not think it worth while to wait for the other important guests to make their speeches. A fellow-Scot of the Prime Minister, Mr. Percy Phillip, ran after the Prime Minister and caught him up and made a laudable effort to accompany Mr. MacDonald to his motor car. Mr. MacDonald paused in his stride and said in a loud, ringing voice: "Isn't Lady Londonderry coming?" and then marched on.

When I went in the *Berengaria* with the Prime Minister on his first official visit to the United States, when he was to meet President Hoover, Mr. Mac-Donald had one great preoccupation what he should wear when he landed. He kept on sending wireless messages to the Foreign Office in London to know whether he should wear a top-hat and a morning coat. He did. Poor Mr. MacDonald, what a fine handsome head, and what a fine speaking voice, but what a muddled mind there was within that fine looking head. He seemed to make a complete muddle of everything he did, and he died, as he lived—at sea.

## A Lovely Lady

A lovely lady lay on a divan in her bedroom. Like the lady in the song: her golden hair was hanging down her back. She wore a silk nightdress which was very *décolleté*, and over the nightdress was a cherry-coloured *peignoir*. The lady was Queen Marie of Rumania.

She apologized, as if any apology were needed, for receiving me in this manner, but as she explained, she was not well. I had met Queen Marie a few weeks previously in the royal train, between Paris and Belgrade, where she was at that moment staying with her son-in-law, the late King Alexander. The Queen, hearing that I was going to Athens, asked me to try and find news of her daughter and son-in-law, King George, who then was on the throne of Greece, and who in a few weeks time was not. The Queen told me that she had heard that her daughter and son-in-law were virtually prisoners in the Palace. She gave me a letter to her daughter and asked me to try and deliver it. I did so, and brought back news of the Queen of Greece.

Queen Marie of Rumania, granddaughter of Queen Victoria of England! My! My! what worlds in between.

## THREE PRESIDENTS

The best way to judge the character of a public personage, I believe, is to see that personage both in private and in public. One must be able to see his or her reactions to other people and then to note how the personage reacts to questions. It has been my privilege to meet three Presidents of the United States publicly and privately. The first President I met was Herbert Hoover, and I met him at a moment when he did not even dream of being President, he was Secretary of Commerce, and a very fine one he was. Then he talked freely about his co-citizens and about his country. He told me, as a considered thought, that the United States did not wish for the destruction of the British Empire; he said that the future of the United States was bound up with the British Empire.

The next time I saw Hoover, he had been elected and was in the White House, and he was waiting to see Mr. Ramsay MacDonald. This time he was receiving the American and British Press. He was gay and jolly, although it was not very long before he underwent a complete change. Wall Street saw to that.

The last time I saw Hoover was when he had been defeated, and it was a few hours after President Roosevelt had been installed. I saw him leave Washington with his wife, tears were rolling down his cheeks. I think Hoover will go down to posterity as the President who was most unfortunate.

I wonder how History will deal with Calvin Coolidge, that dry little red-headed man who, if he never said much, never said anything which can be held up by History against him. Experience has taught me that those whom we call the strong silent men are usually silent because they have nothing to say. I do not know whether this was the case with Coolidge, because when I saw him in private, the first time I ever saw him, he said nothing at all but "How do you do," "How long are you staying" and "Good-bye." The big business men of the United States liked Coolidge, because he never did anything to prevent their doing what they wanted. Yet it must be remembered that Coolidge was President of the United States during the years which preceded the Wall Street crash. The crash from which the world has not even yet recovered. His responsibility must be great, but perhaps "silent Cal" did not know what it was all about. In public Coolidge gave one the impression of having both feet on the floor and intending to keep them there. When he said he did not choose to run for another term of office, maybe he was wiser than even he himself knew.

When a man triumphs over a grave physical disability, he is pretty sure of having the world on his side, no matter what his politics may be. In 1932, Franklin Delano Roosevelt was hailed as the Messiah of the United States. In 1939 people called him other names. Yet, it is the same Roosevelt, the same good-looking, affectionate-looking man who triumphed over infantile paralysis, and that is something which should be remembered as long as the name of Franklin Roosevelt is remembered. What he has done to the United States may be good, may be bad, but nothing can prevent Roosevelt's name being inscribed in History as a very great man.

Roosevelt knows how to "get" his public. When he received me alone, he had just been elected President, but he was still Governor of New York State. He sat in a swivel chair before an ordinary flat-topped desk. On the desk was a package of cigarettes—one of the most famous popular brands in the country. In a wire basket, the President called my attention to what he termed his fan mail. He might have been a film-star; in fact he did look like a film star; he has just that form of face. Naturally neither he nor I referred to the fact that he could not stand alone, in the physical sense. But he threw his chair back, swayed from side to side and did everything that a normal man could and would do. Yet, when he wants to stand up he has to go through the painful process of fixing sort of iron guards which are along his legs into sockets round the knees. He cannot stand unless he holds on to two supports, and that is why on the right-hand side of his desk, hidden in a box of ferns, is a steel handle. Somebody, a secretary or friend, can help him stand up, and then he grasps this hidden handle, and so receives visitors to the White House. In every house in which the President resides, there is a lift; in every house there is a ramp, because the President of the United States cannot raise his feet even half-an-inch from the ground; but he shuffles along, so I think, to immortal fame.

### Père la Victoire

Georges Clémenceau thrust out a grey-cotton gloved hand. His shrewd little eyes twinkled. He had been made Prime Minister by his ancient enemy, Raymond Poincaré, his eyes twinkled with glee. Though he had never seen me but once in his life, he told me within half an hour of this particular meeting, that he was going to jail Joseph Caillaux, and jail him he did, on the very day he said he would, on the following Saturday.

It is impossible to put Clémenceau into a miniature, little as he was, he is too big for that. Often people wonder why Clémenceau wore those gloves. It was because he suffered from a particular form of diabetes which made his hands perfectly numb. Every morning he would plunge his hands into a soup bowl filled with talcum powder. First of all his valet had rubbed his hands with a special ointment which Clémenceau obtained from a near-by chemist: he lived for years in a ground-floor flat in the rue Franklin. The talcum powder and the ointment enabled Clémenceau to hold a pen and to shake hands, and the cotton gloves—

he bought them a gross at a time—prevented the ointment from soiling the documents or, for the matter of that, other people's hands. Because Clémenceau never had any sort of feeling in his feet, he always refused to go to the theatre; unless he could see where his feet were, he could not tell whether they were on a step or not. Some two years before Clémenceau died, he was persuaded to go to the Opera, but he fell down a whole flight of steps. To the credit of the French newspapers, it must be said, that this incident was never reported.

During the last few years of his life, particularly during the last fifteen months, I used to go and see the old man very often indeed. He spoke excellent English although he spoke it slowly. He liked to talk English, and he would tell me stories in English about Mr. Lloyd George and President Wilson and I can only say, with great regret, that they are unprintable.

## FATHER AND SON

My professional life has brought me into touch with all kinds of people, kings, queens, knaves, clowns, confidence-men, prime ministers, presidents the world over, so it is very difficult to make even a random choice of portraits. One of the most pathetic men I ever met was the late King Constantine of Greece. I met him for the first time in Lucerne, when he was finishing his long exile. We often hear of a prize-fighter or sometimes an actor seeking what is known as a come-back. This was to be a kingly come-back, and it was just like a come-back that one could imagine some old-time actor participating in. King

Constantine was worried. He wanted to know what the public was going to say. That nobody could tell him; everybody sort of said: "It will be all right on the night."

I have, close to my hand as I write, a signed photograph that Constantine gave me on this occasion. I see him as a tall man with very large ears. He spoke fluent English but with a strong German accent. The burden of his song was: "Why do your newspapers call me Tino?" I remembered that the name had been mentioned in published correspondence between the Ex-Kaiser and the Tsar of Russia. This did not seem to matter much to King Constantine, because at the end of our meeting, when we said good-bye, he said to me: "Please don't refer to me as Tino."

King George of Greece, who likes to spend so much of his time in London, I saw as I have already related when he was a prisoner in his own palace. I saw him in the garden. He wore a well-fitting white drill suit and a blue yachting cap and a monocle. He looked a king, I mean to say what we are taught to think of as looking like a king; but if his father had been unhappy in Lucerne, how unhappy was this young man in Athens. He asked me to tell him what was going on. He heard that Corfu had been bombarded by Mussolini, but he was not allowed to know the details. They would not tell him anything at all and all he knew was that there were plots to remove him from his throne. Now he is back again, and I hope, for his sake, that he will stay put.

# CHAPTER V

LOOKING BACK on life, I find that the years have magnified some events and reduced the dimensions of others. The mere recording of happenings is not sufficient; when one has seen History made, one should try to fit History into one's own philosophy of life. Maybe it is better to make one's own philosophy fit into History, but then, I always like to try and be different.

In the merry month of May, 1927, Paris was just a little bit crazy. The financial depression which started from Wall Street was still two and a half years away. Paris was full of Americans making whoopee. Then came Lindbergh.

## PARTIES ARE THROWN

Mary Borden, in a book called *A Woman with White Eyes*, aptly sums up the Paris scene. She writes in part as follows: "And there was Marcella to keep things going when our spirits sagged. Marcella Mackintosh was born in Kansas City and struck Paris at the end of the War. She organized our lives for us; all you had to do was to ring up Marcella and say: "I am bored to death," and your house would fill instantly with people. Negroes and harlequins and clowns would

251

pound on your doors; wizards and conjurors would pop out of taxis; barmen would set up a bar in the hall, and an orchestra would set up its music racks round the piano. Princes and Grand Dukes, cocottes and midinettes, English lords and American millionaires would pour in, take the floor, and Marcella, round as a pumpkin, terrible to behold in her mannish coat and skirt, with a face like a suet pudding and eyes like currants, would slump herself down on the piano-stool and then—well, then madness would fill the room. It came from her fat fingers, that pounded out, pounded out the irresistible, insistent, syncopated rhythm of the tom-toms. Faster and faster, louder and louder, wizard fingers, wizard hands, monstrous, magical, they scrambled like fat white mice over the ivory keys, but they were made of iron, they had the strength of steel hammers. They galvanized the saxophones, and the Swanee whistles of the drummers into a frenzy. The people clustered round Marcella, swayed and sweated, and shook; and we shook. Everyone began shaking, everything in the room would begin to shake, the floor, the pictures on the wall, the flowers. The crystal pendants of the lustres began dancing, and Marcella would shout through the din, as more and more people arrived: "Hello, hello there! Hello Reggie, hello Sally, and Annabelle and Charlie; hello there! Hello!"

We did not look quite like savages. We weren't black and we weren't quite naked. The men looked almost like men, those who didn't look like young women. The women looked almost like young women, those who didn't look like men; and we were all decently masked, or partially disguised; and we pretended quite well on the whole, even when

Marcella was not at the piano, to be happy, to be fond of each other. Marcella told us we were happy, and kept telling us we adored each other. She went about Paris yelling the news: "Hello! isn't this fine? isn't this bully? Hello! isn't it great? Don't you adore that woman? don't you think he is grand, this man? Isn't she the most beautiful thing you ever saw? Hello, hello there!"

"She drove us to it, whipped us on, spurred us on and kicked us on. Like a herd of cattle she drove us out across France to Biarritz, into Italy, and back again through the streets of Paris; sex-ridden hags with faces painted to look young, languid youths without sex who were ready to pretend to be lovers; waiters who pretended to be Spanish grandees, and Spanish grandees who pretended to be waiters, Jews out of Russia and dressmakers from the Champs Elysées who pretended to be Princes of the Blood, and Grand Dukes who pretended to be dressmakers; thieves who endowed charities, murderers who wept when their lap-dogs got stepped on, others who made love to old men with big bank accounts; we were a merry, motley crew." Then came Lindbergh. He came to Paris on Saturday, May 21st, 1927, and he arrived at Le Bourget late in the afternoon, and I was there. We all know Marcella Mackintosh, of course, and were it not for the law of libel, I would name her. She is graphically described by Mary Borden. Marcella lives on, but she comes to Paris less often than she used to do. The days when Paris was mad are over. Lindbergh helped in his way to put an end to the madness.

# I HATE TO-MORROW

## THE FLYING FOOL

The Atlantic had been flown successfully and there had been many unsuccessful attempts to fly from East to West and from West to East. True stories of many of the unsuccessful Atlantic flights have not yet been told. In most cases, particularly in the case of the Frenchman, Captain Nungesser, and the English Captain Hinchcliffe, it was a question of a lack of money, of pressing debt, and an opportunity to make a big killing. Millions made romance out of a man and a woman trying to fly the Atlantic together. There was perhaps less glamour when two or more men set out on the perilous quest. Then, when it was reported that a young American was going to try and fly solo, there was a shiver of delightful excitement. This tall, pale young Charles Augustus Lindbergh, an unknown, would he succeed, when he set out to fly alone from the United States to Europe? I have no illusions about my fellow men and women. I know them. I know that the crowds which went to Le Bourget that Saturday afternoon set out much in the same spirit the old Romans felt when they filled the arenas to see the Christians and the lions; much like the Spanish crowds which fill the bull-rings to watch the matadors kill or be killed.

## SATURDAY AFTERNOON

The New York *Times* had purchased the story of Lindbergh's flight, subject of course to the successful accomplishment of it. The *Daily Express* had bought the British rights from the New York newspaper. I merely went to see the landing of Lindbergh, but naturally I had to organize a service of news for the *Sunday Express*. I tried to lease a telephone line from Le Bourget to my Paris Office, but was unable to do so. I therefore left my chief assistant, Francis Tuckfield, in the Paris office with instructions to keep a line with London open as long as possible, principally so that we could learn if London heard of the approach of the American flyer. I took with me to Le Bourget my second assistant, an American, Raymond Fendrick, who during the War had been with the American Flying Corps. Believing there would be a very large crowd and the road to Le Bourget would be blocked with traffic, with subsequent parking difficulties, I decided not to take my own car, but to hire a taxi. Fendrick and I started from the New York Bar in the rue Daunou where we found Charlie, an English-speaking French taxi-driver. He knew all the tricks.

We told Charlie that he had to take us to the flying field at Le Bourget as quickly as possible, and how much more important it was to get us back as quickly as possible and to stay at some place where we could find him. "O.K., gents," answered Charlie.

There was a long line of traffic heading for the aerodrome, but Charlie dodging in and out and round about got us out as quickly as he could. There was a crowd which might have stepped out of the pages of *A Woman with White Eyes*. They had come to see the fun. They had come to see a young American of Swedish ancestry fly to Paris, or maybe not.

# I HATE TO-MORROW

## CHAMPAGNE AND CAVIARE

A good time was being had by all. The restaurant at Le Bourget was a devastated region; fortunately the picknickers, seventy-five per cent American, had thoughtfully provided food and drink for themselves. There was plenty of champagne, plenty of *pâté de foie gras* and caviare sandwiches. Plenty of joy, plenty of happiness, was not the dollar ace high, and over in Wall Street, the sky was the limit.

## NEWS

Every now and again Fendrick or I would go and see whether Charlie could be found; then we would try and get through to Paris and ask Tuckfield if he had any news. Charlie was always on the job, but as regards Tuckfield, it was always a case of "Sister Anne, sister Anne, do you see anyone coming?" Tuckfield reported there were plenty of rumours, but no definite news. The crowd continued to enjoy itself. It laughed and it sang and it drank and it ate. Everybody was in a merry, merry mood. Walking about the gravel paths, I met the Correspondent of the Brooklyn *Daily Eagle*. "Hallo, Greenwall," he said, "you know everything (sarcastically); got any news? I suppose the fish are nibbling his eyebrows by now."

It grew dark on this fine spring afternoon, and flares were lit round the flying field; "just in case". Again I got through to my Paris office. This time there was news. Tuckfield reported that Lindbergh's aeroplane had been sighted off the coast of Devonshire. As I came out of the telephone box, I met Edwin James, then Paris correspondent of the New York *Times*. I told him what I had just learned. Like everybody else he was rather sceptical. So was I, but one could not afford to take chances. It was quite dark now, and I suggested to Fendrick that as Lindbergh was supposed to be heading for France, and if he did arrive, we had better try and reckon out how long it would take for him to get to Paris. That we worked out and as it happened we were almost correct. About half-an-hour before the time we anticipated the arrival, if arrival there was to be, I said to Fendrick we had better start walking out across the field. If and when Lindbergh arrives, there would be such a stampede that we should not see anything at all. Except for the flares round the field, everything was in darkness. Fendrick agreed that we should try and get away from any rush of people. It must be understood that amongst the thousands at Le Bourget, there were not two dozen people who had any idea that Lindbergh had been sighted off the coast of England. Hundreds of people had already left, thousands stayed to continue the good time.

### LINDBERGH ARRIVES

As Fendrick and I walked away from the enclosures, we could hear the voices of hundreds of people uplifted in the song of the moment, "Yes Sir, that's my Baby". They sang merrily. Fendrick began to discuss with me one of his pet subjects: Christian Science. He claimed that his belief had once saved his life when he was flying in France. His was a romantic story. He learnt to fly somewhere down in the south-west of France. One day his plane stalled and he crashed on to a house where there were several daughters. He was nursed back to health and married one of the daughters.

While he was telling me this story once again, I interrupted him. I thought I heard the throb of a motor.

"Hear that?"

Fendrick cocked an ear. "That's a motor bike somewhere out in the lane."

We walked on. Once again I heard the hum of an engine. I was certain. I clutched Fendrick's arm. I was insistent. He listened intently. "Yes," he shouted excitedly, "I hear it, I hear it." . . . "There it is."

We both looked up. He pointed to something in the sky I could not see. The hum and the throb of the motor became louder and louder. The voices way back were still singing the chorus: "Yes Sir, that's my Baby, that's my Baby now." Nevertheless, some people must have heard the noise that we heard, because the singing died away.

Fendrick and I were all alone walking through the lush grass of the flying field; the dew was falling.

While the noise grew louder, and just as I saw for the first time Lindbergh's plane coming out of the sky, I also saw a workman trundling a bicycle through the grass. He was going home, his day's work at the aerodrome over. Within a few feet of the man with the bicycle, Lindbergh landed. The French workman, used to seeing aeroplanes arrive at the flying field, merely glanced up and went on walking. As the aeroplane came to a standstill, Fendrick and I began to run. Often the most dramatic moments of life appear, to me at least, as if they were arranged in the best legend of the theatre, more true to the theatre than to the reality of life. Just as the motor stopped turning, a searchlight, a white arm of fire which had been playing round the sky, searching vainly enough for Lindbergh, struck the halted plane, and as the pale young American stood up in the cockpit, the arm of light hit him full in the face.

He removed his flying helmet, he called to the passing man with the bicycle who wheeled round. Fendrick and I still running could not at the split second hear what Lindbergh said; we saw that he was making gestures, pointing downwards with his finger and trying to make the Frenchman understand. At that moment we reached the plane and we heard Lindbergh say this: "Is this Paris?"

"*Ah! oui Paris,*" smiled the Frenchman.

Thousands had seen the light and hundreds began to run. In less time than it takes to relate the story, Lindbergh and his plane were surrounded by a milling excited crowd who began to snatch souvenirs. Lindbergh's first thought was for the safety of his plane, and his second question, which he kept on repeating was: "How much gas is there left in the tank?" When they told him he smiled, and said he could have gone still further.

Chaos, chaos, chaos. Everything went wrong. All the best laid plans of the New York *Times* went agley; They did not get Lindbergh's exclusive story, and neither did we. The late Myron T. Herrick, American Ambassador to France, hospitably took the young airman to the American Embassy, and always having a liking for newspaper men, he invited the whole corps to come along too. I want you to picture the scene. Lindbergh talking shyly and bashfully to the newspapermen, and Carlisle MacDonald, representative of the New York *Times*, trying to "get" Lindbergh's exclusive story, trying to shoo them all away.

### Journey's End

Fendrick and I found the faithful Charlie and dashed back to Paris. It was a dash, because now and then Charlie even drove us across ploughed fields in his endeavour to get us back to the office as quickly as possible. I was too excited and busy to pay Charlie but told him to meet me next day where I had found him, at the New York Bar. For hours and hours Fendrick and Tuckfield and I worked. We finished about two in the morning.

Next day I went round to the New York Bar to keep my appointment with Charlie and to give him rich recompense. "Oh! Didn't you know," they told me, "Charlie met with an accident. His steering wheel broke and he was killed."

# CHAPTER VI

## A BESSARABIAN NIGHT

A FEW years after the Armistice was signed, Russia was still the Bad Boy of Europe. Russia laughed at the League of Nations, Russia threatened Poland and threatened all countries near to her frontiers, including Rumania, dreaming that one of these days she was going to take back the province of Bessarabia, which had come to Rumania as one of the spoils of the victory she did not win. To Rumania I went to see what it was all about.

An American newspaper man I met in Bucharest and I decided to go along to Kishnev, the capital of Bessarabia and take with us an English-speaking Rumanian journalist, because neither Jack nor I could speak a word of Rumanian and practically no Russian. The journey itself was eventful enough, because we counted nine railway smashes before we ourselves became involved in the tenth. In the middle of the night we ran into a goods train, fortunately we were not travelling faster than a Rumanian express and we did not hurt anybody, but there was a considerable amount of damage done and we had to collect our clothes, jump out into the night and follow a flickering lantern for a mile or so until we found another train which carried us on to Kishnev.

# I HATE TO-MORROW

## The Crows of Kishnev

Once upon a time Kishnev must have been a very prosperous Russian city; when the Rumanians came they started to knock it about a bit. Every Russian had his name Rumanianized; every statue to a Russian was knocked off its pedestal; people were in great fear of a Russian invasion. The whole city and the surrounding country was black with crows. One is accustomed to seeing crows in many parts of the Balkans, but never in my life have I seen them in such millions. They blackened the sky; they filled the trees, and I will not say what else they did to us as we walked through the streets.

## I Lunch with the General

General Radianu asked us to lunch with him. He was a famous Rumanian General who died a few years ago. He had been appointed to take up the command of what was considered a very difficult district. He told us during lunch that if the Russians showed any signs of moving, he would immediately march into the Ukraine and seize Odessa and cut Russia off from her "bread-basket". I remarked that this was very interesting and quite innocently I inquired the distance between Odessa and Kishnev. The General snapped his fingers, apparently to assist thought, and then he sent an aide-de-camp to fetch a book to see what the distance was. After lunch the General drove me out to the Russo-Rumanian frontier, which was the River Dniester. The General wore many rows of medals. We left the motor car and walked to the river bank. On the other bank we could see the Soviet soldiers patrolling. There had been reports of shots being fired in the night. The General and I walked on a little way, and then General Radianu turned his back on Russia and slapping his chest so that the medals clanked, he exclaimed: "See, I'm not afraid."

### THE WORST HOTEL IN THE WORLD

The American, the Rumanian and I obtained three rooms in what professed to be a hotel. The hotel appeared to be run by the porter with whom I managed to converse in German. After leaving the General I thought I would go back to my room and wash before going out to see the town. But this was not just a question of turning a tap. Life in a Bessarabian hotel was much more complicated than that. First of all one obtained the services of one of the two chambermaids, neither of them could have been a day under seventy. Then one gave the chambermaid a small coin, and the chambermaid went out somewhere or other, certainly out into the street and eventually came back with a small pitcher of warm and dirty water.

It was a very hot night, so I decided that after all I would not go out and see the town, but that I would go to bed and read. My bed was close to the door. The American and the Rumanian went out, while I went to bed. In an hour or two they came back with two girls; they said they were investigating local conditions. One girl worked in a post-office and the other in a Government office. They all four came into my bedroom; I rang for the porter and he produced two bottles of Rumanian white wine; we sat down and listened to the story of local conditions as translated by the Rumanian who spoke Russian, the language of the two girls. When the wine had been drunk, the four went out, and the American said that after he had taken the girls home, he and the Rumanian were really going to see the city, but apparently there was nothing for them to see and they came back and went to bed. I rolled up the sleeves of my pyjama coat to the shoulder, it was so terribly hot, and I went on reading.

## I RECEIVE A VISIT

It was between one and two in the morning when I felt rather than heard the door slowly open. I turned round and saw the head of a rather pretty brunette peering round the door. I looked again and I saw behind her the grinning face of the porter.

"What the hell do you want," I yelled at him in German.

"Don't you like the lady?" he queried sorrowfully.

"No," I shouted.

Evidently the lady spoke a little German and understood that the offer of her services was declined with no thanks. She opened the door wider, leant over me and bit me hard in the arm. I jumped out of bed, pushed her into the corridor, closed and banged the door.

Next morning, after I had drunk a cup of coffee, I went to see my American colleague. He also had found the night hot and had removed his pyjama coat. I looked at his body. "A funny thing happened during the night," he said musingly, "a woman came in here and bit me."

# CHAPTER VII

## THE INDIA I KNOW

INDIA INFURIATES me. It is a monument to the futility of mankind. For generations school children in England have been taught that India was the brightest jewel in the Crown! There is not one India, but a thousand Indias; it is not a country but a continent. Hundreds of thousands of English people have devoted their lives and their health and their ambition to the betterment of India, but the Indians are not grateful. Famine has been stamped out and the dreaded plague has been reduced to a minimum, but those who have accomplished these things, where are they; on what scroll of fame and honour are their names engraved?

There were to be forty candles on my birthday cake, and it was also to be the very first birthday cake that I had ever had, because in the days of my youth such extravagances were barred by my stepfather. Not only was I to have a cake, but there was to be a dinner party to celebrate my fortieth birthday. Alas and alack! there was no cake and no dinner party, because when my birthday came round I was at sea on my way to India, to try and get there before Gandhi was arrested. Just as my ship was about to enter the Suez Canal, a wireless message said that Gandhi had been arrested. I left the ship at Port Said and raced to Cairo to catch the Imperial Airways plane to Karachi.

265

There new complications arose, because I was lacking numerous visas. Persia asked for a visa, and Iraq wanted a visa, so I had to make another dash, this time to Aden to pick up a ship. A collision with a water buffalo in the dawn nearly made me miss the ship but I was able to scramble aboard just as she was about to sail away.

During my first visit to India, I travelled some five thousand miles and visited every province under British rule. I visited native states and journeyed as far as the Afghan frontier. I talked with Gandhi in his village and was in Calcutta when it looked as if the whole of Bengal was going up in flames. I was in a Bombay police jail when it was encircled by rioters and an attempt was made to set it on fire. I journeyed down the Ganges and I escaped shooting in the Khyber Pass. I stayed with the Viceroy in Delhi and with the head men of several Indian villages. I saw India, but it was not the India of which they teach in the schools of England. That India is the India of long ago; the India of fabulous legend, swaying elephants and nautch girls, of temple bells and all the colour and glory of the past. Not that in many native states there is a lack of romantic glamour; there is plenty of it, but in many native states there is also corruption and vicious living of which echoes only occasionally reach the West. Then we hear that such and such a prince has been deprived of his prerogatives and has gone to live with a lady for consolation in some nice town on the French or Italian Riviera. All that, however, I insist is not India at all. The India that is and the India that infuriates me is the India ruled by underpaid Englishmen. During the troubles that led up to Gandhi's arrest and other troubles which followed, British rule in India was badly shaken. At that moment I happened to meet in Delhi a political officer whose knowledge and experience made him one of the key men in the situation. He at that very moment had to take into his bungalow a paying guest in order that he should be able to send his young son to a small public school in England.

There are thousands of young men in India in the Police and the Civil Service doing grand jobs, but their recompense is so small and their future so clouded that one is left wondering what their to-morrows are going to be like. The English have killed India with kindness. The English encouraged education in India and that was the beginning of the ruination of the races. Universities turn out graduates of both sexes who are unable to find suitable jobs, either in India or outside of India. It is very uncomfortable to have one's shoes shined by an Indian barrister.

A young man calls at one's hotel and presents his card: on it one finds the words "failed B.A." The leaders of the Gandhi movement and indeed of the whole Indian Congress are intellectuals, graduates of universities without any to-morrow.

In the old days of "John Company", India was ruled. Conditions it is granted were bad, but they were bettered when India was taken over from the East India Company. The betterment of conditions, that is to say the improvement in hygiene and in secondary education and in various municipal matters would have developed in any case, whether India was given Dominion status or not. In fact, all the improvements which have been made in India were carried out long before there was any question of giving India any change in the form of the Government. With the hand-ing over to Indians of public utilities, matters have not even remained as they were, but they have fallen away in efficiency. The Indian is a most charming person, but a most inefficient one. He is fundamentally an idealist, but his idealogy he cannot apply to matters of everyday life.

I once asked an English official who had spent a good many years in a native state how long England could stay in India. His considered reply was: "So long as he could sleep out at night without getting his throat cut." That answer has always been in my mind when I have been thinking or writing about India.

## I Meet Gandhi

Mahatma Gandhi is not a bloodthirsty individual. In fact, apart from some of the younger members of the so-called Bengal Republican Party, I have never met an Indian who had any desire to shed blood in his fight with the English. It is purely a fight between two sets of idealists. The Englishman thinks that he has a good job to do in India and I may say that I am thinking now of the thousands of young men who rule India and not necessarily of the few who are merchants in India. The Indian idealist on the other hand says: India for the Indians, by every means and by every power which can be used, but when he says that he does not think in terms of machine guns and rifles; by power he means the power of intellect and the ballot-box. I daresay many who read these lines will shrug their shoulders and say poor fool, if he really believes what he says; but I do believe what I write and my belief is based on personal observation.

Gandhi is one of those Indian idealists who shrink at the very thought of shedding blood. The power that Gandhi wields in India is based on the same form of admiration which the pious Roman Catholic feels for a God-fearing good-living man. I imagine that twenty-five years hence, historians writing about India will discard Gandhi almost entirely as a great figure; they will refer to him as the man who led a movement, but he led it nowhere at all. My conversations with Gandhi showed me how entirely futile the whole question of India is. In the first place Gandhi never answers a direct question. He hates anything which is really constructive. He will make a speech which entirely contradicts the first speech. By fasting and by organizing campaigns of what is called Non-Co-operation Gandhi and some of his followers believe they can shame the English into doing what the Indians want; but the English know now the strength or rather the weakness of Gandhi, and their only fear is that Gandhi, who is now very old, may die during one of these "fasts unto death". That would be very tragic indeed because immediately there would be an outbreak of trouble throughout India. It is known now, however, that there is not any likelihood of the Indians themselves going to extremes. When I met Gandhi I tried to talk to him in the form of question and answer, but though Gandhi listened very politely to my questions, he did not answer any of them directly. He was most evasive. When I asked Gandhi how he interpreted freedom, all I could get him to say was: "There are many ways of interpreting Freedom." Gandhi's manner of evasion is practised throughout India, not only by his followers but by many who are not interested in his teaching. There are members of

Gandhi's party who will tell you that despite Gandhi's
spiritual leadership over the Indian mind, he has no
leadership in practical politics and knows nothing
about economics and finance.

## Miss Slade

Miss Slade, the famous Mira Bel, was with Gandhi
in his *ashmed* when I saw him. A little later I was
present when she was tried in Bombay. The relations
between Gandhi and Miss Slade are interesting. She
was with him when I first saw Gandhi when he came
to London for the Round Table Conference, but when
I saw them together in India, I noticed that there
was a decided difference in their relationship. While
Gandhi was spinning and talking and evading questions, a number of flies were buzzing round his head
and Miss Slade was trying to swat them. Every time
she did this, Gandhi would say quite gently: "Don't
do that, Mira Bel, Don't do that, Mira Bel," but she
did not take any notice and went on. Suddenly
Gandhi snapped out: "Miss Slade, shut up."

## How India is Held

The old order has indeed changed and the soldier of
Kipling's day, the drunken, swaggering private is no
more. The young soldier of to-day in India drinks
lemonade and goes to the pictures. Yet, although the
age of the average soldier one sees appears to be so
very young, one soon begins to realize that India is
held and will be held by the English civil servant and

the English members of the police force. There you have the real backbone of India. The old men, the tired old men will gradually pass away and leave the ruling of India, so I hope at least, to younger men who have a different appreciation of what is necessary. Nevertheless, as I said in the beginning, India infuriates me because of this huge waste and mismanagement. Nothing happens; so little progress is made to reach any sort of objective. Life merely ambles along in a shiftless manner.

We hear in the West such a lot about the caste system in India, but we hear very little of the caste system of the British in India. There are castes right through British society in India. The Indian is not the only victim of the castes of his own race, but also the castes of the British race. It is the fashion in India either to flatter and fawn upon an Indian or else to bully him, and I think that of the two methods the Indian prefers to be bullied. In a fragment of a book it is almost impertinent to try and deal with such a vast subject as India. I once wrote a book about the country after being warned that I must not do so, but I wanted to do so; I wanted to tell all I had seen.

Nothing in my life has given me greater thrills than travelling through the Khyber Pass, knowing that if one stopped for a moment one would be shot at; hundreds of snipers with nothing to do hide behind huge mustard coloured boulders and pick off any stray European driving along the most romantic thoroughfare in the whole wide world. On the North-West frontier of India there is a thrill every minute of the day.

In Calcutta I found the staff of one newspaper office all mobilized as if for war, and they had been living

like this for months on end. The editor's blotting pad
was a sheet of thin armoured plate. Members of the
editorial staff strapped revolvers round their waists as
they went on duty. When the Governor of Bengal
went out to play golf, there were detectives in every
bunker and he was followed by an armed guard.
When the Governor went out to dine, armed police
were in the house of his host for two days before his
arrival, and machine guns were posted on the roof.

In Bombay a newspaper friend and myself were
dining at the Taj Mahal one night when my native
servant brought me a message to say that the rioters
were trying to fire a police station in a distant quarter.
We were in evening dress and just going into dinner,
but we went off to try and find a story. In the
darkened streets we groped our way along and then
at the end of one street where we knew the jail was
situated, we saw a tram-car on fire. We spent a night
of horror in this "chowky" while stones came hurtling
and in one moment armed police were sent outside to
fire on the crowd. Then in the early hours of the
morning, in order to clear away the rioters, the police
had to charge and we charged with them.

We two civilians of course were unarmed, but we
raced along, our dress shirts as limp as handkerchiefs
and our patent leather shoes torn to shreds by the
sharp cobbles. We were soaked in perspiration but we
had one of the most exciting nights that either of us
had ever known.

# BOOK IV

# CHAPTER I

I HAVE pitched my tent at so many cross-roads of the world that I find myself faced with an embarrassment of riches when trying to sort out impressions, shaking them as it were through a sieve, letting the significant things stay to hand, and the chaff blow away.

The United States of America undoubtedly gave me more mental stimulus than any other country has ever done, and yet, apart from my earliest days in France, I have never been so utterly dejected and miserable as I have been in New York and Washington D.C. Happiness can be obtained from self-contentment, but unhappiness usually arises entirely from external influences. The first time I went to the United States, in the summer of 1926, I went around New York very apologetically; we were so poor and they were so rich. I tried to get rich myself by buying American stocks while the Americans chanted the sky was the limit, but in 1929 I was sort of strapped to the third rail and yelling for mercy. I wish though I could remember the name of the man who foretold it all, everything, just as it happened, the high spots and the crack o' doom. I know I had a letter of introduction to this soothsayer, but then I had about two dozen letters of introduction; I used this letter one very hot afternoon when I was tired of drifting about the city, and finding myself in Times Square I walked over to the block where Keith & Proctor's offices were and was then carried up into the skies and deposited in the office of a man who had some sort of connection with the theatrical business, and a very pretty secretary who was wearing grey silk stockings rolled below her dimpled knees.

The soothsayer and I sat side by side on a divan while he chewed a cigar and spoke works of wisdom about the futility of thinking a nation could be prosperous by mortgaging its income and hoping for the best. I remember him saying: "First they buy a car and then they buy a second car for the wife and if there is a son or daughter they buy another car, all on time. Then they put a sleeping porch on the house, and all the while they are getting stock dividends and think they are getting real money, but it can't last, you will see that within three years (he was right to three months) it will all blow up, sky high. Yeh, I know, the sky's the limit, but the bump is going to be pretty goddam awful, son."

It was. I was there when they were jumping off roofs and wobbling about like drunken sailors. During those three years Europe was plunging about, too, but the United States seemed to be getting along all right and so it was in the late summer of 1929 when I was rushed off to accompany Mr. Ramsay MacDonald on his visit to President Hoover, the first British Labour Prime Minister to make such a trip. How he loved it, poor man; he was not worried about naval equality or the Debt to America, not he; what worried the Prime Minister was, as I tell elsewhere, what he should wear when he landed in New York. He kept on sending wireless messages to London asking what the well-dressed man was wearing. It was terribly cold and blowy when we reached Quarantine and the Premier's party went ashore in the cutter. The Premier looked swell. I shivered behind the smoke stack, then seeing a door I opened and swung neatly down into a large and cosy cabin and was immediately yanked out again by a New York plain clothes policeman because I had entered the holy of holies, the cabin reserved for the Premier.

A number of English newspapermen accompanied the Premier; most of them had never been to the States, indeed, judging by their behaviour I would hazard a guess that Brighton was about as far as they had ventured. The man who caused me so much distress was a former engineer who somehow had managed to become attached to the Parliamentary section of a Left Wing paper. I suppose he got the job because he was a Socialist. Innocently he accepted the offer of two rival American news agencies to work for them, too. The last night at sea it was announced that the United States Government was sending two cruisers to escort the *Berengaria* in. The young reporter said to me that night in the bar: "I suppose they are manned by British deserters?" to which I replied that as the two cruisers were the crack ships of the Fleet, I hardly thought so.

"Well," he commented, "all I can say is I hope they are damn' spies," which for a young man on a goodwill tour with the Socialist Prime Minister of Great Britain, was quite a thought.

Some of these strange journalists who had never been abroad previously thought they could and should operate just as they did at home. They began by thoroughly despising their American colleagues and tried to talk to them in what they considered was the

American language, from out of date comics, right back to the Mutt and Jeff days. It was not so good. They formed committees and shouted: "Chair, chair." Owing to the lucky circumstance of having been in New York myself and knowing the ropes and realizing that time was all important, I was able to have my dispatch, reporting the Premier's arrival, in London in time for all editions, whereas my greatest rival caught the last edition only, and besides, I was lucky in having a colleague like J. W. T. Mason in whose office located in the old United Press offices, I wrote my dispatch. Mason took my story sheet by sheet off the typewriter and carried it a few feet away where there was a Western Union operator putting it on the cable direct into the Fleet Street office of my paper; the first sheets were already in the office before the last sheets had come from my typewriter. Mason had already earned my undying gratitude earlier in the day by saving me from being thrown out of the City Hall reception to the Premier. I had driven up Broadway in the traditional procession, when office tenants in the skyscrapers tear up telephone directories and scatter the pieces so that Broadway looks like some mountain fastness in a snow storm, but I had omitted to put my ticket in my hat band, like a good New York reporter; I had mine in my pocket, just like an effete "limey" would do. The reporters marched into City Hall, and I marched, too, carrying my portable typewriter, when a gimlet-eyed "cop" picked on me and threw me out. I started to argue, but he would have none of it; at that moment Mason appeared, like a tubby little cherub, with his ticket in his hat band, and I was saved. That night we all went to Washington.

The English journalists held their committee meetings, but I was too busy meeting old friends to bother about procedure and so forth. Then the Premier announced he was going to meet the English correspondents at the British Embassy, and it was to be very secret. The Prime Minister read out an official communiqué which contained the words "all questions concerning the two nations (Great Britain and the United States of America) were discussed." The late Sir John Foster Fraser sitting in a corner spoke up and piped out: "Prime Minister, you say all questions; people at home will think you mean War Debts; were *they* discussed?"

Mr. MacDonald thought the question over for a few seconds, then he said: "Yes, they were, but on account of that stupid Balfour Declaration (giving our debtors any benefit accruing from a reduction of the Debt to the U.S.A.), it is no use discussing the matter." Sensation amongst the correspondents. Although this meeting was so very secret, there was, as there nearly always is, a leakage; some of the American newspapers obtained a garbled version of the conversation. There was a great commotion among the correspondents; they held more meetings and shouted: "Chair, chair," very violently indeed. There was another secret meeting but I did not attend it, indeed I never attended any more of the Prime Minister's secret press conferences after that first one, but nevertheless, I was charged with having violated the secrecy of all of them, that is to say the one I attended and two or three I did not. It was not until years later that one of the high Foreign Office officials who had accompanied the Premier told me that the person who had caused the leakage, and very innocently, (he

279

10

thought very likely he was drafting a blue print) was the young Left Winger who hoped the crew of the American cruisers were damn' spies.

I can write light-heartedly now, but what misery I went through in those days. My colleagues shunned me as if I had plague! One of those who almost groaned when he saw me approaching was the journalist whom Sir Nevil Macready had said used to mess with him in Ulster and then go and write scurrilous stories about him.

Time marches on. I went again and again to New York after the "Crash" and was unhappy because everybody else was so unhappy; my friends who used to be so well off were now living in despair. Unless one walked fast it was impossible to escape being pestered by men whining "brother, can you spare a dime?" And I drank too much. I drank Prohibition out and Repeal in. I kept the Campbells coming and going. It was fun while it lasted. I had heaps of fun. But often I used to go to bed hating that inevitable to-morrow and its post-alcoholic depression. I tried to get interested in work, but as Beaverbrook once told me, no sooner did I start something but I wanted to be doing something else. That is me all over.

When I was told to go to the States to cover the Roosevelt Inauguration, I was just as glad as I am always when America comes my way, but once again I landed myself into trouble. Among the American correspondents I met at the White House in Washington was a man named Boettiger and another named Stevens, the second one a pleasant looking little fellow and a favourite of the President who calls him Stevie. Both these men, for reasons I swear I do not know, took a very active dislike to me. The night before

Inauguration, I am speaking of the first term of office, I was staying at the Mayflower Hotel in Washington; the President and his family had reserved a whole floor there. That was the time when a lot was heard of the "Roosevelt Brain Trust," of which the most prominent member was a young college professor named Raymond Moley. One of the correspondents present was Harold Horan, the same who was expelled from France because of the alleged breach concerning the Franco-British Naval Treaty (where is that Treaty now?) A number of us were sitting around in the bedroom of one of the correspondents, drinking Prohibition whisky and working and talking. I happened to say how much I would like to meet Moley, and good friend Horan said he would go and get him. I thought it was a joke, but Horan went out and came back—with Moley. We sat and talked, and the other correspondents, including Stevens and Boettiger, listened. I was discreetly trying to find out what the President was going to say in his Inauguration speech; I knew well enough that even if Moley knew he would not tell me, but I kept on talking. Then Moley said he had to go back to the President. When the door closed hell broke loose. Boettiger, a big hulking sort of a fellow, very different from his friend the light weight Stevens, came for me, metaphorically and physically. All through the uproar I kept asking what they were so sore about; what had I *done*? "You're a goddamned British spy," hissed Boettiger. At that time President Roosevelt's daughter was a Mrs. Dall. She divorced her husband and married again; a journalist whose name as I recall it is John Boettiger.

Once I pitched my tent, almost in the literal sense,

IOA

in the Sahara and knew greater peace than I had
known for years. It was my first meeting with a desert
and I thought I had never seen anything so
marvellous as these unending miles of seemingly
petrified sand. Then I started to de-bunk it, beginning with the Garden of Allah, in Biskra, where the
shrewd old sand diviner will divine almost anything
one likes. Yet, in the end, the desert "got" me again,
and all the magic of Africa too. I have been, at various
times, all over North Africa, from Morocco to Egypt,
and the drumming of the tom-toms is still in my ears.
I have watched the fires flicker at night outside the
tents of the nomads, and a nomad myself, I have
wandered on, through the street of the Ouled Nails,
the painted ladies of the desert, who sit and watch for
the soft padding sons of the desert; clutching at their
burnous as they pass. When a lady of the Ouled Nails
tribe has amassed a dowry, she returns to her tribe
and marries and I hope lives happily ever afterwards.

I have sat for hours watching the squatting Arabs
playing dominoes while they listen to a gramophone
churning out the whining airs which are sweet music
to them and just plain hell to me. I have shared a hut
for a night with a Liberian murderer, in West Africa,
and shared a battleship with Mussolini *en route* to
Libya; in Aden I have sought the elusive donkey of
which all travellers have heard and never seen, and in
Kobe, of all places, I committed hara kiri, but of it
I shall tell later.

## Go East, Old Man

Before Japan began spreading culture and all that,
the finest spot in the world for adventure was the

East, what is usually referred to as the Far East, and by that I personally mean China. I think the Chinese are the finest people among those we call the coloured races. The usual idea of a Chinaman, especially among those who have never met one outside of a Chinese restaurant, is a cunning, cruel fellow. The Chinaman is a gentleman, and a Chinese gentleman is a person worth knowing. The Chinaman is such a gentleman that he even allows us to address him in detestable "pigeon English". "You catchee me glass water," you say to your Number One boy, when I am perfectly sure he would be able to comprehend just as easily: fetch me a glass of water. When I paid off my rickshaw boy in Nankin, he said to me: "Good-bye, sir, good health and God bless you." "Why," I exclaimed amazedly, "you speak English!" He shook his head. The words he had uttered in a deep cultured voice was all the English he knew. What a life, that of the rickshaw coolie; he wears a cotton shirt and shorts; his legs and feet are bare. He is yours, morning, noon and night for about six shillings a week. I never feel more humble and lowly than when I sit in a rickshaw, jog-trotted along by a coolie, the bobbing head and the swaying shoulders and an occasional growl from the unseen mouth; the growl just means get the hell out of there and is applied to anything ranging from a stray mongrel to another coolie. The coolie lives just one jump ahead of starvation; give him a penny and he immediately buys a bowl of rice. He does not know when he is going to get another. In Dairen, in South Manchuria, there is a coolie's brothel where the inmates charge the coolie a penny. The age of the inmates ranges from sixty to seventy. It is the low standard of living of the Chinaman which makes China a paradise for white men, or rather did, before the Japanese came. In China a bank clerk could live like a prince, in fact there are many princes who never lived so well: a fine house and plenty of servants to look after one's comforts; plenty of amusements and only once a month does one have to put one's hand in one's pocket. Life for white men in China, and to a lesser degree in India, is built up on the chit system; you sign a chit, for your food, your drinks, your taxi fare, your rickshaw boy, if you pick up a stray one; for your hair-cut, your clothes, your theatre or cinema, for anything that in the West you pay cash for, out East you pay with a piece of paper. I have heard the system derided, and very likely there are economic reasons that may be held against it, but every white man feels he can always shake hands with a millionaire.

I have often played with the idea of where I would like to live, I mean for ever and ever. Would I like New York or London or Paris? Big cities? U'um, I'm not so sure. What about New Orleans? Well, there you have a city, not too big, not too small. One side of the canal is a hustling sort of place, and then you cross over into the past, Old French, with just a dash of Old Spanish. Patios with splashing fountains, masses of purple bougainvillia, and the singing negroes waiting on the levees almost like in the song. Alas, the only show boats left on the Mississippi are really for show; no longer do the play actors steam along the river in paddle boats churning up the brown waters. A lovely city is New Orleans and lovely people live there, but I would not like to be there for ever and a day.

New York, the acme of sophistication, its continual

urge to be doing something, provides too much of a strain, to have Manhattan always wrapped around one; and yet, when I think of the wet streets at dawn, the sirens echoing from East River, I confess something tugs at my heart strings and I want to go back. New York is the ideal of a newspaperman's city; there is always something going on. One returns to one's apartment feeling tired out, and then there is the shrill hoot of a passing police patrol wagon and instinctively the reporter inside one, the fellow who never sleeps, begins to be alert and copying Old Bill asks: "I wonder where that one went?"

When it was certain that Hauptmann, who was sentenced for the kidnapping of the Lindbergh baby, would go to the chair, I thought I would try and buy his last story, written in the death house. I telephoned his lawyer, Lloyd Fisher, at his New Jersey home and asked if I could see him. Fisher gave me a mysterious appointment. I was to go at six that evening to the Hotel New Yorker, and there by the news stand I would find a bell hop and I was to ask him to conduct me to Lloyd Fisher's apartment; the lawyer was not going to register officially. When I was taken up to his room, Fisher asked if I remembered him, but I thought he was mistaking me for somebody else and I told him that so far as I knew I had never seen him in my life. Fisher asked if I remembered who used to change my money for me in Berlin during the Black Bourse period when pounds and dollars were eagerly sought. There would be mysterious tappings on one's bedroom door and the voice of the money changing bootlegger would be heard in sibilant whisperings. Of course I remembered. Frank Keeney used to change *my* money, I said, "Whispering Frank" (he had a roar like a bull); "he's over at the Chatham, I saw him this noon. Polish Jack! too," I added as an afterthought. Polish Jack later went to do a stretch in Frankfurt. Fisher smiled slightly. "I was there in Berlin too," he said.

Hauptmann's defender, it can be told now, did not believe his client a hundred per cent guilty, although he was convinced he had played his part in handling the ransom money. Lloyd Fisher did not defend the convicted man in the first part of the trial, and for hours that evening he held me spellbound while he told me what he had discovered and how he would have defended him if he had had the chance. Even now it is not possible to relate very much concerning the many mysteries of that mysterious kidnapping which will puzzle many crime experts to the end of their days. The mysterious suicide of the Lindbergh butler is just one factor in that strange story which has never been fully explained, but Lloyd Fisher particularly drew attention to the story of the finding of the remains of the baby; he considered that the identification was not sufficient because the remains were found on the edge of a garden belonging to a foundling's home, where unwanted children were often abandoned.

When I made a bid for Hauptmann's story, his lawyer accepted, but we argued at great length about the payment. I wanted the story written to my specification, which he agreed. I offered two thousand dollars; Fisher agreed, but I wanted to deposit the money in a bank and pay it over only when I had seen the story. Lloyd Fisher did not agree, and that is why no last story from the death house was ever obtained. I hope I have explained why New York is such a fine newspaperman's city? If I have not, I will add just a few lines to this Hauptmann story. The night he was to go to the chair, a Saturday night, I think it was, I was in Floyd Gibbons' apartment to listen to the running commentary on the execution, which was being broadcast. The commentator began his story, then broke it off to announce that the execution had been postponed. I went out into the streets to hear the newsboys calling to-morrow mornings papers, you can always buy them in New York around midnight, announcing the acquittal of a woman who had murdered her doctor lover. New York, lovely city of paradox. I like you, I love you, but I don't think I want to live with you for ever.

I am not sure I do want to know where I want to live, outside of Europe. Pekin? perhaps, although I have not been there since the Japanese have overrun North China in the name of freedom. The lure of Pekin, or Peiping as it should be called now, is magical. It is the last of the really Imperial cities, even though it is years since the Manchu Dynasty was overthrown. Pekin is a city for philosophers who like to speculate that life never really changes; it is we who change. In the one main broad thoroughfare which crosses Pekin, a name I insist on calling this ancient capital of China, one sees life in all its aspects. Side by side, moving with the nonchalance of the twentieth century and the weariness of age, one sees clanging tramcars, slowly padding and flea bitten camels, tooting American motor cars, bullock carts creaking with the piled up years, hustling motor omnibuses, Europeans bent on their pleasures or business, on foot or in rickshaws, and Chinese men and women wearing their inevitable blue gowns.

Occasionally one may meet with adventure in China; there are bandits bent on kidnapping and pirates infesting the Chinese seas, and smugglers galore, but the lure of China once it has caught you, will never leave you; it twists its fingers into the stuff of which you are made and whispers: will you no come back again? Sitting very likely at this very moment in a back room in Henrietta Street, London, is a venerable old publisher. I was lunching with him one day in the Devonshire Club when a casual mention of some Eastern custom put him in a sort of trance. He has been a publisher, it seems, for a thousand years, but before that he was "Number One" in a business out in China. I thought he was going to cry.

## Hara Kiri in Kobe

It was out East, in Japan, that I wilfully closed my career as a Special Correspondent. Small things, very small things sometimes, change the flow of one's life . . . the flick of an eyelid, the toss of a chin. . . . When the moment came for Mr. Ramsay MacDonald to acknowledge that even his misplaced optimism could not carry on any longer with the W-u-r-r-l-d Economic Conference, when all the lies had been told, the Premier decided to convoke the English journalists covering the Conference to a meeting at 10, Downing Street, in the famous library. I suggested to Beverley Baxter, editing the *Daily Express*, that he should go with me. The ubiquitous Mr. George Stewart, the Premier's personal Press attaché, who had been such a source of innocent merriment to the correspondents during the Conference, cast worried looks at my companion. I asked Stewart what was the matter. He asked me who my companion was, and appeared much relieved when I told him it was only the editor!

On our way back along Whitehall, Baxter made a sensational confession: he was leaving the paper. I was not very much surprised, friction between him and the "Little Man" (Beaverbrook) had been growing. Baxter asked me not to tell anybody for the moment and added kindly: "Don't you go because I am going . . . you are there as long as you like to stay." It was a kindly gesture and I appreciated the advice and the way in which it was given, but there and then I saw the red light ahead and made up my mind to avoid it. One of my colleagues, Mr. Collie Knox, in his autobiography, says he does not know why he left the *Daily Express*. Well, my last months made me feel I might have breakfasted with the Borgias.

We had a new editor and a new foreign editor. Then I suggested I should go to Japan, a place almost as far away as it was possible to go. I told myself, however, that this would be probably my last trip for the paper, so I might as well make the most of it, travelling at somebody else's expense. I went first to New York, then drifted through the south to California and fell in love with the sunshine of Hollywood, then went to San Francisco and so to Japan.

Japan was on every front page in England, that was why I was sent to Japan. A Japanese trade delegation had arrived in England to discuss the swamping of British markets with Japanese goods. I spent a day in a textile factory to see how it was done, and then wrote a long cable which I calculated would hit the front page to coincide with the opening of the Jap-English meeting. It did. The editor then launched his own little offensive. He cabled me: "Good story but not worth cable tolls" (a few weeks later in China I discovered the foreign editor had spent £7 cabling the correspondent that if he wanted to see the *Daily Express* he must buy his own copies.) Then the foreign editor cabled me to go immediately to Vladivostock. All members of the editorial staff at that time were barred from Russia, on account of a series of articles written by a Canadian woman journalist. I cabled back it was impossible to go to Vladivostok. The editor cabled himself, thus: "Stephens Delmer Panton all risking their lives stop Please get on with the job."

It was not until I returned to London that I discovered from Lord Beaverbrook that neither of these two pocket Napoleons knew that Vladivostok was in Russia; they thought it was in Manchuria. For the uninitiated I may as well decipher the editorial cable. Stephens meant Pembroke Stephens, who was afterwards killed (when working for another newspaper) in the fighting in Shanghai; Delmer is the name of a Berlin born English journalist whose early dispatches from Germany gave such pleasure to Lord Beaverbrook; Panton is a young Australian journalist. I did not know and do not know where or why they were risking their lives at the moment of the editor's melodramatic cable which caused me to review matters when I left the Kobe Club and went to bed.

I had had twenty years of the *Daily Express*, twenty years of hard work and good fun. I had ruined my health for them during the strenuous months I had spent in Berlin, directly after the signing of the Armistice; when my dispatches had added hundreds of thousands to their circulation.

I had contracted smallpox in Constantinople while on active newspaper service. I had written the best I had in me. I had slept for years with a telephone next to my bedside, answering questions which were rained at me during the night hours, and now the fun seemed over. I had no grievance, but the time had come to commit hara-kiri and I did, by cable, which cost me £12. I enjoyed writing every word of my resignation dispatch, especially the last sentence: "Don't bother about cost this cable stop Its on me." Then I continued my tour round the world.

I had made one bargain with the editor, or thought I had. I said if he would not make my resignation public, I would not; we are prima donni, we newspapermen, and I did not want to prejudice my journalistic future. When I reached Colombo I met two newspaper friends, one Trevor Wignall from my own paper, and Tom Clarke from the *Daily Mail*; they had come to meet the Australian cricketers on their way to England. Both men hailed me: "Why have you resigned?" All Fleet Street knew, they said. I continued my journey late the same night. I did not know it until a year or more later, when Tom Clarke told me in London, but both he and Wignall hid behind barrels and saw me sail that night in the *Conte Verde*. They did not trust my story that I was sailing on; they thought I had some nefarious business connected with the cricketers; if they had only known what I thought about cricket!

I kept running into stories on my last trip. Barbara Hutton and her Mdvani husband were travelling in the same ship and I had the first story of their estrangement. In Singapore the police arrested a number of Japanese spies, one of whom poisoned himself and dropped dead just as he crossed the threshold of the police station. In Penang I found a great state of excitement because a number of Japanese had been arrested on charges of alleged spying; they were members of the crew of a Japanese salvage ship belonging to a company which had secured the contract to raise a Russian cruiser sunk by the *Emden* in Penang harbour during the War; the officers from the cruiser were drunk ashore and the crew asleep when the raider dashed in and out. I cabled the new foreign editor to ask if this story of the Japanese had already been reported, because I had been weeks at sea and had no means of knowing. He cabled back asking if the story would not keep until my return. So far as I know it is still exclusive.

## ALL THAT FOR NOTHING

All good fun comes to an end. I arrived back in London and went to the Fleet Street office ready to work for six months, according to the terms of my contract. I was told they did not want me to work. I then asked for a cheque for six months salary, a request which was met by a ringing boyish laugh from the general manager who begged me not to be silly, because my salary would be paid "indefinitely". That sounded very nice. Then I went along to Stornaway House to bid good-bye to my Lord Beaverbrook who asked me to cancel my resignation and to return to the paper. He said he had inquired about the cables which had been sent me while I was East and he had told the editor he should not have sent them. He said he would meet me in Paris in two days time. I have never seen him since.

All heads of departments were paid monthly "so as to preserve secrecy". My salary was paid as usual for six months, the term of my contract, and then it continued for another three months, which I discovered was the meaning of the word "indefinitely", because at the end of the third month I received this letter:

"Dear Sir,
I have paid this day into your bank the sum of XYZ pounds and I am instructed by the directors to thank you for your long and valuable services."

And there ended a very good lesson.

# CHAPTER II

## LIBERIAN LULLABY

I WENT on a trip to Liberia because I needed the publicity and the money. After leaving my newspaper I went and buried myself in the South of France and wrote the biography of Willie Clarkson, which was a smash hit. It sold out before publication. Then the lawyers got busy and that was the end of that.

I picked on the Negro Republic on the West Coast of Africa, because right across the other side of the Continent we call dark there was a war but I always like to do the unexpected. While many of my colleagues were flocking to Abyssinia, I and another white man started an expedition into the Liberian jungle.

Since the League of Nations fell out with the Liberian Government, the Government of Great Britain had withdrawn diplomatic recognition from the Negro Republic. Great Britain had a Legation in the coast capital of Liberia, Monrovia, but the British Minister had no official standing. Nevertheless one day when he was on leave in Southport, I went to see him and spent hours arranging matters. There are no hotels in Liberia, in fact one could write a whole page of things that are not. One has to arrange to stay with a trader. The general manager of the largest European trading concern in Liberia was on sick leave in England and I went to see him and made definite arrangements to stay with a member of his staff. In October 1935 I sailed from Liverpool for Monrovia.

The monthly arrival of the steamer from home is the greatest event of the Liberian capital. There is no harbour, so a motor boat puts out and comes alongside the liner. Over the side came the British Minister. Eagerly I recalled myself to him. Vaguely he groped in the past and eventually brought up the remark that he thought he had met me somewhere before; had we not travelled home together? Then I sought for the man with whom I was to stay a month as a paying guest. He had never heard of me. A young American, a bank clerk, who looked like a male version of Mae West, was the most helpful white man. He saw to things. He introduced me to the Secretary of the Treasury and the Minister of the Interior. We all had a drink and then we went over the side into a motor boat, and put off for the shore. Then we hit a sand bank and the members of the cabinet, the American and myself had to get out and push the boat out. Late in the afternoon I landed on the shores of Liberia.

In Liberia there are no newspapers, no theatres, no municipal government, no telephones, no street cars or buses, no taxi-cabs, no public sanitation, no fire-engines and in fact one could continue for quite a long time in this strain. There is a Postmaster General, but there is no post office. There are no railways. To ride from the customs offices to the bank—an American bank—where the members of the Government and myself were to go for a drink, might have been a problem if the young American bank clerk had not had the brilliant idea of commandeering the British Minister's motor car. In the whole country there are perhaps eight or ten motor cars. All belong either to members of the Government, or to foreign consuls, except two cars which belong to traders.

Before I had been forty-eight hours in Liberia, I found that a man is judged in that country by his lavatories. I had made a bad picking.

The two nicest houses to visit were the British and German Legations. The British Consulate was a setting sometimes for midnight drama. Softly padding up the garden in the moonlight would come a nude and dripping wet black man, who had slipped overboard from his dug-out canoe; a Kru "boy" messenger from the rebels down the coast.

I wonder what has become of dear old Herr Hermans, German Consul, with the student day scars on his cheeks. Hermans had three portraits on his study: the Kaiser Wilhelm, Hindenburg, Hitler. For myself, I have little doubt whose face he preferred. You see, Hermans was formerly a Governor in a German African colony, and he had his dreams.

I stayed exactly one month in Monrovia. All Europeans have to wear mosquito boots at night. In the so-called "dry season", which is from October until about February, it does not rain incessantly, but it rains every day. Otherwise it rains all day. There is one road in Liberia, about eighty miles long, which starts from the capital and runs into the jungle. Most explorers in Liberia go eastwards towards another coast town called Basza. Just to be different, I went into the south-westerly part of Liberia, where no white man had been seen for the past two years. I tramped 350 miles on my flat feet and eventually arrived at the frontier of Sierra Leone. The only food Liberia knows

and I am referring of course to the European population, is canned food purchased from the local traders,
plus some fresh food which steamers bring and which
can be kept a little while by any of the lucky people
who possess a refrigerator. My travelling companion
and myself took into the interior with us twenty-five
native porters. The most important things we took
with us through the jungle were quinine and whisky
and a lavatory seat; we took far too much quinine but
far too little whisky, but the lavatory seat was the
sensation of the jungle. We managed, after days
of bargaining to obtain the use of a motor lorry
which took us the eighty miles to the end of the
road, and there dumped us. Our boys had walked,
all except those who did not report for duty, so we
had to recruit some more. I had meant to purchase
a compass in Monrovia, but there were no com-
passes in Monrovia, and the only map I found
was in the United States Legation, and that had
been made in 1916 by the State Department at
Washington and was about sixty per cent incorrect,
as I found. Rivers were flowing the wrong way,
according to the map, when I reached them. Dis-
heartenedly I plunged into the jungle and three
days later was down with malaria. I lay in my cot
in the palaver house of a native village which during
the morning was used by the chief as a court. Then
when the fever abated, we were off again, sometimes walking, sometimes carried in a hammock.
The trail through the jungle is not more than two feet
wide. For days and days we never saw the sky, except
when we reached a native village which was cut in a
clearing. The popular picture of an African jungle
is a forest of green trees teeming with animal life. In

point of fact, it is like walking through an endless overheated conservatory. The foliage on either side is so thick that it is not possible to see anything at all. The trees in West Africa, mostly very tall cotton trees, often over sixty feet high, hide the grey sky. There is no sun, but a damp heat. An hour after dawn, I had to stop and change my khaki shirt, because it was black with sweat. The Liberian jungle teems with leopards, but they only prowl at night. The only animals I ever saw were monkeys and parrots and snakes and millions of ants, ants which are so ferocious that they eat live chickens and even small babies if they are left unattended in a native village.

## THE TRUTH ABOUT A JUNGLE

The truth about the African jungle is that it is the most boring place on earth. There is no variety of scenery and every mile travelled is just like the mile left behind; every mud village is just like another mud village. In every village we were a sensation when at night or in the early morning we carried the lavatory seat, we went down the trail and tried to dodge natives and snakes.

Two weeks from London, and we were in an entirely new world. A world in which there are secret societies which live by the rule of the witch doctor.

We reached a blank space on the map which had the word "cannibals" across it. These cannibals eat human flesh, but not as nourishment; they drag out the heart of a dead warrior in order to eat it and become lion-hearted. We came across all kinds of curious secret societies, one of the most curious of which is the "Fish" people who worship catfish. We went through the Elephant country, but never saw an elephant. We came to villages where children screamed at the sight of white men. While I was in one native town, they killed an eighteen foot boa-constrictor.

Perhaps one of these days, some nation will discover Liberia and find out what an abundance of potential wealth there is there. Anything and everything grows. There is copper, there is gold and some diamonds, and tropical fruits of all kinds, and plenty of iron ore. Up in the north in the high lands, I found cotton and tobacco growing.

Although there is a properly constructed Liberian Government and a black President and a Constitution based on the Constitution of the United States, forty miles away from the capital, there is no rule whatsoever. The chiefs rule the country, or at least their own districts, and as long as they make occasional contributions to the Government, they are not troubled.

Cannibalism and witchcraft, all kinds of strange and secret rites are practised—two weeks from London!

# CHAPTER III

## GOOD-BYE, VIENNA

I SAW Adolf Hitler's back for the first time in 1924. I see in my diary that it was on Tuesday, February 26th. The occasion was when General Ludendorff and Hitler and six other people were put on trial in the Infantry School, Munich, on a charge of the attempted overthrow of the Bavarian Government in the previous November. The Court was surrounded with barbed wire and helmeted soldiers. Ludendorff was wearing that day a shiny double-breasted blue suit, a black tie and a wing collar. I noticed that the prisoners appeared like a Board of Directors about to attend the final meeting of a bankrupt company. The case was heard in camera. While the Court was open I noticed that Hitler, under cross-examination, had phrases put into his mouth by the President of the Court, and this enabled Hitler to say what a fine soldier he had been. Hitler said he would like to make a long speech, and the President, undoubtedly thinking of his lunch, said hastily, that there would not be sufficient time; the Court then adjourned. When the Court reassembled in the afternoon, Hitler covered Ludendorff, saying that he was not implicated in the November revolution because he knew nothing about it until it had started. Edgar Mowrer was with me when we both saw Hitler for the first time. Mowrer writes: "Was this provincial dandy, with slick dark

hair, his cutaway coat, his awkward gestures and his
glib tongue, a terrible rebel? He seemed for all the
world like a travelling salesman for a clothing firm!"
I could not better that description. I particularly
remember Hitler's awkward gestures as he filed into
Court. The next time I saw Hitler, it was his face I
saw, and that was on Sunday, March 13th, 1938,
when he drove in triumph into Vienna. During those
fourteen years, Hitler had turned round both
physically and metaphorically. The pinchbeck hero
of the brewery *putsch* had become a great national hero
and an international figure; in the meantime Vienna,
city of romance and glamour and legend, had been
wiped off the map of Europe.

## I GO TO VIENNA

In November, 1918, while I was in Berne waiting to
go to Berlin via Vienna, I met a curious little woman,
named Rosika Schwimmer, who some years earlier
had organized the famous Henry Ford Peace "Ark".
She was now in Berne trying to get some Swiss journalists to go with her to Budapest to write stories
about the sufferings of Hungary.

At this particular time Lord Northcliffe owned
both the *Times* and the *Daily Mail*. A high official in
Geneva was closely connected with both newspapers.
The official having heard through his own spies that
I intended leaving for Austria, telephoned to me from
Geneva and asked me to arrange to pick up a certain
letter in Zurich and to deliver it to Mr. J. N. Jeffries
of the *Daily Mail* who was said to be in Vienna. An

official from the British Consul in Zurich met me as
I passed through that city and gave me a large and
heavily sealed envelope. That night sitting up with
Thierry, my travelling companion, he persuaded me
that I had no business to be taking any sort of document into enemy territory, without knowing what I
was carrying. I had been told that the letter contained
instructions only. Thierry persuaded me to open the
envelope and to transfer the contents to another;
when I did, I almost fell off my chair with surprise;
I found £100 in Bank of England notes and a letter
instructing Mr. Jeffries to proceed immediately to
Berlin. I was furiously angry at the deception and that
I should be helping a rival newspaper; I had little
enough money, goodness knows, and no prospect of
getting any more from London, also I was taking great
personal risk in trying to reach Berlin. Nevertheless, I put the money and the letter of instructions in
another envelope and carried them with me when
Thierry and I started off the next morning.

Almost as soon as I crossed over into Austria, we
found an Italian Army Corps marching through to
occupy Bavaria; they were commandeering everything as they went. In Buchs we found a dilapidated
train, the windows all broken, the cushions torn from
the seats, and ribald jests scribbled all over the panels
by Austrian soldiers. There were no civilians in the
train but hundreds of soldiers who had broken away
from the defeated Austrian Army and were trying to
get home. The train crawled along, stopping at every
station and between every station. At one small place
an Austrian Colonel and his wife entered our compartment. It was so thick with smoke I could hardly
see them. The men looked at the Colonel but took no

notice of him. He glared. His wife timidly found a seat between two soldiers. The men went on laughing and joking, talking a dialect I did not understand. Presently the Colonel said in a parade ground voice: "Men, stop smoking." The soldiers took no notice. The woman tried to check her husband, but again he told the men they were not to smoke. Then a man over in a corner said in a loud ringing voice: "If she does not like it, tell her to get the hell out of here." The Colonel lurched across the compartment and tried to seize the soldier, but all the other men jumped up and a free fight started. The Colonel was flung out on to the track and that was the last we saw of him. The woman sat still until the train reached the next station and then she left.

At the next station, Thierry and I were so hungry that we also decided to leave the train, and try and find food. We left our typewriters and our bags and set out to search the village, but there was nothing to eat. We walked miles and whenever we saw anybody we stopped and begged them to sell us a little food, but nobody had any food to eat, let alone to sell. While we were wandering on in the bitter cold we met some Italian officers in a motor car and told them we were trying to get to Vienna. They drove us back to the station, fetched our luggage and then drove us over a long stage of our journey. During the night it was way down below freezing point, and as we went through a large forest driving towards Voralberg we counted twenty-one forest fires which the Italians, drunk with victory, had started. One division said it was marching to Munich. We went on towards Innsbruck. In every village the peasants seemed to be in an advanced stage of starvation. The Italian

Cavalry divisions had gone so fast that many of their horses had died; the peasants had lived for days on these dead Italian horses. In at least six villages near Innsbruck we found parties of villagers going out to collect the carcases. In Innsbruck also a committee insisted on us addressing them. They were drafting a cable to President Wilson begging him to send food. The Innsbruck people had no food to offer us, except a little black bread and butter which tasted like linseed oil, but there was plenty of wine. We found a train we were told was going to Vienna. It was a long, long journey, and the news of our arrival had gone on ahead from Innsbruck. To our great surprise, there was an enormous crowd waiting for us in Vienna. We were received with cheers for England and cheers for America and people gathered round us begging to be told when the Allies were going to send food.

Like everybody else, I had imagined Vienna a great gay city. It was beautiful enough but the Viennese were like nightmare figures in a Gustave Doré picture. Men and women, officers and civilians were rolling down the Ring as drunk as drunk could be. They danced, they sang and they fell on the pavement, perhaps not so much drunk as weak from hunger. They were dying so fast that at one time there was a shortage of wood for coffins. I was taken to a place where I saw a number of coffins made out of *papier maché*, and although there was not enough wood, there was enough for sawdust to thicken the soup which was all the poor had to eat. I went around the soup kitchens, sometimes more horrifying than any horror one could ever imagine. It was in the early morning, but already a line of women and children more than a quarter of a mile long, had been standing for hours in the snow waiting for the door of the soup kitchen to open. Everybody in the line received half a pint of soup. It consisted of hot water, thickened with sawdust and flavoured with the sweepings from the vegetable market. On Sundays, as a special treat, a small piece of horse-flesh was dropped into the soup, but not enough for any person to receive more than sufficient to fill an egg-spoon. The woman who took me into this soup kitchen insisted I should taste the horrible mess, because she said it was only then that I should know what the British Fleet had done to the Viennese.

And yet, as compared with the hunger, the squalor and the misery, the fashionable shops in the Ring still had numbers of luxurious articles for sale, and in the cafés and hotels, women were well-dressed. During the day, the streets were quiet enough, but as soon as night fell, orgies of drunkenness began. Once when Thierry and I were walking along the Ring, we were overheard to be talking English; a group of officers and women joined hands and danced round us singing "Tipperary". We stayed in the Krantzler Hotel, close to Frau Sacha's famous restaurant, where there was absolutely nothing whatsoever to eat. Every hotel warned visitors not to put their boots outside to be cleaned, because they would be stolen. In all the cafés in the centre of the city, there were notices saying: "Watch your overcoat."

I tried to find Jeffries, but nobody had ever heard of him. Eventually I met a Colonel Summerhayes who said that he had taken Jeffries with him to Vienna, but Jeffries, anticipating that he might have to go to Berlin, had preferred to go to Warsaw. Then I tried to get the Colonel to take charge of the £100, but he refused. Eventually I sent a message to the editor of the *Daily Express* asking him to pay the *Daily Mail* £100; I said I would use the money for *Daily Express* purposes.

While I sat in my bedroom in Vienna trying to write, I was interrupted every few minutes by people coming up and asking me if I could get them their old jobs back in London. I could, of course, do nothing for any of these people, but the interruptions prevented me from working; at last, in desperation, I telephoned the reception office and said to the head clerk: "Please do not allow any more people to come up." The clerk was most polite, he would certainly prevent people from coming up. Within five minutes there was a knock at the door. It was the head clerk himself asking me to help him get his pre-war job back. He had worked at the Carlton Hotel in London.

There was a lot of minor fighting, but nothing very serious during this time I was in Vienna. The hotel was guarded with machine guns, but the Viennese were far too weak to fight; they were longing for food and they did not care anything about politics.

In a brief space of four years, Vienna provided the world with two political martyrs: Dr. Dollfuss and Dr. Schuschnigg. Dollfuss is dead and a martyr. Whether Dr. Schuschnigg is dead or alive, nobody knows. I have yet to meet a person who can tell me that he has seen Dr. Schuschnigg since that afternoon on Friday, March 11th, when the Chancellor of Austria finished his speech over the air. Those who listened carefully heard the Chancellor say after he had closed his speech: "*Ich bin fertig.*" The accepted translation of this phrase is "I am finished." *Ich bin fertig* also means "I am ready", and I do suggest for the consideration of curious students of politics, that Dr. Schuschnigg may at that moment have been addressing his jailers or his executioners. In any case Dr. Schuschnigg has joined Dollfuss among the martyrs.

Dollfus has many political enemies, even to-day; I am one of them, because of his brutal treatment of the Socialists; his bombardment of the Socialist tenement dwellings finished his almost world-wide popularity. Had he not been murdered by German Nazis, who knows what his end might have been? However ifs and ands do not take us very far.

## GOOD-BYE, VIENNA

I saw the Austrian capital in many phases, but I regret I never knew it in its great and glamorous days, when the lilt of the waltz and the swish of the silken petticoats formed the appropriate background to the political intrigue which kept European Chancellories guessing. I went to Vienna when it was starving and I said good-bye to it when the curtain fell for the last time on all that was left of this great city of once upon a time.

It was Donald Duck who assisted me in my dash to Vienna to be present at the funeral of Austria. Reginald Simpson, editor of the *Sunday Graphic*, was my lunch guest in the Savoy Grill on Friday, March 11th. He telephoned me to say he would be a few minutes late; I bought the midday edition of the *Evening Standard* to help me pass the time. I noticed that there was a crisis, another crisis in Central

307

Europe. I also noticed the *Evening Standard* proposed to do something or other about Donald Duck. Though I have the greatest admiration for the Walt Disney comics, European politics did seem more important. When Simpson arrived, I wanted to talk about Austria and he wanted to talk about Donald Duck. It was Donald Duck that had delayed him. He had put through a big deal and from the following week the *Sunday Graphic* was going to be bigger and better than ever. It was all due, I gathered, to Donald Duck. I happened to say casually that the *Evening Standard* was going to publish a Donald Duck picture. Simpson said that was impossible. I told him I had just seen it. When we left the Savoy and were walking along the Strand, we bought another copy of the *Evening Standard* to see who was right. In the middle of Aldwych, Simpson said: "My God, look at this"—a crisis in Europe. The Germans are going to Vienna." "Yes," I said calmly, "I have been trying to tell you for the last two hours."

Simpson said I had better make arrangements to fly to Vienna immediately for the *Sunday Graphic* and the *Daily Sketch*, and I did.

As the Dutch plane which I had picked up in Prague taxied along the airfield at Vienna, I counted 114 German planes, wing to wing, parked around the aerodrome. Over Vienna German planes flew low. German tanks and armoured cars and cavalry, and infantry and artillery poured in to the city. I had the leisure and the opportunity to examine this German equipment. The young soldiers looked fine, but the officers were not of the World War vintage. They were older men, more the college professor type and looked kind of worried. The tanks seemed good enough, but the armoured cars had a very tinny appearance, and I doubt, even although I am only a layman, whether this equipment could stand up to a long campaign.

It was said that Hitler was to arrive that Saturday afternoon. For hours thousands of people lined the streets and waited. I believe that on that Saturday at midday Hitler had not made up his mind whether he would go to Vienna or not. He was not afraid of any hostile demonstration, but he had only made up his mind to go as far as Linz, where he slept on the Saturday night. When France and Great Britain made no hostile move whatsoever, Hitler must have said to himself: "That's all I want to know." Then he set out for Vienna.

My bedroom window in the Grand Hotel looked out on to the Ring. I saw the crowds gather from early morning. Policemen had been brought from Germany to keep back the milling throng. The policemen were tied together wrist to wrist, one facing the crowd and one facing the roadway. They were there from midday until six in the evening; never stirring. And after an interval of fourteen years, I saw Hitler again. He had filled out; he had become podgy. The ill-fitting cutaway coat had been exchanged for a khaki tunic and a flat peaked cap. He was standing up in a motor car with his right arm outstretched from the shoulder. The car drove slowly; his podgy figure swayed. There was a fixed smile on his face, while behind, in semi-circular formation, were numerous cars full of black-uniformed Storm Troopers, with drawn revolvers and rifles pointing at the Viennese. They did not mind, the Viennese; they shouted, they screamed; they had hysterics, especially the women.

# I HATE TO-MORROW

From any window in the Ring, anybody could have tossed a bomb into that open motor car.

But after *Der Tag* there is a price to pay. I left Vienna when the first instalments were being handed over. Shop windows were smashed; places of business wrecked. There were horrible atrocities, and looting. The martyrdom of Vienna, alas, was only beginning.

THE END

# INDEX

# INDEX